Cover Letters That Blow Doors Open

By PREP Publishing

Business and Career Series:

RESUMES AND COVER LETTERS THAT HAVE WORKED

RESUMES AND COVER LETTERS THAT HAVE WORKED FOR MILITARY PROFESSIONALS

RESUMES AND COVER LETTERS FOR MANAGERS

GOVERNMENT JOB APPLICATIONS AND FEDERAL RESUMES

LETTERS FOR SPECIAL SITUATIONS

COVER LETTERS THAT BLOW DOORS OPEN

Judeo-Christian Ethics Series:

SECOND TIME AROUND

BACK IN TIME

WHAT THE BIBLE SAYS ABOUT...Words that can lead to success and happiness

A GENTLE BREEZE FROM GOSSAMER WINGS

BIBLE STORIES FROM THE OLD TESTAMENT...Stories that uplift, educate, and inspire

Cover Letters That Blow Doors Open

Edited by Anne McKinney

PREP PUBLISHING

FAYETTEVILLE, NC

PREP Publishing

1110 ½ Hay Street
Fayetteville, NC 28305
(910) 483-6611

Cover design by David W. Turner

Library of Congress Cataloging-in-Publication Data
McKinney, Anne, 1948-
    Cover letters that blow doors open / Anne McKinney.
    p. cm.
    ISBN 1-885288-13-1 (trade paperback)
    1. Cover Letters. I. Title
HF5383.M225   1999
808' .06665--dc21   98-52224
                                       CIP

Printed in the United States of America

Table of Contents

Part III: Cover Letters for Special Situations: Sixteen Commonly Asked Questions About Cover Letters (and Job Hunting)

Cover Letters That Blow Doors Open

Many people are aware of the importance of having a great resume, but most people in a job hunt don't realize just how important a cover letter can be. The purpose of the cover letter, sometimes called a **"letter of interest,"** is to introduce your resume to prospective employers.

"A Picture Is Worth a Thousand Words."

As a way of illustrating how important the cover letter can be, we have chosen to show you on the next two pages the cover letter and resume of a young person seeking her first job in the teaching field. If the employer received only her resume without a cover letter, this promising young teacher would look like a cook and restaurant worker! A busy principal would probably not be motivated to dial her telephone number to suggest an interview time. In her case, the cover letter is probably more important than the resume she has been asked to submit. What the cover letter allows her to do is to explain that she worked as a cook, closing manager, and cashier full time while going back to school to earn her college degree. This puts her work experience in a different perspective.

• The cover letter is the critical ingredient in a job hunt such as Marcia Vivero's because the cover letter allows her to say a lot of things that just don't "fit" on the resume. For example, she can emphasize her commitment to the teaching profession and stress her talent for teaching mathematics to people who find the subject difficult.

• One of the things that sets her apart from other new graduates in her field is that she is a mature professional who, at age 27, is accustomed to a demanding work schedule. She's no "old lady" but she is five years older and wiser than the typical 22-year-old college graduate. In the high-stress profession which high school teaching is often considered to be, many principals will perceive of her age and experience as a positive factor.

• Although the general rule is that women do not mention how many children they have in their resume and cover letter, there are exceptions to every rule, and Ms. Vivero breaks that rule for a good reason. She points out that she is a wife and mother and would bring to the classroom an in-depth understanding of the learning styles of children.

• Finally, the cover letter gives her a chance to stress the outstanding character and personal values which she feels will be a positive influence on the high school students to whom she wishes to teach mathematics.

You will see on the next two pages that the cover letter gives you a chance to "get personal" with the person to whom you are writing whereas the resume is a more formal document. Even if the employer doesn't request a cover letter, we believe that it is *always* in your best interest to send a cover letter with your resume. The aim of this book is to show you examples of cover letters designed to blow doors open so that you can develop your own cover letters and increase the number of interviews you have.

Date

Exact Name of Principal
Exact Title
School Name
School Address
City, State Zip

Dear Exact Name: (or Dear Principal if you don't know the Exact Name)

With the enclosed resume, I would like to introduce myself and initiate the process of being considered for a position as a Mathematics Teacher in your high school.

As you will see from my resume, I recently graduated from the University of Rhode Island with a B.S. degree in Mathematics which I earned **magna cum laude**. I am especially proud of graduating with honors since I was combining a rigorous academic curriculum with a demanding work schedule which involved me in handling a variety of managerial, accounting, and customer service responsibilities.

Although I graduated in May 2000 with my B.S. degree, I am 27 years old and offer considerable experience in working with children of all ages. Since I am a wife and mother, I would bring to the classroom much understanding of the learning styles of children. I feel I would be skilled in classroom behavior management, and I would offer a maturity which younger college graduates might not have. I am a responsible individual known for my well-organized work habits and disciplined style.

I am deeply committed to a career in the teaching profession, and I intend in my spare time to earn my Master's degree in Mathematics and then a Ph.D. I am a highly motivated hard worker, and I feel my own strong values could be an inspiration to high school students. Although I have earned my degree in Mathematics with high honors, I am fully aware of how difficult mathematics is for many people, and I excel in translating abstract concepts into understandable language.

If you can use a vibrant young teaching professional who could enhance the fine reputation of your school, I hope you will contact me to suggest a time when I could make myself available for a personal interview. I can provide outstanding personal and professional references.

Sincerely,

Marcia Vivero

MARCIA VIVERO

1110½ Hay Street, Providence, RI 28305

(910) 483-6611 • preppub@aol.com

OBJECTIVE	To contribute to a high school that can use a dedicated mathematics teacher who is attuned to the varied learning abilities and styles which students bring to the classroom.
EDUCATION	Earned B.S. degree in **Mathematics,** University of Rhode Island, Providence, RI, May 2000.

- Graduated **Magna Cum Laude** with a GPA of 3.754.
- Received the Certificate of Excellence and was named to the Chancellor's List.
- Excelled academically while working part-time to finance my college education.

Graduated from Eastern Senior High School, Pawtucket, RI, 1990.

- Participated in track and intramural sports.

EXPERIENCE

CLOSING MANAGER, COOK, CASHIER. Chuck's Chicken & Barbecue, Providence, RI (1997-present).

- Was singled out to handle a variety of management responsibilities, and became known for my trustworthiness and cheerful disposition while simultaneously earning my college degree **with honors.**
- Refined my interpersonal skills working with all types of customers and with other employees.
- Trained other employees; assigned tasks to junior employees and supervised their work.
- Expertly operated a cash register, and was known for my accuracy in handling large amounts of cash; trained other employees to use the register.
- As Closing Manager, was responsible for closing the store at the end of the business day; accounted for financial transactions and oversaw end-of-the-day maintenance and security matters.
- Was frequently commended for my gracious style of dealing with the public and for my courteous approach to customer service.

COMPUTER OPERATOR/CLERICAL AIDE. Clear Lake Elementary School, Pawtucket, RI (summer 1990).

- In the summer after my high school graduation, excelled in an office position handling numerous responsibilities related to record keeping for students in summer school.
- Operated a computer in order to input data and maintain records.
- Filed and typed as needed.
- Was known for my attention to detail and accuracy when handling large volumes of work under tight deadlines.

PERSONAL

Have aspirations to earn my Master's degree in Mathematics, and believe I could be a great asset to the teaching profession. Can provide outstanding references. Have taught in Bible School Programs. Believe all students can learn, and am skilled at communicating difficult mathematics concepts to students who find math difficult.

Resume

Although this is not a book in which you will find resumes, we had to show you one resume in order to help you see how important a cover letter can be in a job hunt. Without the cover letter, this young person seems lacking in the raw ingredients which lead to success in the teaching field.

Date

Exact Name of Principal
Exact Title
School Name
School Address
City, State Zip

Dear Exact Name: (or Dear Principal if you don't know the Exact Name):

With the enclosed resume, I would like to introduce myself and initiate the process of being considered for a position as a Mathematics Teacher in your high school.

As you will see from my resume, I recently graduated from the University of Rhode Island with a B.S. degree in Mathematics which I earned **magna cum laude**. I am especially proud of graduating with honors since I was combining a rigorous academic curriculum with a demanding work schedule which involved me in handling a variety of managerial, accounting, and customer service responsibilities.

Although I graduated in May 1999 with my B.S. degree, I am 27 years old and offer considerable experience in working with children of all ages. As a wife and mother, I would bring to the classroom understanding of the varied learning styles of children. I feel I would be skilled in classroom behavior management, and I would offer a maturity which younger college graduates might not have. I am a responsible individual known for my well-organized work habits and disciplined style.

I am deeply committed to a career in the teaching profession, and I intend in my spare time to earn my Master's degree in Mathematics and then a Ph.D. I am a highly motivated hard worker, and I feel my own strong values would be an inspiration to high school students. Although I have earned my degree in Mathematics with high honors, I am fully aware of how difficult mathematics is for many people, and I excel in translating abstract concepts into understandable language.

If you can use a vibrant young teaching professional who could enhance the fine reputation of your school, I hope you will contact me to suggest a time when I could make myself available for a personal interview. I can provide outstanding references.

Sincerely,

Marcia Vivero

Alternate final paragraph (could be substituted for the final paragraph above):

I hope you will welcome my call next week when I try to arrange a time when we might speak briefly in person about your upcoming needs and my desire to become part of your teaching staff. I understand your busy schedule and appreciate in advance any professional courtesies you can extend.

Date

Exact Name of Person
Title or Position
Name of Company
Address (number and street)
Address (city, state, and zip)

Dear Exact Name of Person: (or Dear Sir or Madam if answering a blind ad)

I would appreciate an opportunity to talk with you soon about how I could contribute to your organization through my proven accounts management, customer service, and public relations skills.

You will see from my resume that I began working with Revco when I was 16 years old; I continued my employment with Revco while attending college and was promoted to Pharmacy Technician while earning my Bachelor of Business Administration degree. After college graduation, the university where I earned my degree recruited me for a job in its admissions office, and I excelled in handling a wide variety of administrative and public relations tasks.

Most recently I have worked full time as an Account Representative while going to school at nights and on the weekends to earn my M.B.A., which I received in May 1998. I was handling key accounts worth more than $2 million annually for my employer and was being groomed for rapid promotion into a higher management position.

I have, however, relocated permanently to the LaFayette area because I recently married and my husband owns and manages his own business in this area. I am seeking an employer who can use a highly motivated individual with very strong communication, sales, customer service, and public relations skills. Because I earned both my undergraduate and graduate degrees while excelling in demanding professional positions, I have acquired excellent organizational and time management skills which permit me to maximize my own productivity.

If you can use a self-starter who could rapidly become a valuable part of your organization, I hope you will contact me to suggest a time when we might meet to discuss your needs and how I might serve them. I can provide excellent personal and professional references.

Sincerely,

Louise Patton

cc: Thomas Crane

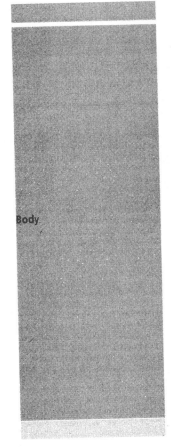

Semi-blocked Letter

Date

Three blank spaces

Address

Salutation

One blank space

Body

One blank space

Signature

cc: Indicates you are sending a copy of the letter to someone

All-Purpose Cover Letters, Career-Change Cover Letters, Cover Letters for Entrepreneurs, and Cover Letters for People Seeking Their First Job in Their Field

In this section you will find cover letters which are "cousins" of each other. In general, the cover letters in this section are written for people who need a very creative and resourceful cover letter. These cover letters are designed to accompany resumes of individuals trying to embark on a course of employment which is different from what they have been doing most recently.

The All-Purpose Cover Letter: In a job hunt, the all-purpose cover letter can be a time saver because it can serve as a "standard" or "model" or "template" which you can use each time you send out your resume. You may wish to modify it from time to time, but the all-purpose cover letter is there, already written, often in your computer, when you see an ad you want to answer or when you identify an employer whom you wish to contact in order to explore suitable opportunities for someone of your skills and abilities. The all-purpose cover letter can be used for employers in your current field or for employers in other industries.

Career-Change Cover Letters: Career-change cover letters are designed to help you find employment in a new field or industry. In this type of cover letter, you must "make sense" of yourself to the prospective employer. Otherwise, the prospective employer may look at your resume and ask himself, "Why is an air traffic controller writing to me about this marketing job?" The career-change cover letter is the employer's first impression of you and can explain why you are approaching him or her.

Cover Letters for Entrepreneurs: Entrepreneurs and self-employed managers in a job hunt are viewed with respect (everyone knows how difficult it is to start up a company) and with suspicion (most employers suspect that entrepreneurs really want to work for themselves and would have a hard time having a boss). Their cover letters must reach out personally to prospective employers and explain why the prospective employer's business is of interest. The entrepreneur is seeking to establish credibility and trust in this type of cover letter.

Seeking First Job in Field: Most people know the frustration of not having any experience in the field in which they are seeking employment. There are particular techniques that should be used when writing a cover letter to try to obtain the first job in one's field. This type of cover letter "builds a bridge" to a new field. Ms. Vivero's cover letter, which was used as an example on page 2, is an example of this type of cover letter.

Date

Exact Name of Person
Title or Position
Name of Company
Address (number and street)
Address (city, state, and zip)

ALL-PURPOSE
COVER LETTERS

Cover Letter that can be used
to approach any field
Notice how this young
professional emphasizes his
management skills and
versatility while pointing out
that his experience has been in
law enforcement and security.
Even to employers outside the
law enforcement and security
field, this background tends to
imply an honest and clean-cut
individual and may inspire
some confidence on the part of
prospective employers.

Dear Exact Name of Person: (or Sir or Madam if answering a blind ad)

With the enclosed resume, I would like to make you aware of my background as an experienced professional who has excelled in managing human, fiscal, and material resources as well as in motivating, supervising, and instructing personnel.

As you will see, while my experience and education have been predominately in law enforcement and security, I have recently earned a bachelor's degree in Business Management. I earned this degree–and associate's degrees in Business Management and Criminal Justice Administration–while simultaneously excelling at meeting the demands of positions in the hectic and pressure-filled environment of military law enforcement and security. My time management and organizational skills have been refined as a Loss Prevention Associate for Simon's Department Store, and I have polished my communication skills teaching on a part-time basis as an instructor for the Basic Law Enforcement Training program at Smyrna Technical Community College.

Throughout my career I have been handpicked for highly visible leadership roles and singled out to act in various capacities as an investigator, inspector and advisor, developer of training, and supervisor. I believe that my greatest strengths are the ability to motivate others and lead them to work together, along with my talent for being able to develop good working relations with people of all ages and skill levels.

If you can use an experienced and mature professional who is adaptable and offers sound judgment and decision-making skills, I hope you will contact me to suggest a time when we might meet to discuss your needs. I can assure you in advance that I could rapidly become an asset to your organization.

Sincerely,

Gerald Utley

Date

Exact Name of Person
Title or Position
Name of Company
Address (number and street)
Address (city, state, and zip)

Dear Exact Name of Person: (or Sir or Madam if answering a blind ad)

Can you use an articulate, enthusiastic, and self-motivated young professional with a strong interest in entering the pharmaceutical sales field?

As you will see from my enclosed resume, I earned my B.S. in Biology from Michigan State University in 1996 and maintained a 3.5 GPA. During my senior year I worked as many as 50 hours a week as a Research Assistant in the university's chemistry lab. I conducted research which resulted in a manual that was distributed at a national conference.

This all-purpose letter emphasizes the communication skills and versatility of a young professional with teaching experience as well as a distinguished military record.

In my most recent job as a middle school science and math teacher, I refined communication, organizational, and time management skills while involved in numerous projects. I planned the school's first science fair as well as a Christmas play and a musical. My greatest accomplishment during this period was in taking a student who was working two grade levels below his classmates and developing an individualized plan to use while tutoring him. I spent four months working closely with him and brought him up to his proper grade level.

Lack of experience in a particular field is not a main reason why employers choose not to interview applicants. Employers are looking for a track record of accomplishment in whatever you have done so far.

Earlier while serving for four years in the U.S. Army, I earned both an Army Commendation Medal and an Achievement Medal for my performance as a supervisor, dental office administrator, and assistant during dental surgery procedures. I quickly took the initiative for clearing up a logistics backlog and was singled out for my role in producing well-trained and skilled X-ray technicians, surgical assistants, and clerical staff members.

I am confident that through my education, experience, and strengths in working with and communicating with others, I could rapidly become an asset to your organization. I hope you will contact me to suggest a time when we might meet to discuss your needs.

Sincerely,

Julie M. Vogel

Date

Exact Name of Person
Title or Position
Name of Company
Address (number and street)
Address (city, state, and zip)

Cover Letter addressed to a
particular company which
could easily be modified into
an all-purpose letter

An all-purpose cover letter can
be personalized to a specific
company by mentioning the
company name in the first and
last paragraph of the letter. So,
with just a couple of changes
in a standard letter which you
can maintain in your computer,
you will have a letter which
seems personally prepared for
each company you approach.

Dear Exact Name of Person: (or Sir or Madam if answering a blind ad)

With the enclosed resume, I would like to make you aware of my strong desire to become permanently employed by Advanced Technology, Inc., in a role in which I could benefit the company through my computer knowledge, sales skills, and customer service experience.

As you will see from my resume, I am currently excelling as an Operations Clerk working for Advanced Technology in Miami, where I am employed in a temporary full-time position through Man Hours Temporary Service. In this job I am involved in a wide range of activities involving computer operations, customer service, and administrative support. I have become proficient in using Beyond Mail, in utilizing the LAN system, and in researching and coordinating service orders in the most efficient manner while applying my knowledge of Advanced Technology's internal telecommunications operations.

In my previous job in Orlando as an Administrative Aide, I became a valuable employee and was entrusted with many complex responsibilities because of my demonstrated initiative, intelligence, and customer service skills. Since I am bilingual in Spanish and English, I conducted new hires of employees in both Spanish and English and frequently translated communication between production workers and office personnel.

My computer skills are excellent, and I enjoy learning new software. While in my previous job I completed a major project in which I computerized data entry for all production workers' payroll. I am knowledgeable of software including Microsoft Word, Excel, Lotus 1-2-3, and PowerPoint.

Please consider me for a position within Advanced Technology which can utilize my excellent communication, problem-solving, and decision-making skills. I can provide outstanding personal and professional references including very strong references from regional and district office Advanced Technology personnel with whom I work.

Sincerely,

Maria Sanchez

Date

Exact Name of Person
Title or Position
Name of Company
Address (number and street)
Address (city, state, and zip)

Dear Exact Name of Person: (or Sir or Madam if answering a blind ad)

With the enclosed resume, I would like to make you aware of my interest in discussing the possibility of employment with your organization. As you will see from my enclosed resume, I have been excelling in a track record of accomplishment while utilizing my skills in communication and customer service.

Both during the process of earning and after receiving my A.S. degree in Theater Arts from the University of New Mexico, I have distinguished myself in sales, public relations, customer service, and management roles.

As you will see from my resume, I offer a proven ability to work with and satisfy sophisticated customers of high-end products while handling responsibilities related to collections, refunds, accounts payable and receivable, and other areas.

In my previous job as a Sales Manager in Beverly Hills, CA, I was responsible for hiring and training 19 sales associates in a store which catered to high-end customers of designer bridal gowns, evening wear, and lingerie. When I recruited sales professionals, I always looked for individuals with strong personalities who demonstrated a proven ability to be resourceful in customer service and problem solving while gaining the confidence of customers in a sales situation. Although I am only 23, I have succeeded in positions which often were filled by a much more senior individual because of my exceptionally strong communication skills, common sense, and ability to skillfully handle customers. My communication skills have enabled me to tactfully resolve difficult customer problems, find creative remedies for employee issues, as well as aggressively develop new accounts.

Please give me every consideration for a position in your company where my superior customer service, sales, and public relations skills could benefit your organization. Thank you in advance for your time.

Yours sincerely,

Joy Van de Hoef

Date

Exact Name of Person
Exact Name of Company
Exact Address
City, State Zip

· **Cover Letter highlighting transferable skills in sales and accounting**
This all-purpose cover letter acquaints prospective employers with sales and accounting skills which could be utilized in versatile ways by a variety of employers in multiple industries. Notice how she emphasizes her strong personal qualities of initiative and congeniality while citing bottom-line accomplishments.

There is a tendency for employers to think, "If she did this for her previous employer, she could do this for me, too."

Dear Sir or Madam:

With the enclosed resume, I would like to make you aware of my interest in joining your organization in some capacity which could use my strong background in sales and customer service as well as my solid training in accounting and bookkeeping.

Sales Distinctions

I am 24 years of age and have worked since I was 18 years old for AAFES, the Army and Air Force Exchange Service. During that time I have excelled in every assignment and have received numerous cash bonuses as well as several Sales Recognition Awards (SRAs). I am proud to say that I have increased sales in every department in which I have worked, and while in Ft. Irwin, CA, I earned the distinction of the #1 camera sales representative in the U.S. while leading my department to a 25% sales increase.

Accounting and Bookkeeping Knowledge

In my spare time, I have nearly completed an Associate's degree in Accounting and Bookkeeping, and my degree program included coursework in financial reporting, accounts receivable and payables management, budget analysis, financial statement analysis, and other similar areas. I excelled academically while also performing with distinction in my full-time day job. My experience with AAFES includes some accounting and bookkeeping, as I have handled responsibilities as a Head Teller and Cashier. In one assignment, I was responsible for balancing all money received daily from 16 cash registers, and it was my job to assure the correct balancing of more than $75,000.

I am a very well-organized individual with superior problem-solving abilities who rapidly masters new tasks and activities. I am certain that you would find me in person to be a congenial individual who would represent your company with poise and professionalism. I hope you will contact me soon to suggest a time when we could meet to discuss your needs and how I might be of service to you. I can provide outstanding personal and professional references at the appropriate time.

Yours sincerely,

Olivia N. Crosby

Date

Exact Name of Person
Exact Name of Company
Address
City, State Zip

Dear Sir or Madam:

Can you use a resourceful manager who offers proven skills in the area of automated information systems, financial management, and personnel administration?

Budgeting and Program Management Experience

While rising to the rank of Major in the U.S. Army, I had an opportunity to positively impact the lives of the many employees I supervised while making significant contributions to organizational effectiveness. In my most recent position, I was specially selected as Chief of a Budget Division in a critical transition phase. I managed a budget in excess of $160 million and supervised a 14-person staff while overseeing the strategic allocation of resources needed by 120 university ROTC programs and 490 junior ROTC programs. In my previous position as a Division Chief, I expanded the number of ROTC programs in 16 states from 160 to more than 400 programs. Simultaneously I instituted Lotus and Excel spreadsheets to track variable and fixed expenses, and I created numerous efficiencies which permitted the purchase of computer equipment needed to set up a badly needed information system.

Quality Control and TQM Experience

Prior to that I functioned as a top-level consultant and Quality Control Inspector. I reported to a Commanding General while organizing and supervising the work of inspectors conducting detailed analyses of the systems and procedures of a 10,000-person organization. I became an expert at the practical application of Total Quality Management principles.

Line Management and Consulting Experience

I have excelled in "line" management positions, including Company Commander of a 100-person organization, and I have also served in "staff" roles. Once I served as a Project Officer on a top-level strategic planning task force responsible for designing the communications-electronics products and information systems of the future.

With an outstanding reputation, I can provide excellent references at the appropriate time. If my background interests you, I hope you will contact me to suggest a time when we might meet in person. Thank you in advance for your time.

Yours sincerely,

Calvin P. Donatelli

Cover Letter of a military officer with diversified experience

An all-purpose cover letter helped this military officer explore job opportunities in various industries. It is not always easy to decide what you want to do, and this accomplished individual with multiple talents wanted to use his resume and cover letter to "go fishing" in various fields and industries. His accomplishments in budgeting, programming, consulting, and management should interest numerous employers and introduce him as a multitalented and versatile executive.

Date

Exact Name of Person
Exact Name of Company
Exact Address
City, State Zip

Dear Sir or Madam:

**Cover Letter emphasizing
youth combined with an
excellent track record**
This all-purpose cover letter is
from a young person who is
emphasizing her positive
attitude and customer service
skills. There are many
employers who will take a
hardworking young person
with a good attitude and train
them, so don't think that you
"have nothing" if you are
young and lack extensive paid
work experience. You are just
the kind of "raw material"
many employers are seeking!

With the enclosed resume, I would like to express my interest in working for your company and acquaint you with the experience and skills I have to offer.

Although I am only 20 years old, I have been working for the same employer since I was 16 years old and have earned a reputation as a versatile and valuable employee. On my own initiative and in my spare time, I have gained proficiency with several popular software programs and operating systems, and I am also taking courses at Louisville Technical Community College to improve my skills.

On numerous occasions, my employer has commended me for my sunny disposition and "willingness to go the extra mile" to provide outstanding customer service. I have proven my ability to excel as a team player as well as in handling total responsibility for a key activity. I have enthusiastically worked hard to help my employer in fundraising efforts related to raising money for juvenile diabetes, muscular dystrophy, and March of Dimes.

Although I am highly regarded by my current employer and am being groomed for advancement into higher levels of responsibility, I would like to work in an office environment in which I can utilize and strengthen my administrative and computer operations skills. I am a quick learner and a self starter and feel that I could rapidly become a valuable part of any organization. If you can use a hardworking and dependable young person, please contact me to suggest a time convenient for you when we could meet. Thank you in advance for your time. I am a single (no children) and stable individual and can provide excellent references at the appropriate time.

Yours sincerely,

Mollie Poindexter

Date

Exact Name of Person
Exact Title
Exact Name of Company
Address
City, State Zip

Dear Exact Name of Person: (or Dear Sir or Madam if answering a blind ad):

With the enclosed resume, I would like to make you aware of my interest in exploring employment opportunities with your company and to acquaint you with my skills and talents.

Excellent analytical and communication skills
As you will see from my resume, I have recently earned my B.S. degree in Political Science from Western Carolina University. Since this major requires extensive reading and writing, I have developed excellent analytical and communication skills.

Extensive customer service experience
In jobs which I held during the summers in order to finance my college education, I learned the importance of doing the small, behind-the-scenes jobs to the best of my ability because that is what often determines the customer's satisfaction. In all of my jobs, I played a key role in ensuring customer satisfaction. In a summer job at Applebee's Restaurant, I was selected to train new servers and was encouraged to join the company's management trainee program after college graduation.

Experience in public relations and computer operations
In two of my summer jobs, I worked at prestigious country clubs and (in addition to improving my golf and tennis games!) was commended for my ability to graciously interact with executives, club members, and their guests. In another summer job, I operated a computer while performing customer service at a small business.

Reputation for personal initiative
If you can use a highly motivated young professional with unlimited personal initiative as well as strong personal qualities of dependability and trustworthiness, I hope you will contact me to suggest a time when we might meet to discuss your needs. I can provide excellent personal and professional references, and I am eager to apply my strong customer service orientation and versatile skills to benefit an organization that can use a cheerful hard worker. Thank you in advance for your consideration.

Sincerely,

Brian Fenton

Date

Exact Name of Person
Title or Position
Name of Company
Address (number and street)
Address (city, state, and zip)

**Changing Careers from the
profit-making sector to the
human services field**
Changing careers can be easier
if you make sure your cover
letter is specially designed to
help you accomplish that
purpose. This individual is
changing from profit-making
activities to the human services
field. Notice how her cover
letter helps her potential
employer understand why
someone with her background
is applying for the Community
Employment Specialist job.
Remember, you are trying to
get in the door for an
interview, so the employer
must be persuaded in the cover
letter that it is worth his or
her time to interview someone
outside the field.

Dear Exact Name of Person: (or Sir or Madam if answering a blind ad)

With the enclosed resume, I would like to make you aware of my strong interest in the position as Community Employment Specialist which you recently advertised.

As you will see from my resume, I am excelling in my current job in the profit-making private sector, but it is my desire to make a career change into the human services field. I am confident that my high-energy personality and sincere desire to help others could be of great benefit in the job you advertise. After reading your advertisement, I believe I satisfy all of the requirements you are seeking and in addition offer a sincere desire to be of service to the developmentally disabled population.

In my current job, I am highly respected for my ability to establish and maintain smooth working relationships. I am certain I could excel in identifying and developing job training and placement sites in local businesses and I believe my business experience would be an asset in that regard.

I can provide excellent personal and professional references at the appropriate time, but I would prefer that you not contact my current employer until after we have a chance to talk. I hope my versatile talents and experience will interest you, and I am confident I could become a productive and caring member of your professional team at Maryland Community Services at Annapolis. Thank you in advance for your time.

Yours sincerely,

Michelle Chan

Date

Exact Name of Person
Title or Position
Name of Company
Address (number and street)
Address (city, state, and zip)

Dear Exact Name of Person: (or Sir or Madam if answering a blind ad)

With the enclosed resume, I would like to formally make you aware of my interest in your organization.

As you will see from my resume, I have excelled in jobs which required originality and creativity in prospecting for new clients, business savvy and financial prudence in establishing new ventures, as well as relentless follow-through and attention to detail in implementing ambitious goals.

I was recruited for my current job when the company decided that it wanted to set up a new commercial division and needed someone with proven entrepreneurial skills and a make-it-happen style. Under my leadership, we have set up a new commercial division which has targeted the healthcare and pharmaceutical industry as a primary customer base in addition to major financial institutions and large corporations. Although I now manage several individuals, I personally prospected for the initial accounts and I discovered that my extensive training and background related to chemicals and microbiology was of great value in interacting with healthcare industry decision makers.

Although I can provide outstanding personal and professional references and am being groomed for further promotion within my company, I have decided that I wish to transfer my skills and knowledge to the healthcare industry. You will notice from my resume that I have been a successful entrepreneur and previously started a company which I sold to a larger industry firm. I succeeded as an entrepreneur largely because of my ability to communicate ideas to others, my strong problem-solving skills, and my naturally outgoing and self-confident nature. I am certain I could excel in the healthcare industry in any role which requires extraordinary sales, marketing, and relationship-building abilities.

If my background interests you, and if you feel there is a suitable position in your organization in which you could make use of my sales and marketing strengths, I hope you will contact me to suggest a time when we might meet to discuss your goals and how I might help you achieve them. Thank you in advance for your consideration.

Yours sincerely,

Douglas Schlegel

CAREER-CHANGE
COVER LETTERS

Changing Careers from commercial sales to healthcare industry marketing
In this letter, a talented individual is attempting to change from commercial sales to the healthcare industry. His cover letter points out that he has excelled in jobs which require creativity and a highly disciplined nature, and those qualities could also be critical to success in the field he is trying to enter.

Date

Director of Human Resources
Charlotte Community College
2200 Airport Road
Charlotte, NC 28374

**CAREER-CHANGE
COVER LETTERS**

**Changing Careers from
government to the academic
community**
In this letter, a city engineer is
attempting to make a career
change from government to
the academic environment. He
has some part-time teaching
experience in addition to
experience in training others as
a military officer. Every
employer knows that attitude
is a critical factor in job
performance, so this individual
is stressing his strong desire to
share his vast experience and
technical knowledge with
others in what for him will be
a second career.

Dear Sir or Madam:

With the enclosed resume describing my qualifications and experience, I would like to respond to your advertisement for a Civil Engineering Technology Instructor.

As you will see from my resume, I offer skills and experience that would be of great value to your students. After earning a B.S. in Civil Engineering and then completing one year of graduate studies, I served as a U.S. Army Engineer Officer. After military service, I excelled as the Chief of the Master Planning Branch at Fort Bragg. Since 1995, I have excelled as a Staff Engineer with the City of Charlotte. Although I am held in high regard by my colleagues and am considered a valuable asset of the city, I enjoy teaching and would relish the opportunity to share my vast experience with students at the beginning of their careers.

You will also see from my resume that my teaching credentials are top-notch. For the past 10 years, I have served as an adjunct instructor with Charlotte Technical Community College and have taught courses including Surveying, Topographic Surveying and Aerial Photography, Astronomical Calculations and State Plane Coordinates, Highway Surveying, and Construction Staking and Layout.

I am conversant with the latest thinking in my field as continuous professional development has been a routine with me throughout my career. Indeed, my current job requires that I remain abreast of environmental issues such as wetlands and erosion control. I have attended numerous review courses offered by North Carolina State University, Clemson, and the University of North Carolina's Institute for Technology Transfer. In addition to teaching at adjunct colleges, I also excelled as a Senior Engineer Instructor while serving as an Army officer.

You would find me in person to be a congenial individual who takes much pleasure in sharing my technical knowledge with younger colleagues. It would certainly be a pleasure to talk with you in person to discuss how my unique background could benefit your academic program and enhance the Civil Engineering career path of your undergraduates. I hope you will contact me to suggest a time when we might meet in person to discuss your needs and how I might serve them. Thank you in advance for your time.

Yours sincerely,

Jason Bessemer

Date

Exact Name of Person
Exact Title of Person
Exact Name of Organization
Address
City, State Zip

Dear Exact Name: (or Dear Sir or Madam if answering a blind ad)

With the enclosed resume, I would like to make you aware of my interest in utilizing my outstanding sales, marketing, communication, and management skills for the benefit of your organization.

Although I most recently have been working in the aviation field and am excelling in my current position, I have decided to embark on a radical career change. I have a strong desire to work in a professional position in which I can combine my extroverted personality and "natural" sales ability with my customer relations and problem-solving ability.

My recent experience in airport management, air traffic control, and in piloting advanced attack aircraft may not appear relevant to your needs, but my stable work history also includes several jobs which, I believe, illustrate my versatility. In one job I excelled as a Juvenile Counselor and thoroughly enjoyed the experience of providing a strong role model for troubled youth who had essentially been kicked out of their homes and labeled as "uncontrollable." In another job in California, I was part of the movie-making industry as I worked as a double for Tom Cruise. I also worked previously as a professional model. A wine expert and gourmet cook, I grew up in an Italian family which was in the restaurant business so I learned customer service at a young age!

In my current job involved in managing people and key areas related to airport management at one of the military's busiest airlift centers, I am continually using my problem-solving and decision-making skills. I am confident that my management ability, resourcefulness, and ability to relate effectively to others are qualities which could transfer to any field. In one of my jobs in the aviation industry, I managed a $3.5 million budget with outstanding results, and I offer a strong bottom-line orientation.

If you can use a highly motivated self-starter known for unlimited personal initiative and a creative problem-solving style, I hope you will contact me to suggest a time when we might meet to discuss your needs. I am single and would relocate and travel extensively as your needs require, and I can provide outstanding references at the appropriate time. Thank you in advance for your consideration.

Yours sincerely,

Mason Jensen

CAREER-CHANGE COVER LETTERS

Changing Careers from air traffic control to a sales or marketing role
In this letter, an Air Traffic Controller is seeking to change fields and move from aviation into an industry which can utilize his strong sales, marketing, and communication skills. Notice how he tries to make the employer understand why someone with his specialized technical background is approaching companies that need generalists and communicators. In a career change, experienced professionals often must sell their personality and potential more than their actual work experience in order to "blow the door open."

Date

Exact Name of Person
Exact Title of Person
Exact Address
City, State Zip

CAREER-CHANGE COVER LETTERS

Changing Careers with a cover letter that emphasizes financial knowledge
In this letter, a young person completing his bachelor's degree reaches out to employers in various fields. He emphasizes his track record of accomplishment with his current employer. Although this is an all-purpose cover letter, Mr. Ferdinand is mostly interested in accounting, financial, or management activities, so there is a subtle emphasis on his skills and interest in those functional areas within this all-purpose framework.

Dear Sir or Madam:

With the enclosed resume, I would like to acquaint you with the considerable accounting, financial, and management skills I could put to work for your organization.

As you can see from the enclosed resume, I am continuing to excel in a "track record" of promotion with a food industry corporation. I began with the company as an assistant manager, was promoted to store manager, and advanced in 1997 to my present position as supervisor overseeing the operations of 11 stores in five cities.

While utilizing my strong communication and problem-solving skills in guiding store managers at 11 locations throughout New Hampshire, I am continuously involved in financial analysis and budget preparation. You will see from my resume that I hold an A.A.S. degree in Accounting and I am currently pursuing completion of my Bachelor's degree. I have acquired practical work experience as well as formal course work in areas including management and program analysis, auditing, budget preparation, and quantitative analysis.

My computer operation skills are highly refined. I offer proficiency with numerous popular software products including Lotus 1-2-3 and offer the ability to troubleshoot and repair various types of equipment problems. While previously serving my country for two years in the U.S. Army, I received extensive training in computer operations and telecommunications operations/repair.

You would find me in person to be a dynamic young professional who prides myself on my ability to rapidly become a contributing member of any team. I can provide outstanding personal and professional references at the appropriate time, and I hope I will have the opportunity to meet with you in person to discuss your needs and how I might meet them.

Sincerely,

Terrell A. Ferdinand

Date

Exact Name of Person
Title or Position
Name of Company
Address (number and street)
Address (city, state, and zip)

Dear Exact Name of Person: (or Sir or Madam if answering a blind ad)

With the enclosed resume, I would like to make you aware of my interest in putting my considerable management and communication skills to work for your organization.

As you will see from my resume, I am pursuing a Master's in Public Administration (M.P.A.) degree at the University of Texas at San Antonio while excelling in my full-time job as an executive with Parke-Davis Pharmaceutical Division. It is my strong desire to transfer my considerable skills into the public sector, and I feel I can make major contributions to a government organization through my strategic thinking skills, management ability, as well as my highly effective approach in training, developing, and managing other employees.

You will notice that I have thus far excelled in a track record of achievement as a sales and marketing executive. I am certain that the planning, organizing, problem-solving, decision-making, and negotiating skills which I utilize daily in my job could be effectively utilized in the public sector. In my prior position with Smith Boyle, Inc., I worked extensively with government officials while servicing up to 700 commercial and government accounts in Utah cities. I am well acquainted with government purchasing procedures and with the steps involved in government decision making.

I can provide outstanding personal and professional references at the appropriate time, and I can assure you that you would find me in person to be a poised communicator who would take pride in contributing to your organizational goals. I hope you will contact me if you feel my considerable management and communication skills could be helpful to you.

Thank you in advance for your time.

Sincerely,

Danny Flanders

Date

Exact Name of Person
Exact Title
Exact Name of Company
Address
City, State Zip

CAREER-CHANGE COVER LETTERS

Changing Careers from retail to an industry that can utilize his proven management ability This letter holds the key to this individual's intense desire to become employed in a sector other than retail. Although he has a background as an accomplished retail manager, he desires a change. Remember that in a career-change situation, your approach simply has to "make sense" to prospective employers and they must feel that you are genuinely interested in leaving the industry you know best— not just "having a bad day."

Dear Exact Name of Person: (or Dear Sir or Madam if answering a blind ad)

With the enclosed resume, I would like to make you aware of the considerable skills I feel I could offer your organization.

As you will see from my resume, I have excelled in a track record of advancement with the Macy's organization, where I started as a management trainee and advanced into a senior management position in charge of 25 individuals. After earning my undergraduate degree in Business Administration with a minor in Economics, I was attracted to the Macy's organization because of its tradition of regarding its managers as profit centers and treating them essentially as entrepreneurs. While hiring and supervising personnel, I handled general management responsibilities including preparing business plans four times a year, reviewing progress monthly toward goals, and performing extensive community relations and public relations. For example, I was active in the Chamber of Commerce.

Although I was excelling in my job and held in high regard, I made the decision to resign from Macy's in late 1999 for two reasons: first, I wanted to spend a few weeks caring full-time for my widowed mother, who had undergone a serious operation, and second, I had decided that I wished to pursue a career outside retailing. I left on excellent terms and can provide outstanding personal and professional references within the Macy's organization including from my immediate supervisor, Crawford McFarland, who would gladly welcome me back at any time.

I feel certain that I could make valuable contributions to your organization through the diversified management experience I have gained as a Senior Manager at Macy's. Although I am only 34 years old, I have controlled buying decisions of more than $5 million annually while refining my skills in prospecting, customer service, public relations, financial forecasting and financial analysis, and budgeting.

I am single and would cheerfully travel as your needs require. If you feel that my skills and background might be of interest to you, I hope you will contact me to suggest a time when we might meet in person. I am a hard worker and have become an excellent problem solver and negotiator through my nearly 13 years in retailing. Thank you in advance for your consideration of my skills.

Sincerely yours,

Christopher Jarvis

Date

Exact Name of Person
Title or Position
Name of Company
Address (number and street)
Address (city, state, and zip)

Dear Exact Name of Person: (or Dear Sir or Madam if answering a blind ad)

    I would appreciate an opportunity to talk with you soon about how I could contribute to your organization through my education in finance as well as through my reputation as a hardworking, knowledgeable, and dedicated professional.

    As you will see from my enclosed resume, I recently received my Bachelor of Business Administration (B.B.A.) degree with a concentration in Finance from The University of Colorado at Boulder. I personally financed my college education by working full time. I am especially proud of the fact that I accomplished this despite having to commute to classes while I was simultaneously advancing in jobs which required expertise in managing human and material resources as well as time.

    The majority of my experience with the retail giant Buy Mart has been in inventory control and support activities, but I have been given opportunities to apply my education and knowledge. Selected for a six-month assignment as a Billing and Data Processing Supervisor, I have also been involved in completing reports and audits which required financial skills.

    Although I have built a track record of accomplishments and have held supervisory positions since the age of 20 with this national retailer, I am ready for a career change which will allow more opportunity to apply my education in finance.

    If you can use a self-confident and self-motivated individual who is persistent and assertive, I hope you will contact me to suggest a time when we might meet to discuss your needs and how I might help you. Thank you in advance for your time.

Sincerely,

Gisela Myshka

Alternate last paragraph:
    I hope you will welcome my call soon to try to arrange a brief meeting to discuss your needs. Thank you in advance for your time.

Changing Careers from managing people to managing finances
In this letter, an individual with a newly minted degree in finance is attempting to move away from responsibilities for managing people to responsibilities for managing finances. With this letter, she will be able to approach Controllers of large companies while also exploring financial planning and financial consulting careers with organizations such as Solomon Smith Barney. She may also approach nonprofit organizations since they often like their top managers to be skilled in financial management.

Date

Exact Name of Person
Title or Position
Name of Company
Address (number and street)
Address (city, state, and zip)

**Changing Careers into the
pharmaceutical sales field**
In this letter, a grocery store
manager is seeking to transfer
her strong bottom-line
orientation and impressive
accomplishments in boosting
sales and profit into a new
industry. She is primarily
interested in the
pharmaceutical industry, and
the letter is designed to
acquaint pharmaceutical
companies with her knowledge
of the territory she would be
covering as well as with her
fine personal and professional
reputation. She is hoping that
the company will be willing to
train a highly motivated
producer who has excelled in
another industry.

Dear Exact Name of Person: (or Dear Sir or Madam if answering a blind ad)

I would appreciate an opportunity to talk with you soon about how I could contribute to your organization through my excellent sales, communication, and customer service skills. I am responding to your advertisement for a Pharmaceutical Sales Representative. I am very knowledgeable of the Dallas, TX, area and offer an outstanding personal and professional reputation in the community.

As you will see from my enclosed resume, I have been highly successful in sales and operations management with a major corporation. Beginning as a Customer Service Manager, I was promoted to manage stores with increasing sales volumes of $7 million, $8.5 million, and $11.5 million annually. In my current position, I have raised total sales by 20%, and profit levels by 25% through my aggressive sales orientation.

Although I am held in high regard by my employer and can provide outstanding references at the appropriate time, I have decided that I would like to apply my sales, customer service, and communication skills within the pharmaceutical sales field. I am certain that my sales ability and strong bottom-line orientation would be ideally suited to pharmaceutical sales. As a store manager, I have become very familiar with a wide range of pharmaceutical products as I have provided oversight of store merchandising, vendor relations, and product mix. I interact with pharmacists and other healthcare professionals with regard to the wide range of pharmaceutical products carried by the store.

With a B.S.B.A. degree, I possess an educational background which complements my sales and management experience. My highly developed communication skills, assertive personality, and time-management ability have allowed me to effectively manage as many as 100 employees. I offer a reputation as a forceful yet tactful salesperson who is able to present ideas as well as products in a powerful and convincing fashion.

I can assure you that this is a very deliberate attempt on my part to transition into the pharmaceutical sales field, and I hope you will call or write me soon to arrange a brief meeting to discuss your current and future needs and how I might serve them. Thank you in advance for your time.

Sincerely,

Gloria Pena

Date

Exact Name of Person
Exact Title
Exact Name of Company
Address
City, State Zip

Dear Sir or Madam:

CAREER-CHANGE
COVER LETTERS

With the enclosed resume describing my qualifications and experience, I would like to initiate the process of applying for a position as a Flight Attendant with your airline.

Changing Careers with the goal of becoming a flight attendant
A change from a small business environment into a major airline company often requires a career-change cover letter. In this case, a talented person with experience in numerous functional areas is expressing her desire to become an airline attendant, and she projects herself as a well-traveled individual with fluency in French who could deal with the public with poise and charm. She'll have to "sell herself" in an interview, but she needs a cover letter that will "blow the door open."

First Aid Knowledge

As you will see from my resume, I am knowledgeable of first aid procedures through my medical and scientific training in the area of anesthesiology.

Fluency in French

An American citizen, I am fluent in French. I have traveled extensively throughout the U.S. as well as in Germany, Greece, France, and the Caribbean. Although I became an American citizen at age 13, I was raised in the South of France in Gandrage.

Modeling Background

During my junior and senior years of high school, I was a part-time model for both a department store and for a meat packing plant which featured me on television commercials. After high school, the Wilhelmina Agency in New York recommended me for a runway modeling job in Paris because of my modeling ability and fluency in French.

Customer Relations and Management Experience

Most recently I have excelled as a small business manager, and I am skilled in dealing with the public, resolving problems in a gracious manner, and managing my time for maximum efficiency and profitability. I have developed my current customer base largely through word of mouth because of the excellent services I provide as well as my public relations skills. You will see from my resume that I have also worked as a hostess and waitress in the Hilton Hotel in Chicago, where I frequently served celebrity customers in an upscale restaurant/bar catering to the affluent.

Please send me information about the Flight Attendant career field with your airline, and I would be delighted to make myself available for a personal interview at the appropriate time. I can provide excellent personal and professional references.

Yours sincerely,

Angela Hapsburg

Date

Exact Name of Person
Exact Title
Exact Name of Company
Address
City, State Zip

Dear

Changing Careers from the
social services field to the
academic environment
Changing careers from social
services to academic
administration is the purpose
of this cover letter. Although
Ms. Bustier has enjoyed her
work in human services, she is
interested in obtaining her
Ph.D. and feels that she would
be better able to pursue this
goal if she were transplanted
to an academic institution.
What she is marketing to
academic institutions is her
managerial resourcefulness and
expertise in staff development.

With the enclosed resume, I would like to make you aware of the background in program management and staff development which I could put to work for your organization.

While excelling in the track record of advancement which you will see summarized on my resume, I have applied my strong organizational skills in implementing new programs, organizing conferences and seminars, training and counseling professional-level employees, and transforming ideas into operational realities. On numerous occasions, I have developed effective formats for formal written documents which have been described as "models."

In my current position, I have served as a Program Manager for the state of South Carolina while spearheading the development of new housing options and employment opportunities for the developmentally disabled and mentally impaired. With a reputation as a vibrant and persuasive communicator, I routinely interface with legislators, state and federal officials, as well as with local program managers. It has often been my responsibility to take a new law and make sure it is efficiently and resourcefully implemented at the local level while assuring compliance with federal and state guidelines. I am continuously involved in teaching and training others—not only the professionals whom I directly supervise but also professionals regionally and locally who turn to me for advice and assistance in problem solving.

I feel confident that my resourceful leadership, expertise in staff training and staff development, and pragmatic approach to operations management and service operations delivery could be valuable to your organization. If you feel you could use my considerable experience in initiating new programs, making existing programs work better, and establishing effective working relationships, I hope you will contact me to suggest a time when we might meet to discuss your needs and how I might serve them. I can provide outstanding personal and professional references at the appropriate time.

Yours sincerely,

Elaine Bustier

Date

Director of Personnel
City of Chesterfield
Grayson Hall, Suite 123
Chesterfield, VT 98231

Dear Sir or Madam:

**CAREER-CHANGE
COVER LETTERS**

**Changing Careers from
manager to fireman**
From store manager to fireman?
It's possible if the cover letter
can "blow the door open."
Notice how this young person
goes back to high school years
to cite a few of his
accomplishments and to market
his strong drive to excel in all
he does. Prospective employers
want to feel that you have the
kind of passion for a new field
that will see you through the
rocky period of intense training
and learning.

With the enclosed resume, I would like to formally initiate the process of becoming considered for a job as a Fireman within your organization.

As you will see when you read my resume, I have excelled in every job I have ever taken on. Currently I am a member of the management team for one of the area's largest and oldest furniture stores, and I have become skilled at problem solving and decision making. I began with the company in a part-time job, was hired full-time after one week, and have been promoted to increasing responsibilities because of my proven ability to make sound decisions under pressure.

While serving my country in the U.S. Army, I was promoted ahead of my peers to a job as Telecommunications Center Operator and earned numerous commendations for my management ability and technical skills. I was praised on numerous occasions for my ability to "think on my feet" and to make prudent decisions under stressful circumstances. I was entrusted with a Secret NAC security clearance.

Throughout my life, I have been known as a highly motivated self starter with a strong drive to excel in all I do. Even in high school, I was on the All-Star baseball team and was elected Captain of the football team in my senior year.

I am sending you my resume because it is my strong desire to make a career in the firefighting field, and I am willing to start in an entry-level position and prove myself. I am always seeking new ways in which to improve my skills and increase my knowledge; for example, I am learning Spanish in my spare time because I feel Spanish language skills will be an asset in any field with our growing Hispanic population. I can assure you that I would bring that same level of self motivation to firefighting as a career field.

I hope you will contact me to suggest a time when we might meet to discuss your needs and how I might serve them. I can provide outstanding personal and professional references at the appropriate time. Thank you in advance for whatever consideration and time you can give me in my goal of becoming a professional firefighter.

Sincerely,

Jorge Perez

Date

Exact Name of Person
Title or Position
Name of Company
Address (no., street)
Address (city, state, and zip)

Entrepreneur who has sold his business and is seeking a new challenge
We have placed the Cover Letters for Entrepreneurs Section next to the Career-Change Cover Letters because the intention of the cover letters in both cases is similar. On this page you will see a cover letter of an Entrepreneur seeking a career change after transitioning his business to new management. Although he has been in the antiques and oriental rugs business, he cites his accomplishments in founding profitable entities as the "fishbait" which he hopes will capture the attention of prospective employers in numerous industries. What employer can't use a savvy individual who could come in and triple sales?

Dear Exact Name of Person: (or Dear Sir or Madam if answering a blind ad)

I would appreciate an opportunity to talk with you soon about how I could contribute to your organization through my business management, sales, and communication skills.

As you will see from my resume, I have founded successful businesses, tripled the sales volume of an existing company, and directed projects which required someone who could take a concept and turn it into an operating reality. While excelling as a retailer and importer of products that included oriental rugs and English antiques, I have become accustomed to working with a discriminating customer base of people regionally who trust my taste and character. In addition to a proven "track record" of producing a profit, I have earned a reputation for honesty and reliability. I believe there is no substitute in business for a good reputation.

I am ready for a new challenge, and that is why I have, in the last several months, closed two of my business locations and turned over the management of the third operation to a family member. I want to apply my seasoned business judgement, along with my problem-solving and opportunity-finding skills, to new areas.

If you can use the expertise of a savvy and creative professional who is skilled at handling every aspect of business management, from sales and marketing to personnel and finance, I would enjoy talking with you informally about your needs and goals. A flexible and adaptable person who feels comfortable stepping into new situations, I am able to "size up" problems and opportunities quickly through the "lens" of experience. I pride myself on my ability to deal tactfully and effectively with everyone.

I hope you will welcome my call soon to arrange a brief meeting at your convenience to discuss your current and future needs and how I might serve them. Thank you in advance for your time.

Sincerely yours,

Desmond Vaughn

Date

Exact Name of Person
Title or Position
Name of Company
Address (number and street)
Address (city, state, and zip)

Dear Exact Name of Person: (or Sir or Madam if answering a blind ad)

With the enclosed resume, I would like to make you aware of my interest in contributing to your organization through my considerable management experience as well as my proven motivational, sales, and organizational skills.

Although most of my business savvy has come from "real-world" experience, I hold an M.S. degree in Business Administration, a Master's degree in Guidance and Counseling, and a B.S. degree. After earning my college degree, I worked as a High School Guidance Counselor, and economics forced me to seek a simultaneous part-time job as a Salesman for used and new cars with a prominent Ford dealership in Detroit. That part-time job opened my eyes to my talent for selling cars and motivating others, and thus began an impressive career in the automotive industry.

After attending Chevrolet's two-year Dealer Trainee Program, I became General Manager of a Chevrolet dealership in Indianapolis, IN. I was successful in turning around that dealership which had experienced multimillion-dollar losses in three previous years, and I led it to show a profit of $500,000—its first profit in four years. Subsequently I served as a consultant to start-up dealerships and to mature dealerships in need of a strong manager to resolve sales and profitability problems.

My first job was as General Sales Manager of Cross Roads Chevrolet, where I played a key role in increasing market penetration by 60%. I was then recruited to serve as President and General Manager of Twin City Chevrolet. I led the company to achieve gross sales of $32 million a year along with a $1 million profit-before-tax income for three consecutive years. We received the Outstanding Dealer's Award for three consecutive years and were recognized as a five-star dealer—the ultimate achievement in customer service—for two years. Most recently, I have managed a successful start-up of a used car dealership which became a major force in the market in less than two years.

I can provide excellent personal and professional references at the appropriate time, and I can assure you that I am a dynamic individual with an outstanding reputation within the industry along with an aggressive bottom-line orientation and a results-oriented style of interacting with others. Thank you in advance for your time.

Sincerely,

J.C. Longenecker

Date

Exact Name of Person
Title or Position
Name of Company
Address (number and street)
Address (city, state, and zip)

COVER LETTERS
FOR ENTREPRENEURS

Entrepreneur seeking to
return to a previous field
This successful entrepreneur is
seeking to return to a career
field he was in more than 10
years ago. At middle age, he
went back to college to earn
his B.S. degree and now wishes
to resume a career as a Golf
Course Superintendent.

Dear Exact Name of Person: (or Sir or Madam if answering a blind ad)

I would appreciate an opportunity to talk with you soon about how I could contribute to your organization through my experience as a golf course superintendent with a reputation as a creative and innovative manager of resources.

As you will see from my enclosed resume, I offer a strong history as a golf course superintendent with more than 15 years of experience at several successful and heavily played courses in the California area. I was highly effective in taking on the challenge of renovating and refurbishing courses which were in need of improvements. For two 150-acre courses located in residential developments and one private club, I brought about significant changes which transformed struggling facilities. While rebuilding these facilities, I applied abilities in areas which included hiring and training personnel, coordinating the renovation of capital equipment, planning for long-range success, and completing design projects for sprinkler layout, drainage, and reconstruction of greens, tees, and fairways. I also oversaw the design and installation of water reservoirs for irrigation, including a 110-acre reservoir at Rolling Hill Golf Course in San Diego.

My organizational and time management skills have been displayed more recently while attending college full-time, excelling academically, and simultaneously creating a successful residential landscape design business. Building on my earlier A.A. degree in Agronomy and Turf Production and golf course experience, I recently earned a B.S. in Agribusiness and Environmental Resources.

I would like to point out that I have relocated permanently to the Pittsburgh area to be near family members. If you can use an experienced golf course superintendent with a broad base of experience and well-developed abilities, I hope you will contact me to suggest a time when we might meet to discuss your needs. I can assure you in advance that I could rapidly become an asset to your organization.

Sincerely,

Reynold W. Krueger, Jr.

Date

Exact Name of Person
Title or Position
Name of Company
Address (number and street)
Address (city, state, and zip)

Dear Exact Name of Person: (or Sir or Madam if answering a blind ad)

With the enclosed resume, I would like to initiate the process of being considered for employment within your organization. I am a recent graduate of Clemson University with an excellent scientific education along with superior technical writing skills, experience in laboratory analysis and instrumental analysis, as well as some knowledge of medicinal chemistry.

While earning my B.S. in Chemistry, I excelled in courses including Medicinal Chemistry, which focused on modern pharmaceuticals, and Instrumental Analysis. I am skilled in operating equipment and devices including fluorescence spectrometers, atomic mass spectrometers, UV/VIS molecular absorption spectrometers, high performance liquid chromatography (HPLC), gas chromatography (GC), as well as IR/Raman spectrometers, NMR, and FTIR.

At Clemson, I was a popular tutor of Chemistry and Calculus, and I acted as a Mentor for 11 Engineering and Science students. During the summers while earning my college degree, I worked in technical environments which taught me much about teamwork. For example, in the summer of 1997 at Cutler Hammer, I worked on an assembly line assembling, inspecting, and packing electrical control panels. In the summer of 1995, I worked as a Procedure Writer for Westinghouse Savannah River Company, where I developed and revised Defense Waste Processing Operations Procedures with special emphasis on chemical processing procedures. In the summer of 1993, I worked as a Production Assistant for Black & Decker.

I feel confident that you would find me in person to be a warm and congenial individual who relates well to others and who offers excellent communication skills. While mentoring other Engineering and Science students at Clemson, I frequently mediated disputes and trained students to utilize conflict management techniques.

If you can use a sharp and astute young chemistry graduate who offers excellent analytical and communication skills, I hope you will contact me to suggest a time when we might meet in person. I am flexible and able to relocate according to your needs. Thank you in advance for your time.

Yours sincerely,

Sonya T. Blasock

First job in field for a Chemistry graduate
Chemistry graduate seeks first job in her field with a cover letter that emphasizes her tutoring experience and summer jobs. Students without experience in their field need to remember that their past work experience is relevant to prospective employers because it still shows the development of good work habits. Notice that this student mentions her unpaid work experience in mentoring students at Clemson.

Date

Exact Name of Person
Title or Position
Name of Company
Address (number and street)
Address (city, state, and zip)

**SEEKING FIRST JOB
IN FIELD**

**Computer Science graduate
emphasizes his maturity and
work experience which he
hopes will distinguish him
from other recent Computer
Science graduates.**
Remember when you are
marketing anything, including
yourself in a job hunt, you are
trying to market what is
unique about the product (or
you). In Mr. Harrell's case, he is
hoping that employers will be
impressed that he completed
his degree while excelling in a
demanding full-time job.

Dear Exact Name of Person: (or Sir or Madam if answering a blind ad)

With the enclosed resume, I would like to make you aware of my background as a versatile and experienced professional with a history of success in areas which include computer operations, logistics and supply, production control, and employee training and supervision.

As you will see, I have completed my bachelor's degree in Computer Science from Devry College. I am proud of my accomplishment in completing this course of study while simultaneously meeting the demands of a career in the U.S. Army. In my current military assignment as a Technical Inspector at Ft. Carson, CO, I ensure the airworthiness of aircraft required to relocate anywhere in the world on extremely short notice in response to crisis situations.

Throughout my years of military service I have been singled out for jobs which have required the ability to quickly make sound decisions and have continually maximized resources while exceeding expected standards and performance guidelines. I have been responsible for certifying multimillion-dollar aircraft for flight service, training and supervising employees who have been highly productive and successful in their own careers, and applying technical computer knowledge in innovative ways which have further increased efficiency and productivity.

I offer a combination of technical, managerial, and supervisory skills which will allow me to quickly achieve outstanding results in anything I attempt. Known for my energy and enthusiasm, I am a creative and talented professional with a strong desire to make a difference in whatever setting and environment I find myself.

I hope you will contact me to suggest a time when we might meet to discuss your needs. I can assure you in advance that I could rapidly become an asset to your organization.

Sincerely,

Rob Harrell

Date

Exact Name of Person
Title or Position
Name of Company
Address (number and street)
Address (city, state, and zip)

Dear Exact Name of Person: (or Sir or Madam if answering a blind ad)

With the enclosed resume, I would like to initiate the process of being considered for employment within your organization.

As you will see from my resume, I will receive on May 10 a Bachelor of Arts degree in English with a minor in French and Writing, and I have excelled academically. I have worked as a Staff Writer for my college newspaper, and I have become skilled at composing copy that requires little editing and in meeting tight deadlines. I have also tutored students in both English and French.

In an internship as an Advertising Copywriter with a respected and award-winning advertising agency, I created copy for the agency's web page, wrote a newsletter aimed at children, and compiled a portfolio of sample ads which was received quite favorably by my supervisor. In a summer job with a magazine in Arizona, I worked in the distribution and circulation part of the business and became a valuable part of the magazine's staff within a short period of time.

Although I have limited hands-on experience simply because I am 20 years old, I can assure you that I am an accomplished writer. I have been published in Tapestries and in The National Book of Poetry. My life experiences have been quite diverse as I have traveled extensively worldwide including in Europe and Africa as well as South America. I lived and worked in India last summer.

I can provide outstanding personal and professional references at the appropriate time, and I can assure you that you would find me to be a hardworking, congenial individual who prides myself on always doing my best. If you can use a hard worker who could become a valuable part of your organization through my creativity and language skills, I hope you will contact me to suggest a time when I can make myself available for a personal interview at your convenience. Thank you in advance for your time.

Sincerely,

Madeline A Pereira

Date

Exact Name of Person
Exact Title
Exact Name of Company
Exact Address
City, State Zip

SEEKING FIRST JOB IN FIELD

History graduate emphasizes that the company he worked for during college had offered him a full-time job upon college graduation. Employers are looking for people who are highly regarded by other employers, because they generally feel that if your current employer thinks highly of you, it is because of your good attitude and excellent work. Notice that a cover letter can make the employer aware of the best times to reach you, if you are often unavailable during the day.

Dear Sir or Madam:

With the enclosed resume, I would like to make you aware of my interest in your organization and to acquaint you with the considerable talents and skills I could put to work for you.

As you will see from my resume, I recently earned my B.A. degree in History from North Carolina State University, and I was offered a full-time management position immediately upon graduation with the company for which I had worked throughout college. In my current position, I manage a wide range of functional areas for a large cinema complex. My responsibilities include training and hiring employees, overseeing cash control and assuring accurate financial management, auditing a wide range of activities, and assuring outstanding public relations and customer service. While working for the company on weekends and during summers and other breaks throughout college, I was named Employee of the Month five times and I earned a reputation as a hard worker known for the highest standards of reliability, integrity, and initiative.

Although I am held in high regard in my current position and am being groomed for further promotion by the company's owners, I am interested in applying my management skills in a more traditional business environment. I can provide excellent personal and professional references at the appropriate time.

Since the cinema business is generally an afternoon and night-time business, I am usually at work from 5 p.m. to midnight, so you would be able to reach me at home most mornings. Thursday is my regular day off, so I could make myself available to meet with you personally on any Thursday or perhaps on another day if arrangements were made well in advance. I feel certain that you will find me to be a dynamic young professional whose abilities could enhance your organization.

Sincerely,

James Ray Watkins

Date

Exact Name of Person
Title or Position
Name of Company
Address (number and street)
Address (city, state, and zip)

Dear Exact Name of Person: (or Sir or Madam if answering a blind ad)

I would appreciate an opportunity to talk with you soon about how I could contribute to WKRG TV-3 as a Salesperson.

As you will see from my enclosed resume, I am an experienced retail salesperson with a college background in Media Journalism and English. Although I have no previous experience in broadcast sales, I feel that my intelligence, educational background, and exceptional written and verbal communication skills would more than make up for any lack of practical experience.

I have a strong history of success in leadership roles and in environments where I have excelled in selling my ideas and concepts to others. Beginning with my days as student body president of my high school, on through college volunteer activities requiring negotiating and communication skills, I have always been highly effective in getting my views across to others in a persuasive and effective manner while still displaying tact and an understanding of their views.

One area that I did not mention on my resume but would like to point out now is that while I was in college, I was given an opportunity to write public service announcements and then represent a writing class by presenting them on the air on a new campus radio station.

I believe that I have high levels of raw talent, enthusiasm, and energy that would translate into successful sales for your station and allow me to become a productive member of your sales force. I hope you will welcome my call soon to arrange a brief meeting at your convenience to discuss WKRG TV-3's present and future needs, and how I might serve them. Thank you in advance for your time.

Sincerely yours,

Rainey L. Crocker

Date

Exact Name of Person
Title or Position
Name of Company
Address (number and street)
Address (city, state, and zip)

Dear Exact Name of Person: (or Dear Sir or Madam if answering a blind ad)

With the enclosed resume, I would like to make you aware of my interest in employment with your organization and acquaint you with the considerable experience and skills I could offer you.

As a Candidate for a B.S. in Nursing, I am maintaining a 3.7 G.P.A. in my Nursing Program at Duke University. I also hold a B.A. in Political Science from Emory University in Atlanta (G.P.A. 3.6) and, prior to transferring to Duke from Emory, I had a 3.6 G.P.A. in Political Science Studies. After volunteering at Emory Medical Center I knew I wanted to pursue a nursing career and I transferred to Duke after two years at Emory.

You will see from my resume that I am currently working as a Nurse's Aide II in the Surgical ICU at University of North Carolina at Chapel Hill Medical Center. I was offered this job after excelling in my summer externship in Surgical ICU at UNC-CH Medical Center. I have tremendously enjoyed my work in Surgical ICU and can provide outstanding professional references from those who have observed or supervised my enthusiastic, caring, and professional approach to caring for ICU patients.

I have also performed seven-week clinical rotations in orthopedic, pediatric, psychiatric, OB/GYN, community health, and surgical ICU environments at Duke Hospitals, Durham County Hospital, Raleigh Health Clinic, and Chapel Hill Medical Center. For two semesters at Emory in 1997, I was privileged to be able to work with a pediatric hematologist/oncologist in setting up a database for patients with neutropenia. After we set up this database, patients with the condition were able to receive very expensive treatment, G-CSF, at no cost while the pharmaceutical company providing the drug conducted research on the condition and the drug's effects. I have also worked in jobs as a bank teller and student assistant during the summers and school years.

Please give me every consideration for employment, as I can assure you that you would be taking on a dedicated young professional who offers a true commitment to the nursing profession. I would be delighted to make myself available for personal interviews at your convenience. Thank you very much for your consideration of my talents, skills, and experience.

Yours sincerely,

Faith A. Staszewski

Date

Exact Name of Person
Title or Position
Name of Company
Address (number and street)
Address (city, state, and zip)

Dear Exact Name of Person: (or Sir or Madam if answering a blind ad)

SEEKING FIRST JOB
IN FIELD

Sociology and Social Work
graduate emphasizes his
internship and peer mentor
experience.

With the enclosed resume, I would like to make you aware of my interest in being considered for employment within your organization in any capacity in which you could utilize my versatile knowledge related to human resources and human services as well as my communication skills, management abilities, and computer operations knowledge.

Since graduation I have been excelling in a job as a Management Trainee but I am seeking a position in which I can utilize my education in sociology and social work. You will see from my resume that I completed a Social Work Internship at Walker Senior High School where I earned a reputation as a highly motivated individual who was most effective in working with at-risk juveniles. Indeed, as an upperclassman during my junior and senior years at Michigan State University, I served as a Peer Mentor helping incoming freshmen transition into college life. Through my experience as a Peer Mentor and as a Social Work Intern, I gained insights into the particular problems faced by first-generation college students and by low-income students.

Although this individual is in a
Management Trainee position
(notice he omits mentioning
the industry in which he is
currently working), he is
yearning to obtain a position
in the field for which he
obtained a college degree. He
is trying to come across as a
young professional committed
to making a difference in his
chosen field, not just making a
living in any type of work.

In a part-time job while earning my degree, I refined my counseling and interviewing skills as an M.A.S. Administrator at the V.A. Medical Center, where I interviewed Persian Gulf and Vietnam veterans.

While in college I had several field experiences relevant to social work and sociology. In one situation I functioned as a Home Assistant, working with Thomas A (mentally challenged) adults and assisting those consumers in acquiring more independence and mastery of their everyday activities. In another situation as an Autism Therapist, I worked with an autistic child in a private home.

I hope you will give me an opportunity to talk with you in person because I am sure that my personal qualities and professional skills could enhance your organization's goals. Thank you in advance for your consideration.

Sincerely,

Leo Martelli

Part II: Cover Letters by Field, Occupation, Profession, and Industry

In the previous section, you saw cover letters for individuals changing fields, seeking their first job in their field, or moving into a different type of work. If you are changing fields or industries, you usually need to "translate" what you've been doing into language that employers in other industries will understand.

In this section, you will find cover letters of professionals in many different fields and industries. Frequently these individuals are seeking to advance in their current field or industry, although there are exceptions. For example, in the "Military Transition" section, some of the letters were written for people who were in career change or who weren't sure what they wanted to do next. Often, however, these cover letters are designed to communicate with other experienced professionals in the field. The cover letters are arranged by alphabetical order by field, industry, profession, or occupation. If you don't find yourself here, consult the Table of Contents and find a category close to the industry or field you are in.

Accounting, Banking, and Finance
Aviation
Clerical, Secretarial and Administrative Support
Computer Operations
Construction
Distribution and Warehousing
Electronics
Engineering
Health Care
Human Resources
Journalism
Legal and Paralegal
Linguists
Logistics and Supply
Maintenance and Production
Management
Manufacturing
Marketing
Media and Public Relations
Medical
Military Transition
Nonprofit Management
Police, Security, and Law Enforcement
Quality & Safety
Restaurants, Hotels, and Food Service
Retailing
Sales
Social Work & Human Services
Sports
Teaching
Telecommunications
Transportation

Date

Exact Name of Person
Title or Position
Name of Company
Address (number and street)
Address (city, state, and zip)

Dear Exact Name of Person: (or Sir or Madam if answering a blind ad)

Accounting Professional
This accounting professional
with payroll expertise is seeking
to advance her career by
moving to a company which
will allow her to assume
responsibilities on a higher
level. Notice how this cover
letter begins with a question.

Can you use an experienced accounting professional with exceptional supervisory, organizational, and communications skills as well as a background in payroll and benefits administration, accounts receivable/payable, and payroll tax regulations in multistate and multiunit environments?

As you will see, I have excelled as Payroll Administrator for the manufacturing division of International Imports furniture company, where I managed a $52 million annual payroll for three facilities employing more than 800 personnel. I created, updated, and maintained employee files, entering new hires and terminated employees into the system. In addition, I acted as liaison between the employees and the garnishment trustees of various organizations, such as the IRS and the bankruptcy courts, and interacted with Social Services and various lending institutions regarding various issues related to the verification of employment, child support, and salary information.

In a previous position with Par For The Course Miniature Golf Courses of America, I managed a $3 million annual payroll for 400-750 employees. I prepared daily sales recaps, state and federal payroll taxes, federal and state quarterly and annual tax forms, and monthly sales tax reports for a multicourse, multistate operation. In a previous job as a Supervising Accounting Clerk, I supervised five accounting clerks and prepared financial statements for the corporation.

Highly computer literate, I am skilled in utilizing popular computer accounting and office-related software, including the ADP payroll software, Access, Excel, QuickBooks, Lotus 1-2-3, and Quicken.

If you can use a self-motivated and experienced accounting professional with extensive payroll and benefits administration experience, I would enjoy the opportunity to meet with you in person to discuss your needs. I assure you in advance that I have an outstanding reputation and can provide excellent references.

Sincerely,

Rita Carvalho

Date

Exact Name of Person
Title or Position
Name of Company
Address (number and street)
Address (city, state, and zip)

Dear Exact Name of Person: (or Sir or Madam if answering a blind ad)

With the enclosed resume, I would like to make you aware of my background which includes a Bachelor's degree in Business Management with a concentration in Finance along with experience in branch banking as well as finance and administration.

Banking Professional
This banking professional is moving toward the financial services area and is communicating the fact that he is currently preparing for his Series 7 and 63 licenses. This shows his commitment to his field.

After earning my degree with honors, I built a track record of accomplishments with National West Bank of Phoenix and Scottsdale, AZ, where I was a Customer Sales and Service Representative. I recently received the "Top Shop Award" and achieved the highest scores in the region following an independent evaluation of sales and customer service processors. Originally hired as a Teller while still attending college, I quickly became the Head Teller for the branch before earning promotion to the Customer Service and Sales Rep position.

Currently preparing for my Series 7 and 63 licenses in stocks and mutual funds, I have become known as a highly articulate, intelligent, and talented professional.

Skilled in dealing with people of all ages and cultures, I have a great deal to offer any organization in need of a highly motivated young professional with a strong bottom-line orientation. I hope you will contact me to suggest a time when we might meet to discuss your needs. I can assure you in advance that I could rapidly become an asset to your organization.

Sincerely,

Gerry Wilkes

Notice the alternate last paragraph, which is a more aggressive way to end the cover letter. It's always better if you call to follow up on the letter you send. This communicates your strong interest and persistence.

Alternate last paragraph:
I hope you will welcome my call soon when I try to arrange a brief meeting with you to discuss your needs and my interest in your organization. Thank you in advance for your time.

Date

Exact Name of Person
Title or Position
Name of Company
Address (number and street)
Address (city, state, and zip)

Dear Exact Name of Person: (or Dear Sir or Madam if answering a blind ad)

Banking Professional
Sometimes professionals who
relocate from other countries
have a difficult time
communicating what they
have been doing, even if they
are trying to remain in the
same industry. This banking
professional has recently
relocated from England
and is seeking a U.S.
banking position.

With the enclosed resume, I would like to make you aware of my interest in joining your organization in some capacity which could utilize my banking industry background.

You will see from my resume that I offer a proven track record of accomplishment with the Bank of the United Kingdom in England, where I began as a Teller and was promoted into management responsibilities which involved selling mutual funds, supervising employees, and managing multimillion-dollar portfolios of mortgages, car loans, and student loans. I have excelled as a Consumer Credit Officer, Assistant Manager of the Consumer Credit Department, and Senior Personal Banking Officer. Prior to relocating to Texas, I was being groomed for advancement to a more senior level responsible for handling liaison with the bank's most valuable customers and managing even larger portfolios.

My husband, who is a Registered Nurse, was recently recruited by Corpus Christi Medical Center, so we relocated to Texas at that time. I have been in the process of establishing U.S. residency and obtaining a work permit so that I can resume my career in financial services.

With a reputation as a versatile professional with a proven ability to profitably manage a loan portfolio and provide outstanding service to VIP clients as well as others, I can provide outstanding personal and professional references. Just as you will notice my history of loyalty to the Bank of the United Kingdom, I am seeking to join a company where I could make long-term contributions and eventually become a valuable part of the management team.

If you can use a knowledgeable financial services professional known for my professional demeanor, commitment to quality service, and total attention to detail in all matters, I hope you will contact me to suggest a time when we might meet to discuss how I might fit into your organizational structure. I am a dedicated hard worker and can assure you in advance that I could rapidly apply my extensive knowledge and experience in ways that would produce valuable bottom-line results.

Yours sincerely,

Gillian Andrews

Date

Exact Name of Person
Title or Position
Name of Company
Address (number and street)
Address (city, state, and zip)

Dear Exact Name of Person: (or Sir or Madam if answering a blind ad)

Controller
This controller with experience
as a Chief Financial Officer is
seeking employment
opportunities in her field.

With the enclosed resume, I would like to formally make you aware of my interest in exploring employment opportunities within your organization.

As you will see from my resume, I have excelled in a variety of assignments which required outstanding accounting, customer service, and management skills. In my current position as Controller, I prepare monthly financial statements and year-end financials while also supervising ten people in the accounting department including an assistant controller as well as the MIS and accounts payable/receivable personnel. I wrote this 30-year-old company's first policies and procedures manual. While in control of $5 million in inventory, I have developed procedures whereby the company will be processing inventory by barcode at its nine locations.

In my prior job, I rose to Chief Financial Officer for a diversified corporation with holdings in the construction industry and restaurant business. For one of the company's divisions, I was personally responsible for leading the limited partnership's reorganization out of Chapter 11 bankruptcy and, after leading the company out of bankruptcy, the company posted a 7% net profit within the first year.

Here's a tip: Try to avoid
starting every sentence in the
cover letter with "I." That
repetition gets boring for your
reader. Notice the technique
used in this cover letter to
avoid doing that. Your cover
letters will sound more
polished if you put this tip
into practice.

Knowledgeable of software including Depreciation Solution, Computer Systems Dynamics (CSD) programs, and Microsoft Office 97, I have demonstrated my capabilities in many areas including: customer service and general management; property development and construction project management; contract development and negotiation; debt structure reorganization; information systems and data processing administration; and computer systems implementation and administration.

If you can use a hardworking and reliable professional with knowledge in numerous operational areas, I hope you will contact me to suggest a time when we might meet to discuss your needs and how I might serve them. I can provide outstanding personal and professional references. Thank you in advance for your time, and I would appreciate your holding my interest in your company in the strictest confidence at this point.

Yours sincerely,

Michelle Bazaldua

Date

Exact Name of Person
Title or Position
Name of Company
Address (number and street)
Address (city, state, and zip)

Dear Exact Name of Person: (or Sir or Madam if answering a blind ad)

With the enclosed resume, I would like to formally respond to your advertisement for a Controller for Jarvis Manufacturing, Inc.

As you will see from my resume, I am a C.P.A. currently working in the firm of Covington, Davis, Young, and Co., LLP. I hold a Bachelor of Accounting from University of Nevada at Las Vegas.

Highly computer proficient, I am skilled in the use of Excel spreadsheets and knowledgeable of numerous accounting software programs. While assisting in audits of nonprofit and commercial statements, I have been exposed to the full range of accounting functions including payables, receivables, payroll, and payroll reports. I am skilled in preparing corporate tax returns.

Although I am excelling in my current position, I am attracted to your ad because of your company's fine reputation. I am somewhat familiar with the reputation of the founder, John Maxwell, and feel that I can make a significant contribution to a profit-making corporation. I offer outstanding personal and professional references.

I would be delighted to discuss my salary history with you in person, and I appreciate your thoughtful consideration of my background as well as my genuine interest in your company.

Yours sincerely,

Sue Hoffman, C.P.A.

Certified Public Accountant (C.P.A.)
This C.P.A. seeks a position as a controller. She indicates in her cover letter that she is selectively exploring opportunities in firms to which she is attracted because of their strong reputation.

Here's a tip: If the ad asks for your salary history, it's usually best to respond in the way that this C.P.A. has responded. Companies will normally interview you anyway if you seem to fit their needs, and it's best for you not to "name your numbers" before the interview.

Date

Exact Name
Exact Title
Exact Name of Company
Exact Address
City, State Zip

Dear Sir or Madam:

With the enclosed resume, I would like to make you aware of the considerable experience in credit and collections which I could put to work for you.

As you will see from my resume, prior to moving to Tulsa to live near my extended family, I was excelling as an Accounts Manager and Collections Specialist with Consumer Sales Finance, Inc., in Oklahoma City. Because of my hardworking nature as well as my skills in negotiating and resolving difficult problems related to past due accounts, I was selected as Team Leader for the agency with the responsibility of training new employees. I utilized the Dialex Power Dialer in making up to 150 calls daily while collecting on electrical, medical, and fitness accounts as well as others. I am skilled at obtaining credit information and in skiptracing delinquent customers. I have handled both voluntary and involuntary repossessions.

In a previous job I handled collections as well as other duties for a medical practice, and I also handled credit and collections for Online Information Services in Oklahoma City. In every collections job I have held, I have always been selected to train new employees and have exceeded all quotas for my personal productivity.

If you can use my considerable skills and experience, I hope you will contact me to suggest a time when we might meet in person to discuss your needs and how I might serve them. I can provide outstanding personal and professional references at the appropriate time. Thank you in advance for your time.

Yours sincerely,

Roni Jeffries

Credit and Collections Specialist

Many companies can use a credit and collections specialist. Ms. Jeffries will be able to use this letter in applying for positions with a variety of companies. Since the most recent job on her resume will be in another state, notice how she explains to prospective employers why she has relocated to Tulsa.

Here's a tip: If you are moving to a new town, and if the last job shown on your resume is in another city, use the cover letter to tell the employer what's going on in your life and why you have moved. See the cover letter on the next page to see how a relocation can be explained in the first paragraph.

Date

Exact Name of Person
Title or Position
Name of Company
Address (number and street)
Address (city, state, and zip)

ACCOUNTING, BANKING, AND
FINANCE

**Consumer Lending Professional
with Credit Union Experience**
Employers are curious about
why people left their last job.
Cover letters provide an
excellent opportunity to satisfy
the employer's curiosity.
In this case, the individual
resigned and has relocated
for family reasons.

Dear Exact Name of Person: (or Sir or Madam if answering a blind ad)

With the enclosed resume, I would like to make you aware of an experienced financial industry professional with exceptional communication, motivational, and supervisory skills and a background in branch management, consumer lending, and account management in credit union environments. Although I was highly regarded by my most recent employer and can provide outstanding personal and professional references at the appropriate time, I have resigned my most recent position and am permanently relocating to Oregon in order to be closer to my family.

As you will see, I have been excelling with Pentagon Federal Credit Union, advancing in a track record of increasing responsibility. In my most recent position as branch manager of the busy Washington location, I supervised a staff of 18 employees, including two loan officers. I developed and implemented an annual operating budget of $700,000 and oversaw the administration of a $2 million change fund. By developing innovative and effective business and marketing plans, I increased membership by 67%, loan dollars by 271%, and number of product sales per visit by 151%.

In a previous job as assistant manager of the telephone call center in Alexandria, I supervised 25 employees handling 1,500 calls per day to provide members with banking services by phone. I acted as manager in my supervisor's absence, and also served as a loan officer, with authority over $90,000 in aggregate indebtedness. In a prior job as an account researcher, I reorganized the work flow to increase the effectiveness of the accounts research staff and created computerized versions of account reports and other documents.

With a Bachelor of Science in Business from the University of Virginia, I supplemented my degree program with numerous finance and accounting courses.

If you can use a self-motivated and experienced financial professional with exceptional communication, motivational, and supervisory skills, I would enjoy talking with you and discussing your needs. I hope I will have the pleasure of hearing from you soon to suggest a time when we might meet in person.

Sincerely,

Carolyn H. Pracht

Date

Exact Name of Person
Title or Position
Name of Company
Address (number and street)
Address (city, state, and zip)

Dear Exact Name of Person: (or Sir or Madam if answering a blind ad)

Controller
This controller has an unusual history since he is a middle-aged professional who has worked for only one employer in his life. His company recently reorganized and he was offered a position in another state, but he has decided to stay in the state where he has put down roots. Notice how a cover letter can provide the employer with your personal history and answer the question, "Why is he no longer with his longtime employer?"

With the enclosed resume, I would like to make you aware of my considerable experience in the area of accounting, finance, budgeting, and controlling.

As you will see from my resume, I have a rather unusual work history since I have worked for only one company. I began with U-Move Truck Rental, Inc., and was promoted through the ranks until I became a District Controller for one of U-Move's 90 districts. For a district with a fleet of 800 vehicles, I received extensive recognition for exemplary performance in accounts receivable management as well as prudent accounting management in all areas.

In the last year, U-Move has been engaged in a process of eliminating administrative services performed at the district level and moving them to a Shared Services Center in Orlando. I have played a key role in helping customers and staff adapt to the new concept. Although I have been strongly encouraged to be part of the restructured organization, I do not wish to move to Orlando. I can provide outstanding references at the appropriate time.

If you can use a professional with extensive experience in managing people while managing the bottom line for maximum profitability, I hope you will contact me to suggest a time when we might meet to discuss your needs. I am confident that I could become a valuable addition to your management team.

Yours sincerely,

Carlos Rodriguez

More aggressive final paragraph:
I hope you will welcome my call soon when I try to arrange a brief meeting with you to discuss your goals and how I might help you achieve them. I can assure you in advance that I have a strong bottom-line orientation and am known for my resourceful problem-solving style.

Date

Exact Name of Person
Title or Position
Name of Company
Address (number and street)
Address (city, state, and zip)

Financial Planning Manager
This financial planning
manager emphasizes sales and
marketing skills as well as
investing knowledge. Notice
how he mentions something
that he did for fun: founding
an investment club. That
might be just the tidbit that
sets him apart from his
competition in this job hunt.

Dear Exact Name of Person: (or Sir or Madam if answering a blind ad)

With the enclosed resume, I would like to initiate the process of being considered for employment within your organization in some capacity in which you can use my extensive knowledge of finance and investing combined with my leadership skills, management experience, and resourceful problem-solving style.

In my most recent position, I have come to be regarded as an astute manager of financial resources while analyzing and preparing financial plans and investment programs for individuals and families. On my own initiative and in my spare time, I have also founded and serve as President of a popular investment club with members from four states, and I have provided the leadership and financial expertise needed to keep the club's bank and investment portfolio and accounts active and profitable. I offer highly refined sales and marketing skills.

Prior to my current job in the financial services industry, I earned a Master's degree in Human Resources in addition to a B.A. in Economics while simultaneously serving as Director of Training and Human Resources for a crisis-oriented medical evacuation company which responded to worldwide emergencies. In that job I worked with international officials and humanitarian relief organizations as I streamlined internal operating procedures to ensure greater efficiency.

Here's a tip: Remember that
you are writing the cover letter
to try to distinguish yourself
from the others in your field.
Try to mention an
accomplishment that will make
you stand out from colleagues
with similar credentials and
background.

If you can use a sharp and experienced young manager with an aggressive bottom-line orientation, I feel certain that my versatile background could be valuable to you. I am accustomed to working in environments where creative "opportunity finding" and resourceful problem solving are the keys to success. I can provide outstanding personal and professional references at the appropriate time. I hope you will contact me soon to suggest a time when we might meet in person to discuss your needs and how my background might serve those needs.

Sincerely,

Robert K. Streight

Date

Exact Name of Person
Title or Position
Name of Company
Address (number and street)
Address (city, state, and zip)

Dear Exact Name of Person: (or Sir or Madam if answering a blind ad)

Financial Planner
Here is a cover letter used by a
financial planner to respond to
an advertisement for a
Financial Analyst position.
Notice that she emphasizes her
creativity in developing and
implementing a new
marketing system that boosted
her client base. Also notice
that she didn't explain or
define the marketing system.
She is trying to pique the
employer's interest.

With the enclosed resume, I would like to make you aware of my strong interest in receiving consideration for the position of Analyst which you recently advertised in the *Atlanta Observer-Times*.

As you will see, I am presently a Financial Adviser and Branch Manager for IFG Network Securities at the Southern Central branch office. When I stepped into this position, I took over a client base of approximately 100 people and, in just over a year, doubled it to 220 clients. With Life & Health and Long-Term Care Insurance Licenses in addition to my Series 6, 22, 63, and 65 Securities Licenses, I manage assets which include stocks, bonds, mutual funds, and partnerships for clients throughout the southeastern region of the country. One of the changes which has allowed me to double my client base so quickly was my development and implementation of a new marketing system which has been highly effective.

Currently pursuing my M.B.A. at the University of Atlanta, I have completed more than half of the degree requirements. I hold a B.S. in Business Administration from Chicago University with a minor in Economics.

Prior experience includes working as a Travel Consultant and Bookstore Manager as well as completing H&R Block training leading to certification as a Tax Preparer/Consultant. You will see that most of my experience has required an individual who can work well independently while displaying strong analytical and problem-solving skills.

I am confident that I possess the skills, experience, and knowledge the City of Atlanta is seeking in candidates for this job. I hope to hear from you soon to arrange a time when we could meet to discuss your current and future needs and how I might help meet them. I can assure you in advance that I have an excellent reputation as a mature and reliable professional and would rapidly become an asset to your organization.

Sincerely,

Terri Cavaness

Date

Mr. David Turner
Chief of Operations
Robins AFB

By fax to: 910-483-6611

Dear Mr. Turner:

Air Traffic Controller
With this cover letter, an experienced Air Traffic Controller is attempting to explore opportunities with an organization that can utilize his experience in budgeting, quality assurance, safety, and management. He wants to stay in his field.

With the enclosed resume, I would like to make you aware of the considerable aviation expertise and quality control experience I could put to work for you.

As you will see from my resume, I have been working as Air Traffic Controller in flight operations at Davis Air Force Base, one of the military's busiest airlift hubs. Through my background as a pilot, I have been able to make significant contributions in staff development and employee training because I have been able to help flight tower and other personnel better understand the concerns of aircrews. By applying my managerial skills, I have cut personnel costs by 35% without compromising our emphasis on safety and quality control. I am skilled at numerous aspects of airport management.

In previous experience with the U.S. Air Force, I gained expertise in quality assurance and inspections while acting as an Aircrew Loadmaster. In another job as an Aircraft Dispatcher with the Department of Defense, I managed a $3.5 million budget subdivided into 204 areas. In addition to gaining expertise in managing a multimillion-dollar budget, I became proficient in managing multiple priorities while coordinating the utilization of human and physical resources in volatile conditions.

Here's a tip: Avoid using a word more than once or twice in the cover letter. Proofread your cover letter to make sure you haven't used the same word numerous times. For words like "skill," for example, you can find synonyms such as "ability," "proficiency," "competence," and so forth.

Throughout my work experience with the Air Force and Department of Defense, I have earned a reputation as a resourceful problem solver and skillful analyst who is capable of functioning with poise during emergencies. In every job I have held, I have become the individual to whom others have turned during crises and situations when many are in panic. I have learned to make decisions and solve problems in circumstances in which there is no room for error.

I would enjoy using my decision-making, problem-solving, and opportunity-finding skills in whatever capacity you feel you could best utilize them, and I hope you will contact me if you feel you have a suitable opportunity in mind.

Yours sincerely,

Jason Knight

Date

Exact Name of Person
Title or Position
Name of Company
Address (number and street)
Address (city, state, and zip)

Dear Exact Name of Person: (or Sir or Madam if answering a blind ad)

AVIATION

Airport Manager
Here is a cover letter for an
airport manager whose
experience has been in military
environments. One of the
things she mentions in her
cover letter is that she is an
experienced pilot.

I would appreciate an opportunity to talk with you soon about how I could contribute to your organization through the application of the human, material, and fiscal resource management abilities I am refining while earning rapid advancement as a military officer.

As you will see from my enclosed resume, I am presently the manager of an Alaskan airport which serves both the military post of Ft. Richardson and the civilian community of Anchorage. One of the most critical aspects of this job is public relations—developing and maintaining open lines of communication with a variety of representatives throughout the community. I am involved in such diverse activities as developing funding plans and controlling a $236,000 annual operating budget as well as supervising air traffic control, refueling, weather, and crash/rescue support functions.

While building a reputation as a calm and resourceful problem solver with sound judgment, I have excelled as a fixed and rotary wing pilot. As I earned rapid advancement to my present rank of Captain in the U.S. Army, I attracted the attention and respect of my superiors for my managerial skills and was selected for highly visible management positions. I have built a track record of outstanding results in every assignment whether developing and overseeing training programs, managing maintenance operations, or developing and implementing physical security programs.

If you can use an experienced and mature professional who is adaptable and assertive with a talent for maximizing resources and finding ways to get the most out of employees by setting the example and expecting only the best from others, I assure you in advance that I could rapidly become an asset to your organization. Please call or write me soon to suggest a convenient time for us to meet to discuss my qualifications and how I could contribute to your organization. Thank you in advance.

Sincerely,

Sharon M. Dobranski

Date

Exact Name of Person
Title or Position
Name of Company
Address (number and street)
Address (city, state, and zip)

Dear Exact Name of Person: (or Sir or Madam if answering a blind ad)

Airframe and Power Plant Mechanic

Here you see the cover letter of an Airframe and Power Plant Mechanic with a background as a Technical Inspector. His background is military and he is attempting to transfer his skills and knowledge to the civilian world.

I would appreciate an opportunity to talk with you soon about how I could contribute to your organization through my experience and training in the areas of aircraft maintenance and technical inspection gained while serving my country in the U.S. Army.

As you will see from my enclosed resume, I have my FAA Airframe and Power Plant License and earned excellent scores in military training programs which evaluated technical skills and knowledge as well as written and verbal communication, leadership, and analytical abilities.

Recently promoted to the position of Technical Inspector after building a reputation as a knowledgeable and productive Crew Chief, I oversee technicians maintaining eight multimillion-dollar OH-58D(I) Advanced Scout helicopters. I have been singled out to receive several medals in recognition of my technical expertise, ability to train and motivate others, and familiarity with support activities such as record keeping and documentation of maintenance activities, hazardous material handling and disposal, workplace safety, and weights and balances.

A hardworking, dedicated professional, I offer a broad range of knowledge and skills related to aircraft maintenance. I am confident that I can make valuable contributions to an aircraft maintenance facility through my mechanical skills as well as my leadership abilities.

I hope you will contact me to suggest a time when we might meet to discuss your needs. I can assure you that I can provide excellent references and could rapidly become an asset to your organization.

Sincerely,

Clyde E. Pearson

More aggressive final paragraph:
I hope you will welcome my call soon when I try to arrange a brief meeting with you to discuss your goals and how I might help you achieve them. I can provide outstanding references at the appropriate time. I can assure you in advance that I have a strong bottom-line orientation and am known for my resourceful problem-solving style.

Date

Exact Name of Person
Title or Position
Name of Company
Address (number and street)
Address (city, state, and zip)

Dear Exact Name of Person: (or Sir or Madam if answering a blind ad)

With the enclosed resume, I would like to make you aware of my interest in becoming associated with Friendly Air Airlines as a pilot.

Currently I am flying the Mexicair Regional Jet for Southeastern Airlines, out of Atlanta. As a native New Yorker, I am interested in offering my abilities to a carrier with a strong presence in that state.

I am interested particularly in Friendly Air because I have observed its expanding presence in the aviation industry and am aware of its reputation for excellence. I would like to be a part of the company and feel I could become a key member of your quality organization.

I hope I will have the opportunity to meet with you in person to discuss my interest in Friendly Air, and I hope you will contact me if my experience and skills are of interest to you.

Sincerely,

Kirk Donovan

This pilot is seeking a flying position with a competing airline which is in an expansion mode.

Date

Exact Name of Person
Title or Position
Name of Company
Address (number and street)
Address (city, state, and zip)

Dear Exact Name of Person: (or Sir or Madam if answering a blind ad)

Aviation Maintenance Professional

Mr. Baiocchi offers a background in aviation maintenance along with diversified experience in the management of personnel, inventory, and support services.

I would appreciate an opportunity to talk with you soon about how I could contribute to your organization through my experience in aviation maintenance with an emphasis on power train repair. In addition to my technical expertise and knowledge, I offer a well-rounded background in employee supervision and support services such as inventory control and safety program operations.

You will see from my resume that I have earned an associate's degree in Supervisory Leadership and completed a one-year Electrical School program as well as attending military training programs in both technical subjects and leadership/supervisory techniques.

I have received numerous awards and medals for my professionalism, dedication to excellence, and technical expertise as an aircraft mechanic. Since 1997 I have been based at Ft. Campbell, KY, one of the largest military bases in the world, and have been selected for task force and special project participation in Saudi Arabia and Iraq.

Here's a tip: Be aware of the special needs and sensitivities of your industry and emphasize your strong qualities in those areas. For example, safety and quality control might be critical factors in the aviation industry. Integrity and customer service experience might be critical needs in the financial field.

I am confident that I possess skills and knowledge which exceed that of many of my peers and that I am a fast learner who would easily transfer my military training, education, and knowledge into outstanding results in any organization.

I hope you will call or write me soon to suggest a time when we might meet to discuss your current and future needs and how I might serve them. Thank you in advance for your time.

Sincerely,

Anthony Baiocchi

Alternate last paragraph:
I hope you will welcome my call soon to arrange a time for us to discuss your current and future needs and how I might serve them. Thank you in advance for your time.

Date

Exact Name of Person
Title or Position
Name of Company
Address (number and street)
Address (city, state, and zip)

Dear Exact Name of Person: (or Sir or Madam if answering a blind ad)

I would appreciate an opportunity to talk with you soon about how I could contribute to your organization through my troubleshooting and technical electronics skills as well as through my motivational and supervisory abilities.

You will see from my enclosed resume that I served my country in the U.S. Air Force where I built a reputation as an adaptable quick learner who could be counted on to motivate others and set the example of dedication to excellence. While meeting the demands of a military career with its frequent temporary assignments, I completed requirements for an A.A.S. degree in Avionics Systems Technology from the Community College of the Air Force.

Upon my retirement from military service, I will be offering an organization my strong background in troubleshooting and functional testing of analog and digital circuits to the system, subassembly, and component level. I am confident that the expertise and knowledge I have acquired will allow me to easily adapt to any situation where personal integrity and dedication to quality are valued.

If you can use a positive, results-oriented professional, I would enjoy talking with you in person about how my talents and skills could benefit you. I hope you will welcome my call soon when I try to arrange a brief meeting with you to discuss your needs. I can assure you that I have an excellent reputation and would quickly become a valuable asset to your company.

Sincerely,

Chuck Yarborough

Date

Exact Name of Person
Title or Position
Name of Company
Address (number and street)
Address (city, state, and zip)

AVIATION Dear Exact Name of Person: (or Dear Sir or Madam if answering a blind ad)

Pilot

This accomplished aviation executive has done it all. He has accumulated more than 3390 flight hours in 26 different aircraft, and he has planned complex operations for aviation organizations worldwide. He will be leaving military service soon, and this cover letter is designed to help him explore suitable opportunities in the aviation industry.

With the enclosed resume, I would like to make you aware of my interest in utilizing my aviation expertise for the benefit of your organization.

A graduate of the U.S. Military Academy at West Point, I have served my country for over 25 years in the U.S. Army while advancing to the rank of Colonel. I hold a Commercial Pilot license—Rotorcraft-Helicopter Instrument and Airplane Multiengine Land Instrument. In more than 19 years as an aviator, I have over 3390 flight hours in 26 different aircraft, with 1500+ as pilot-in-command.

My recent flight experience was as a PA-31 Cheyenne pilot and UH-60 helicopter pilot providing executive transport. This assignment followed two years of tactical aviation duty in the 82nd Airborne Division, piloting both the OH-58D and UH-60 helicopters while serving as the Aviation Brigade Commander. I have served as a Special Operations Pilot (MH-60, MH-6, and AH-6 helicopters) and as an Experimental Test Pilot at the U.S. Navy Test Pilot School. I have been trained twice at Flight Safety International in both Piper Cheyenne and Piper Seminole Airplanes. I offer extensive experience in night vision goggle flight, mountain flight, overwater/shipboard operations, and helicopter external load operations.

Throughout my flying career, I have become known for my emphasis on safety, quality control, and strong interpersonal skills. Once I was specially selected to take over the management of a multinational staff after a fatal friendly fire incident between Air Force and Army aircraft. I provided leadership to a demoralized organization while making changes to assure the safety of flight operations in the war zone of Iraq.

If you can use an experienced pilot with extensive management experience, I would be pleased to make myself available at your convenience so that we could talk about your needs and how I might serve them. I can provide outstanding references at the appropriate time. Thank you in advance for your consideration.

Yours sincerely,

William Smith

Date

Exact Name of Person
Title or Position
Name of Company
Address (number and street)
Address (city, state, and zip)

Dear Exact Name of Person: (or Sir or Madam if answering a blind ad)

This young professional is
pursuing his Airframe and
Power Plant License and he
points out in his cover letter
that he expects to get it soon.

I would appreciate an opportunity to talk with you soon to discuss how I could contribute to your organization through my experience in the aviation field with an emphasis on maintenance, production control, and quality control.

As you will see from my enclosed resume, during my nearly ten years of service in the U.S. Army, I have developed expertise with three aircraft: UH-60A Blackhawk, UH-1 Huey, and AH-1F Cobra. As a crew chief, I have logged approximately 300 flight hours in the Blackhawk and Huey combined. I am pursuing my Airframe and Power Plant License and expect to receive it soon.

I was selected from a pool of 15 well-qualified professionals for my present job as a Maintenance and Production Control Supervisor. As a technical inspector, I oversee quality control for a fleet of 15 Blackhawk helicopters at the largest military base worldwide.

I offer a keen understanding of aircraft maintenance, administrative office operations and computer applications, and quality/production control. If you can use an experienced professional with a reputation as a creative and enthusiastic individual along with the ability to quickly learn and master new technology and procedures, I hope you will contact me to suggest a time when we might meet to discuss your needs. I can assure you in advance that I could rapidly become an asset to your organization.

Here's a tip: If you are pursuing a degree or license in your spare time—and if it is related to your field—it's usually good to mention that in the cover letter. If you are pursuing a degree that is *not* related to your field, don't mention it, because you would be advertising your intention to change fields once you complete it.

Sincerely,

Byron J. Culpepper III

More aggressive final paragraph:
I hope you will welcome my call soon when I try to arrange a brief meeting with you to discuss your goals and how I might help you achieve them. I can provide outstanding references at the appropriate time. I can assure you in advance that I have a strong bottom-line orientation and am known for my resourceful problem-solving style.

Date

Exact Name of Person
Title or Position
Name of Company
Address (number and street)
Address (city, state, and zip)

Dear Exact Name of Person: (or Sir or Madam if answering a blind ad)

Maintenance Technician

This A & P Mechanic and Crew Chief offers experience with both fixed-wing and rotary wing aircraft. He is already "civilianized" because he has moonlighted in a civilian job as Director of Maintenance at a local airport.

With the enclosed resume, I would like to introduce the considerable experience I offer related to aircraft maintenance, both fixed-wing and rotary wing. I have recently relocated to the Arizona area after serving my country with distinction in the U.S. Army.

You will see from my resume that I was promoted ahead of my peers in the Army and earned a reputation as a self-starter known for my unrelenting desire to exceed the highest quality goals, safety standards, and performance objectives. I am known for my attention to detail and was awarded prestigious medals in all of my jobs.

While excelling in demanding maintenance management positions supervising other crew chiefs, I made time to earn my Airframe and Power Plant license. I am both a licensed A & P Mechanic and a licensed pilot.

Most recently I excelled in two jobs simultaneously. As a Crew Chief with the U.S. Army at the world's largest U.S. military base, I trained and supervised three individuals while maintaining and accounting for $24 million in aviation assets. At the city's local airport, I also "moonlighted" six days a week, from 6 pm to 10 pm, as Director of Maintenance maintaining fixed-wing general aviation. Because of my outstanding reputation and technical expertise, I was also responsible for 24-hour-a-day on-call maintenance support for U.S. Air and the commuter airline ASA Airlines.

If you can use a dedicated leader who is known for commitment to safety, quality, and productivity, I hope you will contact me to suggest a time when we might meet to discuss your needs. Thank you in advance for your time.

Sincerely,

Bill Turner

More aggressive final paragraph:
I hope you will welcome my call soon when I try to arrange a brief meeting with you to discuss your goals and how I might help you achieve them. I can provide outstanding references at the appropriate time. I can assure you that I have a strong bottom-line orientation and am known for my resourceful problem-solving style.

Date

Exact Name of Person
Title or Position
Name of Company
Address (number and street)
Address (city, state, and zip)

Dear Exact Name of Person: (or Dear Sir or Madam if answering a blind ad)

CLERICAL, SECRETARIAL, AND
ADMINISTRATIVE SUPPORT

Administrative Assistant
This administrative assistant
offers extensive experience in
computer operations, customer
service, and production
operations support.

I would appreciate an opportunity to talk with you soon about how I could contribute to your organization through my versatile experience and skills in office operations, computer applications, and quality control.

As you will see from my enclosed resume, I am a self-motivated professional who believes in the importance of customer satisfaction and quality products and services. I enjoy the challenge of developing methods of improving productivity and effectiveness while reducing costs. Through my excellent verbal and written communication skills, I have become known as one who can be counted on to prepare accurate and timely reports and correspondence and to work well with others in leadership roles while contributing to team efforts.

In my most recent job as an Administrative Assistant at Jones Fabrications, I handled a wide range of office and production activities. I prioritized work, provided quality assurance support, controlled inventory, and typed/word processed a variety of reports, documents, and spreadsheets. I also filed and answered multiline phones and then directed calls to appropriate personnel.

I am confident that my willingness to meet challenges head on and dedicate my efforts to increasing efficiency and reducing costs would make me a valuable asset to any organization seeking a dedicated hard worker. I hope you will contact me to suggest a time when we might meet to discuss your needs. I can assure you in advance that I could rapidly become an asset to your organization.

Sincerely,

Paulette Vander

More aggressive final paragraph:
I hope you will welcome my call soon when I try to arrange a brief meeting with you to discuss your goals and how I might help you achieve them. I can provide outstanding references at the appropriate time. I can assure you in advance that I have a strong bottom-line orientation and am known for my resourceful problem-solving style.

Date

Exact Name of Person
Title or Position
Name of Company
Address (number and street)
Address (city, state, and zip)

**CLERICAL, SECRETARIAL, AND
ADMINISTRATIVE SUPPORT**

Administrative Aide
This professional in her thirties
was in a jobhunt because her
employer downsized due to a
business downturn and she lost
her job with a Fortune 500
company. She doesn't say in the
cover letter that she was
downsized. Instead, she uses
the space in her cover letter
to cite her numerous
contributions to the bottom
line. Her cover letter is all
purpose, but she wants to find
a similar job in another
engineering environment.

Dear Exact Name of Person: (or Sir or Madam if answering a blind ad)

With the enclosed resume, I would like to acquaint you with my exceptional organizational, communication, and computer skills as well as my background in purchasing and inventory control; customer service; manufacturing; and the supervision and training of office personnel.

As you will see, I have excelled in a variety of positions at the same facility, first with Janson, Inc. and most recently with Burlington Industries. In my last position, I oversaw control and disbursement of the company's travel reimbursement fund as well as the purchasing of office supplies and company shirts. In this capacity, I reduced supply expenditures by 50% without compromising the effectiveness of the department. I also read and analyzed engineering diagrams and entered the data into an IBM AS-400 computer system, and updated information using Burlington's proprietary software.

In previous positions as Coordinator of Administrative Services and Computer Terminal Operator, I refined my computer skills, mastering Microsoft Word, Excel, PowerPoint and Outlook, and the FoxBase engineering program while gaining mainframe computer experience on IBM System 36, System 38, and AS-400 computers. I provided customer service for seven Burlington facilities and was involved in purchasing, processing invoices and receipts, and reconciling discrepant orders and invoices.

If you can use a highly motivated, articulate professional with strong computer, organizational, communication, and administrative skills, I hope you will contact me to suggest a time when we could meet to discuss your needs. I can assure you that I have an excellent reputation and would quickly become a valuable asset to your organization.

Sincerely,

Regina Logan

More aggressive final paragraph:
I hope you will welcome my call soon when I try to arrange a brief meeting with you to discuss your goals and how I might help you achieve them. I can provide outstanding references at the appropriate time. I can assure you in advance that I have a strong bottom-line orientation and am known for my resourceful problem-solving style.

Date

Exact Name
Exact Title
Exact Name of Company
Address
City, State Zip

Dear Sir or Madam:

I would appreciate an opportunity to talk with you soon about how I could contribute to your organization through my experience and knowledge in the areas of data entry and office operations as well as in medical records maintenance and patient services. With a versatile background in customer service, troubleshooting, and problem solving, I have become recognized as an adaptable quick learner.

Customer Service
Although this professional has worked in medical environments in hospital record keeping and admissions, she has also worked in customer service for a credit company. Her skills are transferable to a wide range of industries.

As a Senior Customer Service Representative for American Credit, I was given a great deal of responsibility while entrusted with responding to problem calls. When a customer could not be satisfied through the efforts of the person who originally took their call, I stepped in and defused the situation and found the answer which would satisfy them. In this capacity I had to remain calm, be courteous, and really listen so I could find the answer.

Earlier I served in the U.S. Army as a Patient Administration Specialist in military hospitals and medical clinics both at Ft. Belvoir, VA, and in Germany. I became highly knowledgeable of medical records maintenance, admissions procedures, data entry, and customer service during this period. In 24-hour-a-day hospital environments, I learned to handle the stresses of long hours while working 16- or 24-hour shifts in the admissions office.

You would find me in person to be a vibrant and enthusiastic individual with an ability to establish and maintain strong working relationships. I am known for initiative, sound judgment, and a diplomatic and tactful manner.

I hope you will call or write me soon to suggest a time convenient for us to meet and discuss your current and future needs and how I might serve them.

Sincerely,

Mariann Delaphant

More aggressive final paragraph:
I hope you will welcome my call soon when I try to arrange a brief meeting with you to discuss your goals and how I might help you achieve them. I can provide outstanding references at the appropriate time. I can assure you in advance that I have a strong bottom-line orientation and am known for my resourceful problem-solving style.

Date

Exact Name of Person
Title or Position
Name of Company
Address (number and street)
Address (city, state, and zip)

**CLERICAL, SECRETARIAL, AND
ADMINISTRATIVE SUPPORT**

**Secretary and
Receptionist**
With more than 10 years of
experience in real estate and
legal environments, Ms. Dietz
stresses that she is a versatile
and adaptable professional.

Dear Exact Name of Person: (or Sir or Madam if answering a blind ad)

    With the enclosed resume, I would like to acquaint you with my background as an office clerk, secretary, and receptionist while also making you aware of the strong organizational, interpersonal, and communication skills I could offer your company. I have recently moved to the Waco area, and I am seeking employment with an organization that can use a hardworking young professional with a proven ability to make significant contributions to efficiency and profitability.

    As you will see from my resume, I offer more than ten years of office experience, and I have demonstrated my ability to excel in various environments including the real estate and legal fields. A versatile and adaptable individual with a cheerful personality, I can assure you that my outstanding customer service and time management skills would be assets to any organization.

    Fluent in Spanish, I have earned a reputation as a skilled communicator with a talent for dealing effectively with people. I believe my hardworking nature and ability to work with little or no supervision have been the keys to my success.

    If you can use a motivated professional with strong office and computer operations skills, I hope you will contact me to suggest a time when we can discuss your present and future needs and how I might meet them. I can provide outstanding personal and professional references, and I thank you in advance for your time and consideration.

Sincerely,

Aurelia Dietz

More aggressive final paragraph:
    I hope you will welcome my call soon when I try to arrange a brief meeting with you to discuss your goals and how I might help you achieve them. I can provide outstanding references at the appropriate time. I can assure you in advance that I have a strong bottom-line orientation and am known for my resourceful problem-solving style.

Date

Exact Name of Person
Title or Position
Name of Company
Address (number and street)
Address (city, state, and zip)

Dear Exact Name of Person: (or Sir or Madam if answering a blind ad)

With the enclosed resume, I would like to respond to your advertisement which appeared in the newspaper for an Office Manager.

As you will see from my resume, I offer a unique combination of communication and bookkeeping skills. Most recently I have worked as a Teacher in a child care environment in Korea where the lesson plans had to pass strict inspection by government officials. I completed numerous training modules including CPR, First Aid, and training related to detecting child abuse.

In a prior job after graduating from George Washington High School, I combined college studies in Business Administration with a full-time job. Because of my outstanding high school record, I earned a partial college scholarship. In my full-time job, I earned rapid promotion from a secretarial position to the job of Office Manager which placed me in charge of six office workers and 10 repair technicians in an appliance company which sold new and reconditioned appliances while also providing round-the-clock repair service. In addition to scheduling technicians, I handled bookkeeping including accounts payable, receivable, and payroll. I am skilled at handling multiple tasks and priorities.

My computer skills are top-notch, and I am proficient in handling data entry quickly and accurately. Proficient with most popular software programs, I am experienced in working with spreadsheets and offer the proven ability to rapidly master new computer programs. My customer skills are also excellent and have been refined through my experience in handling a multiline switchboard for an import-export company as well as in scheduling and managing repair services for an appliance company.

If you can use a hardworking young professional who offers a reputation as a thorough, persistent, and highly motivated individual, I hope you will contact me. I can provide strong references.

Sincerely,

Remi H. Morgan

Office Manager
Even when you have been working for a few years, employers are impressed if you had significant academic or other accomplishments in high school. This young professional stresses her track record of accomplishment and her skill in handling multiple priorities and tasks.

Date

Exact Name of Person
Title or Position
Name of Company
Address (number and street)
Address (city, state, and zip)

**CLERICAL, SECRETARIAL, AND
ADMINISTRATIVE SUPPORT**

Office Manager
With this cover letter, a versatile
office professional hopes to find
an attractive opening with a
company that will value her
diversified experience in
customer service, telemarketing,
office operations, and
purchasing.

Dear Exact Name of Person: (or Sir or Madam if answering a blind ad)

With the enclosed resume, I would like to make you aware of an experienced customer service professional and office manager with exceptional communication, organizational, and computer skills as well as a background in telemarketing, office administration, accounting, and purchasing.

In my present position with TeleSales Worldwide, I provide customer service and telephone direct marketing at the large local call center of one of the country's largest telemarketing companies. I contact businesses and individuals to introduce them to the client's products and services, which include several long distance plans and other telephone services such as caller I.D., additional lines, voice mail, and call waiting. Because of my ability to quickly build a rapport with and tactfully deflect the objections of customers, I have frequently been the top producer on corporate campaigns.

As Office Manager for Corrugated Roofing Company, I held final accountability for a number of different operational areas. I processed all accounts payable and accounts receivable, prepared the company's weekly payroll and monthly billing statements, and oversaw all purchasing of roofing materials, office supplies, and equipment. I am proficient in the use of Microsoft Word, QuickBooks accounting software, Microsoft Excel, and Windows 95.

In an earlier job with Sprint Telemarketing, I refined my communication skills as I called on residential telephone customers to explain the benefits, features, and incentives involved in switching their long distance service to Sprint. I became skilled in effectively presenting information on the various rate structures offered for international, domestic, and local calling area service.

If you can use an experienced professional with a strong background in customer service, office administration, telemarketing, and accounting, I hope you will contact me to suggest a time when we might meet to discuss your needs. I can provide outstanding references at the appropriate time.

Sincerely,

Constance Menezes

Date

Exact Name of Person
Title or Position
Name of Company
Address (number and street)
Address (city, state, and zip)

Dear Exact Name of Person: (or Sir or Madam if answering a blind ad)

CLERICAL, SECRETARIAL, AND
ADMINISTRATIVE SUPPORT

Office Manager
This office manager stresses her
excellent communication skills
including her knowledge of
grammar, spelling,
capitalization, and punctuation.
Remember that you are always
trying to "sell" what's different
about you compared to other
office managers.

With the enclosed resume, I would like to make you aware of the considerable clerical and office administration skills which I could put to work for you.

As you will see from my enclosed resume, I offer more than 10 years of experience in all aspects of office management. In my current job, I manage a busy office and am the resident expert on all matters pertaining to reports, correspondence, and memoranda. In previous jobs while serving my country, I received many awards and honors in recognition of my efficiency and productivity. For example, I once received a respected award for my leadership in reducing a large backlog of personnel documents to zero, which made my unit the first of 17 to achieve such a distinction.

My communication skills are highly refined, and I am knowledgeable of grammar, spelling, capitalization, and punctuation. I am proficient in utilizing most popular software programs, and I am well versed with Word, Excel, Lotus, and numerous automated programs used to track inventory and monitor scheduling.

I would welcome the opportunity to put my clerical and office administration abilities to work for you, and I can assure you that I am a dedicated hard worker who offers the determination and persistence necessary to succeed in anything I take on. If you feel that my considerable talents and knowledge could be of use to you, I hope you will call or write me to suggest a time when we might meet to discuss your needs and how I might serve them.

Sincerely,

Charlene Troxler

More aggressive final paragraph:
I hope you will welcome my call soon when I try to arrange a brief meeting with you to discuss your goals and how I might help you achieve them. I can provide outstanding references at the appropriate time. I can assure you in advance that I have a strong bottom-line orientation and am known for my resourceful problem-solving style.

Date

Exact Name of Person
Title or Position
Name of Company
Address (number and street)
Address (city, state, and zip)

CLERICAL, SECRETARIAL, AND ADMINISTRATIVE SUPPORT

Office Manager
This office professional offers experience in accounts management and supply management. Notice that Ms. Schumacher uses the cover letter as the means of informing prospective employers that she has relocated permanently to the area and is seeking an employer to whom she can make a long-term commitment.

Dear Exact Name of Person: (or Sir or Madam if answering a blind ad)

With the enclosed resume, I would like to make you aware of my background in accounts management, personnel supervision, and customer service as well as my strong organizational, interpersonal, and communication skills. My husband and I have recently relocated back to Vermont, where our families are from.

In my most recent job, I began as a Receptionist answering a 30-line phone system for a 1,100-employee company which provided on-line computer services. I rapidly advanced to Accounts Manager and Shift Supervisor, which placed me in charge of eight people. In that job I made hundreds of decisions daily which involved committing the company's technical resources. In addition to dispatching technicians and managing liaison with companies such as The Bank of Chicago, NationsBank, and Kmart, I was authorized to commit company resources valued at up to $500,000.

With my husband's retirement from military service after 19 years, we are eager to replant our roots in Vermont, and I am seeking employment with a company that can use a highly motivated hard worker who is known for excellent decision-making, problem-solving, and organizational skills.

If you can use a resourceful and versatile individual with administrative and computer skills, I hope you will contact me to suggest a time when we can discuss your present and future needs and how I might meet them. I can provide outstanding personal and professional references, and I thank you in advance for your time and consideration.

Sincerely,

Greta Schumacher

More aggressive final paragraph:
I hope you will welcome my call soon when I try to arrange a brief meeting with you to discuss your goals and how I might help you achieve them. I can provide outstanding references at the appropriate time. I can assure you in advance that I have a strong bottom-line orientation and am known for my resourceful problem-solving style.

Date

Exact Name of Person
Title or Position
Name of Company
Address (number and street)
Address (city, state, and zip)

Dear Exact Name of Person: (or Sir or Madam if answering a blind ad)

Office Professional
If you have worked for
temporary companies, you can
still market the names of the
companies for which you have
worked. This office professional
has obtained a temporary job at
MCI but she is using the cover
letter as a means of acquainting
MCI with her desire to become a
full-time permanent employee.

With the enclosed resume, I would like to make you aware of my strong desire to become permanently employed by MCI in a role in which I could benefit the company through my computer knowledge, sales skills, and customer service experience.

As you will see from my resume, I am currently excelling as an Operations Clerk working for MCI in Tucson, where I am employed in a temporary full-time position through MegaForce Temporary Service. In this job I am involved in a wide range of activities involving computer operations, customer service, and administrative support. I have become proficient in using Beyond Mail, in utilizing the LAN system, and in researching and coordinating service orders in the most efficient manner while applying my knowledge of MCI's internal telecommunications operations.

In my previous job in Carson City, NV, as an Administrative Aide, I became a valuable employee and was entrusted with many complex responsibilities because of my demonstrated initiative, intelligence, and customer service skills. Since I am bilingual in Spanish and English, I conducted new hires of employees in both Spanish and English and frequently translated communication between production workers and office personnel.

My computer skills are excellent and I enjoy learning new software. While in my previous job I completed a major project in which I computerized data entry for all production workers' payroll. I am knowledgeable of software including Microsoft Word, Excel, Lotus 1-2-3, and PowerPoint.

Please consider me for a position within MCI which can utilize my excellent communication, problem solving, and decision making skills. I can provide outstanding personal and professional references including very strong references from MCI personnel in the regional and district office with which I work.

Sincerely,

Martina Stavlo Longoria

Date

Exact Name of Person
Title or Position
Name of Company
Address (number and street)
Address (city, state, and zip)

Computer Operations Manager

Preparing for his first full-time job in his field, Mr. Rogaine is using the cover letter as a means of alerting potential employers to the fact that he will be graduating soon with a Computer Science degree, which he has earned while excelling in a full-time job.

Dear Exact Name of Person: (or Dear Sir or Madam if answering a blind ad)

With the enclosed resume, I would like to make you aware of my background as a versatile and experienced professional with a history of success in areas which include computer operations, logistics and supply, production control, and employee training and supervision.

As you will see, I am completing requirements for my bachelor's degree in Computer Science which I will receive this winter from Mercer College. I am proud of my accomplishment in completing this course of study while simultaneously meeting the demands of a career in the U.S. Army. In my current military assignment as a Technical Inspector at Ft. Jackson, SC, I ensure the airworthiness of aircraft utilized by the 18th Airborne Corps which is required to relocate anywhere in the world on extremely short notice in response to crisis situations.

Throughout my years of military service, I have been singled out for jobs which have required the ability to quickly make sound decisions and have continually maximized resources while exceeding expected standards and performance guidelines. I have been responsible for certifying multimillion-dollar aircraft for flight service, training and supervising employees who have been highly productive and successful in their own careers, and applying technical computer knowledge in innovative ways which have further increased efficiency and productivity.

I offer a combination of technical, managerial, and supervisory skills which will allow me to quickly achieve outstanding results in anything I attempt. Known for my energy and enthusiasm, I am a creative and talented professional with a strong desire to make a difference in whatever setting and environment I find myself.

I hope you will contact me to suggest a time when we might meet to discuss your needs. I can assure you in advance that I could rapidly become an asset to your organization.

Sincerely,

Elmer Rogaine

Date

Exact Name of Person
Title or Position
Name of Company
Address (number and street)
Address (city, state, and zip)

Dear Exact Name of Person: (or Dear Sir or Madam if answering a blind ad)

With the enclosed resume, I would like to make you aware of my desire to utilize and expand my knowledge of computer software and business applications within an organization that can use my enthusiastic personality, sales and marketing background, as well as my strong desire to provide expert technical support to others.

As you will see, I am proficient in a wide range of computer software, including most versions of Microsoft Word, Excel, and PowerPoint, as well as Publisher 97, DragonDictate, and Website Developer. In my present position, I utilize all of the above software packages to compile data and produce reports, newsletters, and other documents for distribution to 30 branch offices. I also demonstrated my ability to train others in software operation, allowing the Branch Managers whom I instructed to achieve maximum productivity from their use of the Mobius computer report system.

Through my rapid advancement with Bank of the Midwest, I have been afforded the opportunity to achieve a degree of success rare for a young professional. While I am highly regarded by my present employer and can provide excellent references at the appropriate time, I feel that my strong computer skills and software knowledge would provide greater benefit to an organization with a stronger technological orientation.

If you can use a highly motivated young professional whose personality and technical knowledge could surely enhance your organization, I hope you will contact me to suggest a time when we might meet to discuss your needs and how I might meet them. Thank you in advance for your time.

Sincerely,

Lashalle Curtis

Computer Professional
This young person is actually in career change. Although she works with computer applications for the banking industry as a minor part of her current job, she is yearning to leap from banking into a computer company so that she can take her computer knowledge to high levels.

Here's a tip: Notice how this young professional has figured out the skills she wants to use and is managing her career in order to put herself in a position where she can utilize and refine those skills. She will use this cover letter to launch her career in the computer industry.

More aggressive final paragraph:
I hope you will welcome my call soon when I try to arrange a brief meeting with you to discuss your goals and how I might help you achieve them. I can assure you in advance that I have a strong bottom-line orientation and am known for my resourceful problem-solving style.

Date

Exact Name of Person
Title or Position
Name of Company
Address (number and street)
Address (city, state, and zip)

Dear Exact Name of Person: (or Dear Sir or Madam if answering a blind ad)

With the enclosed resume, I would like to make you aware of my background in the troubleshooting, repair, and maintenance of digital electronic systems and radio communications equipment as well as my track record of success in the supervision and training of technical personnel.

As you will see from my resume, I am completing an Associate's degree in General Studies with a concentration in Electronics. I have completed numerous courses related to electronics repair including communications electronics, electrical maintenance, digital electronics, microprocessor systems, and computer repair. In addition to my college course work, I excelled in numerous technical courses as part of my military training.

In my current position as a Computer Center Supervisor with the U.S. Army, I manage sophisticated laser targeting systems as well as digital and radio communications equipment used to make precise calculations for live-fire training projects. I supervise and train four employees, including one more-junior supervisor. My training efforts have resulted in 100% first-time pass rates for personnel under my supervision.

In an earlier job as a Electronics Equipment Operator, I supervised three employees and trained six personnel in the use of oscilloscopes, multimeters, signal generators, and logic probes to locate faults and troubleshoot malfunctions in a wide variety of digital and analog electronic equipment. I was responsible for the repair of single- and multichannel radios, generators, radar equipment, and weapons control systems on AH-64 Apache helicopters, as well as other types of electronics equipment, microprocessors, and computer systems.

If you can use a motivated, experienced technician with exceptional troubleshooting and repair skills along with the proven ability to train, supervise, and motivate others, I hope you will contact me. I can assure you in advance that my integrity is beyond reproach, and I could quickly become a valuable asset to your organization.

Sincerely,

Willie C. Greer, Jr.

Date

Exact Name of Person
Title or Position
Name of Company
Address (number and street)
Address (city, state, and zip)

Dear Exact Name of Person: (or Dear Sir or Madam if answering a blind ad)

COMPUTER OPERATIONS

Network Engineer
This professional will find herself in great demand as long as she gets her cover letters to the right companies. She is an experienced Network Engineer. Even when getting a job is not a problem, the key is to find a job you will enjoy in the geographical location where you want to live.

With the enclosed resume, I would like to make you aware of my interest in utilizing my background in computer science and my interest in customer service for the benefit of your organization.

As you will see from my resume, I am a Certified Novell Administrator and a Microsoft Certified Professional for NT 4.0 Workstation, and I hold an Associate's degree in Computer Applications and Programming as well as a B.S. in Computer Science and Information Management Systems. I am an experienced Network Engineer.

Although I am excelling in my current position, I am seeking to utilize my technical expertise in an environment where I can also interact with customers and/or users on a more frequent basis. My naturally outgoing personality and strong communication skills would make me very effective in any position which required interaction with others, and I would enjoy an opportunity to develop and maintain strong working relationships as part of my job. I offer a proven ability to translate complex technical concepts into language which can be comprehended by nontechnical individuals, and I believe my technical expertise would be best utilized in an environment which required extensive human interaction.

If you feel that my strong interest in customer service as well as my expertise in network engineering, design, administration, and troubleshooting could be useful to you, I hope you will contact me to suggest a time when we could meet to discuss your needs. I certainly appreciate your time and consideration, and I am confident that I could make valuable contributions to your long-range goals.

Yours sincerely,

Charlisa Reese

More aggressive final paragraph:
I hope you will welcome my call soon when I try to arrange a brief meeting with you to discuss your goals and how I might help you achieve them. I can provide outstanding references at the appropriate time. I can assure you in advance that I have a strong bottom-line orientation and am known for my resourceful problem-solving style.

Date

Exact Name of Person
Title or Position
Name of Company
Address (number and street)
Address (city, state, and zip)

Dear Exact Name of Person: (or Dear Sir or Madam if answering a blind ad)

Training and
Operations Manager
His background is in systems
administration. Since he has
fielded and worked with the
equipment of the major defense
contractors, a logical place to
begin in his job hunt is by
addressing cover letters to the
companies that have
manufactured the equipment
with which he has
become familiar.

I would appreciate an opportunity to talk with you soon about how I might contribute to your organization through my expertise, skills, and knowledge related to computer systems administration and personnel management.

Along with my skills as a systems administrator and troubleshooter, I am known for my ability to master challenges and find the solutions which will keep the systems running and personnel motivated to achieve outstanding results, no matter how difficult the mission.

In my most recent position as Computer Training and Operations Manager, I have continued to build a track record of accomplishments and make valuable contributions. My analytical skills and technical knowledge were critical in a project during which I analyzed automation needs and wrote the five-year plan for 1999-2004 ADP requirements. In this job I also monitored the status of technical training and documented such training for the organization's personnel as well as troubleshooting and training new users of the Sun operating system and Sun Sparc computer. I hold a Top Secret (SCI) security clearance and have experience in translating intelligence data from Spanish into English.

I have excelled in supervising up to 82 people while controlling multimillion-dollar equipment inventories. I have played an important part in the fielding of the latest state-of-the-art ADP and communications systems and have acquired expertise in troubleshooting and in operations management.

If you are in need of a results-oriented professional who specializes in systems administration as well as in developing and supervising motivated and skilled personnel, I am confident that I am the type of fair and honest professional your organization would value.

I hope you will contact me to suggest a time when we might meet to discuss your needs and how I might help you. Thank you in advance for your time.

Sincerely,

Francisco Hernandez

Date

Exact Name of Person
Title or Position
Name of Company
Address (number and street)
Address (city, state, and zip)

Dear Exact Name of Person: (or Dear Sir or Madam if answering a blind ad)

I would appreciate an opportunity to talk with you soon about how I could contribute to your organization through my extensive knowledge of electronics, information systems, and imagery operation/analysis as well as my superior trouble-shooting, problem-solving, and decision-making skills.

As you will see from my resume, I have served my country with distinction while earning a reputation as a skilled supervisor and technical problem solver. I have excelled as a Technical Consultant, Automatic Test Equipment Operator, and Maintenance Supervisor in worldwide locations including Germany, Somalia, Haiti, Korea, and in numerous stateside sites.

In my most recent job I have supervised the maintenance, operation, and deployment of a $7,500,000 ground station. I received a certificate after completing training from the Common Ground Station Training AN-TVQ 178, and I also received a diploma after extensive training on the Joint STARS Medium Ground Station Module AN-TVQ 168. Prior to entering military service, I earned two A.A.S. degrees in Electronic Engineering Technology.

My supervisory skills have been refined and tested in numerous management situations. In one job I trained and supervised 10 employees while supervising two systems valued at $35 million and overseeing the highest quality electronic equipment testing for a maintenance organization. Known as a resourceful problem solver, that job helped me refine my ability to discover the shortest path to the highest quality result.

I hope that this resume will answer your questions about my varied background, versatile skills, and distinguished military record, and I trust that you will contact me to suggest the next step I should take in exploring the possibility of working for your company. Thank you in advance for your time.

Sincerely,

Roberta Podruchny

Date

Exact Name of Person
Title or Position
Name of Company
Address (number and street)
Address (city, state, and zip)

Dear Exact Name of Person: (or Dear Sir or Madam if answering a blind ad)

Network Administrator

Experience in network administration is in demand, so this job seeker is probably in excellent shape. Nevertheless, he is trying to get in the maximum number of doors and negotiate the best package possible.

With the enclosed resume, I would like to offer my extensive computer knowledge to an organization that can benefit from my exceptional communication, organizational, and technical skills as well as my background in network administration, troubleshooting, and installation.

As you will see, I have been excelling in a position as Network Administrator while simultaneously working a second job and completing additional training for the Microsoft Certified Systems Engineer exam. With Memphis Computer Services, I perform hardware and software troubleshooting, configuration, repair, and installation in a client/server environment. In addition to processing new user accounts and updating existing user accounts, I also provide technical support to customers.

I am currently finishing my studies in preparation for the Microsoft Certified Systems Engineer test. I have already completed numerous courses, including TCP/IP Networks, Windows NT Server 4.0/Enterprise, PC Upgrading & Maintenance, and others. I feel that my strong combination of education, technical ability, and experience would be a valuable addition to your company.

If you can use a motivated computer professional with a background in network administration, troubleshooting, and installation, then I look forward to hearing from you soon to arrange a time when we might meet to discuss your present and future needs and how I might meet them. I assure you that I have an excellent reputation and would quickly become an asset to your organization.

Sincerely,

Kyong Chan

More aggressive final paragraph:
I hope you will welcome my call soon when I try to arrange a brief meeting with you to discuss your goals and how I might help you achieve them. I can provide outstanding references at the appropriate time. I can assure you in advance that I have a strong bottom-line orientation and am known for my resourceful problem-solving style.

Date

Exact Name of Person
Title or Position
Name of Company
Address (number and street)
Address (city, state, and zip)

Dear Exact Name of Person: (or Dear Sir or Madam if answering a blind ad)

   With the enclosed resume, I would like to acquaint you with my excellent computer skills as well as my background in computer programming and Web page design.

   As you will see, I have earned an Associate's degree in Computer Studies from the University of Louisiana, and I need only nine more courses to complete my Bachelor's degree in Computer Science. I am already proficient with Pascal and HTML and am currently learning Java. I designed a personal Web page, and am currently designing a Web page for Bob West Real Estate in Mississippi. For the last two years, my full-time efforts have been focused on pursuing my degree.

   In my previous positions, I have been known as a results-oriented, hardworking professional, capable of prioritizing multiple tasks and working with little or no supervision. I am certain that my strong computer skills would be an asset to your organization.

   If your company can benefit from the services of a motivated computer programmer or Web page designer, I look forward to hearing from you soon to arrange a time when we might meet and discuss your needs and how I might meet them.

Ms. DeGaetano does not have an extensive background in the computer field, but she is approaching a booming industry and she has some interest in one of the fastest-growing niches—web page design. Many computer companies will take an employee with limited computer programming skills and train them.

                              Sincerely,

                              Carmen DeGaetano

   More aggressive final paragraph:
   I hope you will welcome my call soon when I try to arrange a brief meeting with you to discuss your goals and how I might help you achieve them. I can provide outstanding references at the appropriate time. I can assure you in advance that I have a strong bottom-line orientation and am known for my resourceful problem-solving style.

Date

Exact Name of Person
Title or Position
Name of Company
Address (number and street)
Address (city, state, and zip)

COMPUTER OPERATIONS

Dear Exact Name of Person: (or Sir or Madam if answering a blind ad)

UNIX Administrator

This computer professional offers considerable UNIX systems experience which he gained while working for the largest training organization in the world—the U.S. Army. He will use this cover letter to explore opportunities in companies which can utilize his problem-solving and management skills.

With the enclosed resume, I would like to make you aware of my considerable experience in UNIX systems administration and network administration as well as in management and accounting.

While serving my country in the U.S. Army, I have completed extensive training in computer operations and am proficient in utilizing popular as well as specialized software of numerous types. For example, I have been designated as a UNIX Systems Administrator and have acquired extensive experience in troubleshooting technical problems. I also offer experience in utilizing popular software including Quick Books for business accounting. I have been entrusted with a Top Secret security clearance with SBI.

My management skills are highly refined. In addition to training and developing networking specialists, I previously gained experience in personnel administration and supply management while serving in the U.S. Army Reserves. In a job as a Sales Representative with an electronics company prior to joining the Army, I advanced rapidly into key responsibilities for customer service and quality control.

If you can use a versatile and hardworking professional with vast knowledge related to computer operations, network management, and accounting, I hope you will contact me to suggest a time when we could meet to discuss your goals and how I might help you achieve them. I can assure you in advance that I have a strong bottom-line orientation and am known for my highly resourceful approach to problem solving and decision making.

Sincerely,

Jack L. Richart

More aggressive final paragraph:
I hope you will welcome my call soon when I try to arrange a brief meeting with you to discuss your goals and how I might help you achieve them. I can provide outstanding references at the appropriate time. I can assure you in advance that I have an ability to creatively apply my versatile knowledge to produce strong bottom-line results.

Date

Exact Name of Person
Title or Position
Name of Company
Address (number and street)
Address (city, state, and zip)

Dear Exact Name of Person: (or Dear Sir or Madam if answering a blind ad)

MIS Manager

This Vice President of Management Information Systems is selectively exploring opportunities in major corporations that can utilize her applications know-how. She will also use the cover letter to explore the opportunities available in companies operating at the forefront of technology and designing the kinds of software applications which she recently has been utilizing. She's not sure what she wants to do!

With the enclosed resume, I would like to make you aware of my considerable background in the management of information systems and in the development of state-of-the-art software and business applications.

As you will see from my resume, I was recruited two years ago by a fast-growing corporation experiencing rapid expansion to oversee the design and implementation of its MIS activities at 80 store locations. I was promoted to Vice President of Management Information Systems in the process of making major contributions to efficiency, productivity, and profitability. We have replaced store computers with a Windows-based system that reduced manual record keeping and since then I have been designing the implementation of the second phase of this reengineering project. We are also developing an Intranet for stores, supervisors, and other office personnel, and I have personally designed and conducted training and support for all job levels, from top executives, to store management, to entry-level employees.

In my prior position, I was promoted in a track record of advancement with a company which developed software products for the building materials and home building industry. During that time I transformed a failing operation which was losing money into an efficient and profitable business while reengineering a product which became the industry's #1 seller.

My software knowledge is vast, as you will also see from my resume, and I offer recent experience with C++ as well as Intranet and HTML.

I can provide outstanding personal and professional references at the appropriate time, and I can assure you in advance that I have a reputation for building and maintaining effective working relationships with people at all organizational levels. If my considerable skills, experience, and talents interest you, please feel free to contact me at my work number during the day at 910-483-6611 ext. 239 or at home at 910-483-2439 in the evenings.

Sincerely,

Lorenza Lopez

Date

Exact Name of Person
Title or Position
Name of Company
Address (no., street)
Address (city, state, and zip)

Dear Exact Name of Person: (or Dear Sir or Madam if answering a blind ad)

Project Manager

Construction industry professionals find themselves in frequent job hunts, since projects end. This project manager and foreman for a major company on the east coast is seeking a new position.

Can you use a resourceful professional with extensive operations and project management experience along with a "track record" of outstanding results in safety, cost reduction, and other areas?

As you will see from my resume, I am currently excelling as a project manager and foreman for a multimillion-dollar company operating all over the east coast. My results have been impressive; I have greatly exceeded my targeted 20% profit margin by actually performing 32% above profit while finishing all jobs within or ahead of schedule and with no accidents.

In both my current job and in a previous job as Manager of Operations with a major fire prevention company working under contract to GE, IBM, and other industrial giants, I have acquired expert knowledge of OSHA, EPA, and other regulations. I have been trained and certified by OSHA in soil testing and I have worked closely with OSHA officials regarding HAZMAT, MSDS, and other areas.

I am particularly proud of the contributions I have made to my employers in the areas of cost reduction. On numerous occasions I have discovered ways to free up working capital by decreasing inventory carrying costs, automating manual functions, and monitoring everyday activities to find new ways to streamline operations and decrease both overhead and variable costs.

You would find me in person to be a congenial individual who prides myself on my ability to get along well with people at all levels. I can provide excellent references from all previous employers, including from my current company.

I hope you will write or call me soon to suggest a time when we might meet to discuss your current and future goals and how I might help you achieve them. Thank you in advance for your time.

Sincerely yours,

Napoleon Radosevich

Date

Exact Name of Person
Exact Title of Person
Exact Name of Company
Address
City, State Zip

Dear Sir or Madam:

CONSTRUCTION

Construction Manager
Responding to an
advertisement, this experienced
construction manager is
pointing out his wealth of
knowledge related to hospital
construction.

I would appreciate an opportunity to talk with you soon about how I could contribute to The Mayo Clinic. I am responding to your ad for a Construction Manager with this *confidential* resume and cover letter to express my interest in receiving your consideration for this position.

As you will see from my enclosed resume, I offer approximately 18 years of progressively increasing responsibility in construction management with the specialized knowledge in a hospital environment that you require.

I would like to point out that I am experienced in working within JCAHO (Joint Commission on Accreditation of Health-Care Organizations), DFS (Division of Facility Services), and Interim Life Safety guidelines through my extensive background in construction management in a hospital environment.

Known for my dedication to high quality and compliance with safety standards, I have always been effective in supervising projects and seeing that work is completed on schedule.

I hope you will welcome my call soon to arrange a brief meeting at your convenience to discuss the current and future needs of The Mayo Clinic and how I might serve them. Thank you in advance for your time. I can provide outstanding personal and professional references.

Sincerely yours.

Christopher Oxendine

Exact Name of Person
Title or Position
Name of Company
Address (number and street)
Address (city, state, and zip)

CONSTRUCTION

Dear Exact Name of Person: (or Dear Sir or Madam if answering a blind ad)

Construction Manager

With a background similar to that of a City Manager, this versatile professional seeks a position which will place him in charge of multimillion-dollar construction projects. He emphasizes his background in quality control and quality assurance.

    With this letter and enclosed resume, I would like to initiate the process of being considered for the job of Senior Buildings Specialist with Seattle Construction Company, which was posted on 08/27/01, Requisition ID 453-00006.

    As you will see from my resume, I have excelled as a military officer and was promoted ahead of my peers to Major while handling extensive fiscal responsibility, project management, and day-to-day coordination of human and material resources. In one job in Germany, I supervised city planning projects valued at up to $100 million, including major renovation and full-scale construction. In that job I functioned in the role of a city planner and senior buildings manager while coordinating maintenance and major facility repairs, including interiors and exteriors, in addition to coordinating contractor support and ensuring that contractor staff were complying with all regulations, policies, and procedures.

    As a military officer, I functioned routinely as an "international diplomat" and gained a reputation as an insightful analyst, prudent problem solver, and outstanding strategic thinker in jobs as an International Analyst and International Consultant. I am accustomed to being held to the highest standards of personal accountability for decisions which affect the lives and well-being of thousands of people in a single project.

    In all my jobs, quality control and quality assurance have been key considerations of mine, and I have developed and implemented policies and procedures including checklists and other tools to assure compliance with established policies and procedures.

    If you can use an experienced leader with proven abilities in the area of strategic planning as well as in managing multiple projects and priorities to assure timely delivery of services and completion of tasks, I feel certain I could contribute to the goals of Seattle Construction Company as a Senior Buildings Specialist.

    I can provide outstanding personal and professional references at the appropriate time, and I would be pleased if you would contact me to suggest a time at your convenience when we could meet in person to further discuss your needs. Thank you.

Yours sincerely,

Louis Savage

Date

Exact Name of Person
Title or Position
Name of Company
Address (number and street)
Address (city, state, and zip)

Dear Exact Name of Person: (or Sir or Madam if answering a blind ad)

With the enclosed resume, I would like to acquaint you with my excellent leadership and technical skills, as well as my extensive background in heavy equipment operation, welding, and crew supervision.

While serving as a Team Leader and General Manager of crews with up to 20 people, I have supervised heavy construction crews of various sizes while being responsible for the accountability of hundreds of thousands of dollars worth of equipment. I have received numerous commendations for my engineering expertise and ability to train others. Even at the start of my career, my skills and leadership ability were quickly recognized, resulting in a rapid promotion after only one year—an unusually rapid rate of advancement into management.

I offer a reputation as a skilled heavy equipment operator and welder with years of supervisory and heavy construction experience. I am proficient in mig and arc welding and familiar with tig; I own my own welding truck with a complete inventory of welding equipment.

If your organization can benefit from the services of a hardworking and versatile individual with extensive supervisory experience, heavy equipment operation skills, and welding expertise, please contact me to suggest a time when we could meet to discuss your needs and how I might serve them. I can provide outstanding personal and professional references.

Sincerely,

David Sanchez

CONSTRUCTION

Construction Manager

Crew supervision is one of the strengths of this Construction Manager who offers a background in heavy equipment operation, welding, and crew supervision. He points out that he owns his own welding truck with a complete inventory of welding equipment—which certainly makes him appear to be a dedicated professional in his field.

Date

Exact Name of Person
Title or Position
Name of Company
Address (number and street)
Address (city, state, and zip)

**DISTRIBUTION
& WAREHOUSING**

Distribution Manager
A Kmart manager with limited
distribution experience is
trying to advance in the field
and persuade his current
employer that his previous
management experience
qualifies him for an internal
opening in the Distribution
Center. Don't forget that
sometimes the best way to
advance is with your
current employer!

Dear Exact Name of Person: (or Dear Sir or Madam if answering a blind ad)

I would like to acquaint you with my extensive experience and knowledge of Distribution Center operations as well as my strong supervisory, communication, and motivational skills.

At Kmart, I have excelled in a variety of tasks through my hard work and willingness to take on additional responsibilities. I have consistently received high marks on performance evaluations and have been honored with nine Distribution Salute awards in the last six months. In addition to my regular duties as an order filler, I train and supervise new employees in the use of forklifts and other heavy power equipment.

As you will see from my resume, I have six years of previous management experience with Quick Lube, Inc., where I supervised eight mechanics. By utilizing my excellent motivational and communication skills, I was able to retrain marginal employees and effectively manage the operations of that fast-paced business. I am certain that with my proven leadership skills, I can make an even greater contribution to Kmart's success at the Little Rock Distribution Center.

I look forward to hearing from you so that we can schedule a convenient time to discuss the company's needs and how I might meet them. Thank you in advance for your time and consideration.

Sincerely,

Chester Armstrong

Date

Exact Name of Person
Title or Position
Name of Company
Address (number and street)
Address (city, state, and zip)

Dear Exact Name of Person: (or Sir or Madam if answering a blind ad)

With the enclosed resume, I would like to make you aware of an experienced operations manager with excellent organizational and supervisory skills along with an extensive background in shipping, receiving, logistics, and support.

Currently excelling as an Operations Manager for the Costco Distribution Center in Delaware, I am responsible for all aspects of the shipping operation for this 1.25 million square-foot regional warehouse which ships up to $4 million worth of inventory daily. I supervise up to 55 employees, including a Billing/Data Processing Manager, a Non-Conveyables Manager, and three Area Managers. I was promoted to this position after serving as Receiving Manager and Shipping Manager at the Dover Distribution Center.

I started with Costco as an Order Filler and was quickly moved into the Area Manager Trainee program on the basis of my exemplary job performance and previous supervisory experience in logistics and supply. After completing the training program, I was promoted to Shipping Manager of the Wilmington distribution center. I supervised 30 people in the shipping department of this soft lines warehouse before moving on to a position as Receiving Manager.

If you can use an experienced logistics and supply professional whose supervisory and organizational skills have been tested and proven in challenging environments both civilian and military, I hope you will contact me to suggest a time when we might meet to discuss your needs. I can assure you in advance that I have an outstanding reputation and would rapidly become an asset to your company.

Sincerely,

Nathan Decker

More aggressive final paragraph:
I hope you will welcome my call soon when I try to arrange a brief meeting with you to discuss your goals and how I might help you achieve them. I can provide outstanding references at the appropriate time. I can assure you in advance that I have a strong bottom-line orientation and am known for my resourceful problem-solving style.

Date

Exact Name of Person
Title or Position
Name of Company
Address (number and street)
Address (city, state, and zip)

Distribution Manager
An experienced manager is
seeking to enter the
merchandise distribution
field with this cover letter
that expresses his relevant
skills and his strong interest
in the field.

Dear Exact Name of Person: (or Sir or Madam if answering a blind ad)

I would appreciate an opportunity to talk with you soon about how I could contribute to your organization through my considerable leadership and management skills along with my experience in inventory control, logistics, warehousing, and distribution. I have a particular interest in merchandise distribution which I developed last year while completing an 11-month "Training With Industry" partnership at Kmart head-quarters.

As you will see from my enclosed resume, I have served my country as a junior military officer while advancing to the rank of Captain. Because of my accomplishments, I am considered to be on the "fast track" and have consistently been recommended for promotion ahead of schedule. Although I am being groomed for further rapid advancement and have received the highest evaluations of my performance in every job I have held, I have decided to resign my commission as a military officer.

I have excelled in both line management and staff consulting positions while serving my country. In one job as a Company Commander in Panama, I transformed a dysfunctional supply support operation into a model of efficiency. That 120-person unit with 145 lines of supplies and $10 million in equipment provided eight widely diverse organizations with all classes of supplies and equipment.

I have been handpicked for critical jobs which required expertise in all phases of receiving, storing, issuing, and distributing supplies as well as a strong bottom-line orientation. I have managed budgets, accounted for multimillion-dollar assets, developed teams of dedicated employees, and trained employees in management techniques as well as supply operations. With the ability to translate ideas and concepts into operating realities, I have acquired a reputation as a creative problem solver and enthusiastic self-starter with unlimited initiative.

I hope you will welcome my call soon to arrange a brief meeting to discuss your current and future needs and how I might serve them. Thank you in advance for your time.

Sincerely,

Luke R. Bishop

Date

Exact Name of Person
Title or Position
Name of Company
Address (number and street)
Address (city, state, and zip)

Dear Exact Name of Person: (or Dear Sir or Madam if answering a blind ad)

DISTRIBUTION
& WAREHOUSING

Distribution Manager
This manager offers an
extensive background in
employee supervision and
training in addition to
experience in improving the
efficiency of distribution
operations.

With the enclosed resume, I would like to make you aware of my extensive experience in distribution, warehousing, and shipping and receiving functions.

As you will see from my resume, I have excelled in management positions with Shop-Mart. In my most recent position as Manager of Non-Conveyable Shipping, I was in charge of 65 loaders, five yard drivers, eight fixed associates, and two supervisors while overseeing the shipping of $1 million in freight weekly to North Dakota and South Dakota stores. My customer service skills are excellent, and it was my responsibility to call all stores once a month and to visit all stores every six months.

In a prior job with Costco, I worked in New Mexico and was involved in establishing and conducting training classes for Costco employees. Previously I supervised shipping operations in a 1.2 million square foot warehouse in Las Cruces, NM, where I also supervised 65 people. I hold numerous licenses and certifications and have trained distribution employees in nearly every job related to warehouse operation.

Prior to my employment with Costco, I also worked in warehousing operations for the federal government in a Civil Service position. I became very familiar with proper warehousing procedures regarding both perishable and nonperishable materials.

If you can use a dedicated hard worker who could enhance the efficiency of your distribution functions, I hope you will contact me. I will make myself available at your convenience and can provide excellent references.

Yours sincerely,

Ross LeBlanc

More aggressive final paragraph:
I hope you will welcome my call soon when I try to arrange a brief meeting with you to discuss your goals and how I might help you achieve them. I can provide outstanding references at the appropriate time. A nonsmoker and nondrinker, I am known for my emphasis on safety and quality assurance in all matters.

Date

Exact Name of Person
Title or Position
Name of Company
Address (number and street)
Address (city, state, and zip)

**DISTRIBUTION
& WAREHOUSING**

Distribution Manager
An experienced manager is
seeking to move up in his field
and is hoping to become
involved in training other
employees within a high-
volume distribution center
environment.

Dear Exact Name of Person: (or Sir or Madam if answering a blind ad)

With the enclosed resume, I would like to make you aware of my background as an experienced shipping professional with strong leadership and communication skills. I offer a results-oriented management style and a history of excellence in the training, motivation, and supervision of distribution center personnel.

With Wal-Mart distribution centers, I started as a Floor Associate in the shipping department and have rapidly advanced to positions of increasing responsibility. In my current job as Shipping Manager at the Drayton Distribution Center, I supervise up to 55 employees including two desk clerks, five yard drivers, and more than 35 shipping associates. I interview, hire, and train all new employees while also conducting annual employee performance appraisals. Previously as a Shipping Supervisor in Marcy, NY, I supervised as many as 45 shipping associates. I developed a load quality auditing system which tracked the performance of each associate, providing personal accountability and raising quality standards for shipping department personnel. In my earliest position with the company, I quickly mastered the essential methods and practices of shipping in a high-volume distribution center environment.

As you will see, I have completed nearly two years of college level course work towards a Bachelor of Science degree in Criminal Justice. In addition, I have excelled in leadership and management courses sponsored by Wal-Mart, including the 40-hour "Training the Trainer" course.

If you can use an experienced shipping manager whose proven leadership and communications skills have been tested in challenging, high-volume distribution environments, I hope you will contact me to suggest a time when we might meet to discuss your needs. I assure you that my integrity is beyond reproach; I have an outstanding reputation and would quickly become an asset to your organization.

Sincerely,

Jorge Goetz

Date

Exact Name of Person
Title or Position
Name of Company
Address (number and street)
Address (city, state, and zip)

Dear Exact Name of Person: (or Sir or Madam if answering a blind ad)

ELECTRONICS

Electronics Technician
Electronics installation and maintenance is the specialty of this professional with experience in quality control and technical supervision.

I would appreciate an opportunity to talk with you soon about how I could contribute to your organization through a strong background in communications-electronics installation and maintenance as well as through my supervisory, project planning, and problem-solving skills.

As you will see from my enclosed resume, I have earned a reputation as a highly skilled technician and leader while serving my country in the U.S. Air Force. With experience in quality control, installation team supervision, and technical instruction, I am a well-rounded professional with versatile skills as well as a proven ability to quickly learn and master new technology. Once I was a member of a team which placed third worldwide in an electronics installation competition. I hold a Top Secret security clearance with SBI/SCI/TK, and I have acquired vast technical knowledge of numerous systems and equipment in the communications-electronics field.

The recipient of five prestigious medals for exemplary performance, I have been singled out for my accomplishments, professionalism, and technical expertise. Recently I earned an Associate of Applied Science degree in Electronics Systems Technology from the Community College of the Air Force, and I have excelled in extensive training related to electronics engineering, installation, and maintenance.

My contributions have included designing improvements to training programs and developing a database, both of which vastly improved productivity and efficiency. I have managed multimillion-dollar budgets, ensured the success of efforts to standardize Air Force communications-electronics products, and was handpicked for several high-visibility roles.

I offer a keen understanding of state-of-the-art communications systems used by the U.S. military worldwide and a reputation as an individual who can be counted on to find a way to get the job done on time, no matter how complex or difficult. I hope you will contact me to suggest a time when we might meet to discuss your needs. I can provide outstanding references.

Sincerely,

Troy K. Deisch

Date

Exact Name of Person
Title or Position
Name of Company
Address (number and street)
Address (city, state, and zip)

ENGINEERING

Dear Exact Name of Person: (or Sir or Madam if answering a blind ad)

Mechanical Engineer

This Mechanical Engineer lost his job because of friction with his boss. He ended up accepting a much better position in another engineering company that was impressed by his ability to develop multiple control designs for use in several industries.

I would appreciate an opportunity to talk with you soon about how I could contribute to your organization through my versatile experience as an engineer in product engineering, product marketing, and project management.

As you will see from my resume, I have excelled in a track record of accomplishment with R. J. Reynolds since graduating with my B.S. degree in Mechanical Engineering (Industrial concentration).

I started my employment with the company as a Design Engineer in Winston-Salem, NC, and earned an Engineering Recognition Award. I have developed multiple control designs for use in several industries. I became a Product Marketing Manager and received a prestigious award for Excellence in Marketing. As a Product Marketing Manager, I played a key role in producing a gross sales increase of $22.6 million over a two-year period.

Last year I was specially selected to act as a Product Engineering Manager and relocated to Lynchburg, VA, where I have handled a wide range of tasks related to the strategic and tactical transfer of products from an assembly plant in Winston-Salem to a Custom OEM assembly plant in Lynchburg. I have set up the engineering department, standardized product production of $20 million in sales, communicated with outside sales professionals and customers during the phase-in process, and created documentation related to the manufacture and assembly of products. While supervising a team of nine design engineers and two drafts people in developing new products and planning production methods, we have added $3.4 million in revenue through recent product development programs.

I am approaching your company because I believe my versatile experience in project management, product development, marketing analysis and sales, and engineering design could be of value to you. I can provide outstanding personal and professional references at the appropriate time. If you can use a superior performer with a strong bottom-line orientation and an ability to think strategically, I hope you will contact me to suggest a time when we might meet.

Sincerely,

Perry M. Whitaker

Date

Exact Name of Person
Title or Position
Name of Company
Address (number and street)
Address (city, state, and zip)

Dear Exact Name of Person: (or Sir or Madam if answering a blind ad)

With the enclosed resume, I would like to introduce you to an educated, meticulous professional with excellent communication and organizational skills as well as a background in medical, surgical, and logistics environments which require careful attention to detail.

I am currently excelling in a rigorous Mechanical Engineering degree program while working part-time to finance my education. My academic excellence has earned me a position on the Dean's List for the last two semesters, and I will receive my Associate's degree in May. I have already completed a number of courses in Computer Aided Drafting and the operation of related software, including: Technical Drafting 1 and II, AutoCAD 1 and II, CAD/CAM (using AutoCAD R12 and R13), and Drafting Design I (using AutoCAD R13 and R14). I have also taken a course on Pro-Engineer, which is a design and production program used to automate the mechanical development of a product from conceptual design through production.

As you will see from the enclosed resume, I have previously worked as a Surgical Technologist, providing operating room support and assistance in surgical procedures from appendectomies to open heart surgery. I gained experience in the use of new instruments, equipment, and procedures as well as in integrating new technologies with the existing equipment and procedures. Prior to my medical career, I served my country in the U.S. Air Force, most recently as an Air Cargo Loading Supervisor and Air Evacuation Medical Specialist. The attention to detail and problem-solving ability required in these positions, as well as my education in Mechanical Engineering, will make me a valuable asset to your organization.

If you can use a self-motivated, meticulous computer-aided drafting professional with excellent communication and organizational skills and a growing knowledge of CAD and related software, I would enjoy talking with you in person. I can provide outstanding personal and professional references at the appropriate time.

Sincerely,

Christina Marie Gautreau

Engineering Student
The best way to enter an industry is to behave and act as though you are already a part of it. This engineering student is marketing her extensive course work in CAD, AutoCAD, CAD/CAM, and drafting design.

Date

Exact Name of Person
Title or Position
Name of Company
Address (number and street)
Address (city, state, and zip)

Dear Exact Name of Person: (or Sir or Madam if answering a blind ad)

Senior Manufacturing Engineer
This Senior Manufacturing Engineer offers an extensive background in quality assurance, safety, budgeting, and manufacturing design.

With the enclosed resume, I would like to make you aware of my background as an industrial and manufacturing engineer with excellent communication and organizational skills along with a background in manufacturing, quality assurance, and safety. I am writing to express my interest in employment opportunities with your organization.

In my most recent position as a Senior Manufacturing Engineer at Crayton Industries, I was responsible for the security and maintenance of more than $9 million worth of equipment while developing and managing a $1.5 million budget for the maintenance department. Through proper process and materials selection, I reduced hazardous waste generated by the plant by 99%. I also oversaw the removal and proper disposal of all hazardous materials from the paint line and paint booth after that operation ceased. In previous positions, I was responsible for training employees on environmental, health, and safety issues and personally addressing any problems in these areas. Through my initiative, the facility drastically reduced its generation of hazardous waste, which resulted in a downgrading of our Hazardous Waste Generator Status to Conditionally Exempt. This change in status greatly reduced our risk of future liability and exempted the facility from certain regulations.

I offer a proven ability to transform a concept into an operating reality. Once I designed a wiring harness for one of our products, resulting in a $100,000 per year reduction in the manufacturing costs for that item.

I hold a Master's degree in Engineering from Texas A & M University and a B.S. in Industrial Engineering from Georgia Tech. I have completed many courses in management, hazardous materials transportation and handling, EHS and ISO auditor training, and other courses through training sponsored by my employer and the Environmental Protection Agency.

If you can use a highly skilled engineer with exceptional communication and problem-solving skills and a background in manufacturing, training and supervision, hazardous materials handling, and safety, I hope you will contact me.

Sincerely,

Barry Sheldon

Date

Exact Name of Person
Title or Position
Name of Company
Address (number and street)
Address (city, state, and zip)

Dear Exact Name of Person: (or Sir or Madam if answering a blind ad)

Director of Nursing

An experienced health care professional is responding to an opening for a Director of Nursing in the facility where she is currently working. She is hoping to change her part-time employment into full time. A cover letter is written slightly differently in tone when you are writing to people you know.

   With the enclosed resume, I would like to make you aware of my strong desire to be considered for the Director of Nursing position with Boise Ambulatory Surgery Center.

   As you may be aware and as my resume shows, I offer extensive administrative skills along with experience in supervisory roles. Although I am currently working only two days a week for Boise Ambulatory Surgery Center, I have been associated for the past two years with BASC and have worked full-time as Staff Nurse in PACU and as Head Nurse in PACU.

   In my previous job, I excelled in a variety of roles with Saul Phillips Memorial Hospital, where I was Head Nurse responsible for a staff of up to 25 medical professionals on a 46-bed surgical floor. I am experienced in all aspects of personnel administration including providing oversight of payroll administration and resolving a wide range of personnel disputes and problems.

   I would welcome the opportunity to serve the Boise Ambulatory Surgical Center as its Director of Nursing.

Yours sincerely,

Penelope R. Wheaton, R.N.

Exact Name of Person
Title or Position
Name of Company
Address (number and street)
Address (city, state, and zip)

HEALTH CARE

Dear Exact Name of Person: (or Sir or Madam if answering a blind ad)

Licensed Physical Therapy Assistant (L.P.T.A.)
Extensive geriatric and rehabilitation experience is the main calling card of this LPTA.

With the enclosed resume, I would like to formally initiate the process of exploring the possibility of joining your organization as a Licensed Physical Therapy Assistant (L.P.T.A.).

In my current position with Logos Healthcare, I am providing my services to geriatric patients, and I have worked with rehabilitation in CVA, hip fractures, general weakness, contractures and orthotic splints, as well with patients in other medical conditions. I am known for my meticulous attention to detail in providing the comprehensive and detailed information needed for reimbursement, and I am also known for my caring attitude and sincere enjoyment of the geriatric patients whom I help. It is truly gratifying to me to see patients become ambulatory again, or to make even small steps in rehabilitation which renew their zest for life.

In my previous position with Moon Hospital, I worked with outpatient, stroke, spinal cord, and geriatric rehabilitation. Prior to that, I was instrumental in establishing Raeford Memorial Hospital's Physical Therapy Department "from scratch." I have been involved in acute, hydrotherapy, and outpatient duties, and I am truly skilled in every aspect of physical therapy.

A highly motivated professional with a proven ability to work with little or no supervision, I am aware of how important accurate and detailed paperwork is so that billing and reimbursements can proceed in a timely and error-free manner. Known as a caring professional who takes great pride in the progress my patients achieve, I pride myself on my ability to develop excellent working relationships with patients and their families, doctors, nurses, hospital personnel, and others.

I can provide outstanding personal and professional references. If my considerable skills could be of value to you, please contact me to suggest a time when we might meet in person to discuss your current and future needs and how I might serve them. Thank you in advance for your time.

Sincerely,

Shila Delfield

Date

Exact Name of Person
Title or Position
Name of Company
Address (number and street)
Address (city, state, and zip)

Dear Exact Name of Person: (or Sir or Madam if answering a blind ad)

With the enclosed resume, I would like to formally enquire about the possibility of joining your organization in some capacity which could utilize my experience as a medical assistant, phlebotomist, laboratory aide, and administrative aide. I am in the process of relocating permanently to the Chicago area with my husband.

As you will see from my resume, I most recently worked as a Clinical Assistant with a respected family practice, and I was known for my compassionate nature and professional attitude. In my prior position, I worked as a Medical Laboratory Aide with the Veterans Hospital, where I worked primarily in the area of venipuncture and specimen identification. I am an experienced Medical Assistant and have assisted doctors in physical exams as well as in minor surgeries and biopsies and other procedures.

You will also see from my resume that I have been active as a Red Cross Volunteer. While working full-time, I have volunteered up to 30 hours per week performing wound care, assisting with asthma patients, and working in numerous other areas to help others and expand my knowledge.

My office operations and administrative skills are highly refined. I proudly served my country as an enlisted soldier specializing in administrative services, and after my honorable discharge I worked at The Pentagon and then at a hospital as an administrative aide. I am knowledgeable of insurance billing.

I can provide outstanding personal and professional references which will, I feel certain, describe me as a highly motivated individual who could enhance any practice. I hope you will welcome my call soon to arrange a brief meeting to discuss your current and future needs and how I might serve them. Thank you in advance for your time.

Sincerely,

Myrna Jimmison

Medical Assistant
Relocating to Chicago is in the cards for this medical assistant who is an experienced phlebotomist and laboratory aide with experience as a clinical assistant.

Date

Exact Name of Person
Title or Position
Name of Company
Address (number and street)
Address (city, state, and zip)

Dear Exact Name of Person: (or Dear Sir or Madam if answering a blind ad)

**Health Care
Systems Administrator**
A strong supervisor with
experience in starting up new
facilities and staffing them is
seeking a position within
a health care organization
that can utilize his
versatile background.

I would appreciate an opportunity to talk with you soon about how I could contribute to your organization through my expertise in health care systems administration.

During my career with the U.S. Army, I applied my proficiency in versatile assignments in medical clinic administration, personnel management, and program development while earning promotion ahead of my peers. Prior to my recent assignment at Ft. Polk, LA, I was a Medical Clinic Personnel Administrator in Germany. In this job I supervised 41 medical specialists, controlled a $3.5 million inventory, carried out reconstruction projects, and trained more than 500 people in emergency medical treatment during a five-month special project.

You will see from my resume that I have been selected to manage important projects and activities. For example, I played a key role in the design process and supervised equipment installation related to the construction of a new medical facility called the Robertson Health Clinic. This clinic was only one of the medical facilities being built during a major medical expansion through the year 2005. I have also played a key role in staffing the 500-bed hospital at Ft. Polk and have managed the training of LPNs, OR Technicians, Physical Therapists, Orthopedic Technicians, and medical office personnel.

With my strong communication, supervisory, and managerial skills, I am confident that I offer experience and knowledge which would be valuable to an organization in need of a strong leader known for unlimited personal initiative.

I hope you will contact me to suggest a time when we might meet to discuss your needs and how I might help you. Thank you in advance for your time.

Sincerely,

Brent H. Umphrey

More aggressive final paragraph:
I hope you will welcome my call soon when I try to arrange a brief meeting with you to discuss your goals and how I might help you achieve them. I can provide outstanding references at the appropriate time.

Date

Exact Name of Person
Title or Position
Name of Company
Address (no., street)
Address (city, state, and zip)

Dear Exact Name of Person: (or Dear Sir or Madam if answering a blind ad)

Medical Office Manager
An office manager with knowledge of ICD-9 and CPT-4 coding should be a worthy addition to some health care organization, especially when she has been involved in the start-up of new facilities.

I would appreciate an opportunity to talk with you soon about how I could contribute to your organization through my versatile skills related to medical office operations and financial services, as well as through my proven sales ability, initiative, and creativity oriented toward improving the "bottom line."

As you will see from my resume, most recently I played a key role in the start-up of a new orthopedics practice. While developing office systems and office procedures "from scratch," including designing all forms, I used and trained other employees to use UNIX software and made valuable suggestions which the UNIX vendor applied to upgrade the system. Skilled in bookkeeping and insurance claims administration, I have filed insurance claims and performed ICD-9 and CPT-4 coding. I also handled accounts payable/receivable and payroll and acted as Credit Manager.

In my previous job at Scotland Memorial Hospital I was rapidly promoted to coordinate business office systems and supervised a large staff while acting as the "internal expert" on the computer system and software problems.

I hope you will welcome my call soon to arrange a brief meeting at your convenience to discuss your current and future needs and how I might serve them. Thank you in advance for your time.

Sincerely yours,

Rosalind Rulnick

Alternate last paragraph:
I hope you will call or write me soon to suggest a time convenient for us to meet and discuss your current and future needs and how I might best serve them. Thank you in advance for your time.

Date

Exact Name of Person
Title or Position
Name of Company
Address (number and street)
Address (city, state, and zip)

Dear Exact Name of Person: (or Sir or Madam if answering a blind ad)

Medical Technology Supervisor
A teaching background in addition to supervisory experience in managing technologists and phlebotomists is what this professional is offering a health care organization.

With the enclosed resume, I would like to make you aware of my background as a medical technologist and supervisor with exceptional communication, organizational, and staff development skills as well as extensive laboratory experience.

In my current position as Medical Technology Supervisor at the Veteran's Administration Medical Centers, I supervise eight employees including three medical technologists and five phlebotomists. In addition to managing a $40,000 supply budget and handling the hiring process, I train all employees on the operation of new laboratory instruments, and write, revise, and update all procedure manuals for Blood Bank, Hematology, Coagulation, Phlebotomy, and Urinalysis. As a Medical Technologist in the Chemistry department, I played a vital role in smoothing the transition when the lab was refitted with newer equipment. I set up and trained the staff on the operation of many of these cutting-edge laboratory instruments, including the Atlas urinalysis machine and the Immuno-I immunoassay device. My contribution was recognized by my supervisor with an award for "Outstanding Performance" and a cash incentive.

At Phoenix Technical Community College, I served as Clinical Chemistry Instructor for the Medical Laboratory Technician Program. I lectured on test methods, chemical reactions, abnormal results, and other testing issues while also administering practicals and written tests and grading students on their performance. I quickly mastered the operation of all the laboratory instruments at Arizona Medical Center in Phoenix in order to train the Clinical Chemistry students during clinical rotations.

As you will see from my enclosed resume, I earned a Bachelor of Science degree in Medical Technology from the University of Colorado at Boulder.

If you can use a highly experienced medical technologist and supervisor with exceptional technical, communication, and staff development skills, I hope you will contact me to suggest a time when we could meet to discuss your needs. I can provide excellent references at the appropriate time.

Sincerely,

Venus Campbell

Date

Exact Name
Exact Title
Exact Name of Organization
Exact Address
City, State Zip

Dear Exact Name of Person: (or Dear Sir or Madam if answering a blind ad):

With the enclosed resume and this cover letter, I would like to make you aware of my interest in being considered for the position of Long-Term Care State Facilitator. In addition to my expert knowledge of nursing center administration and long-term care, I offer a reputation as a highly effective communicator, creative problem-solver, and skilled crisis manager.

As you will see from my resume, I am a Licensed Nursing Home Administrator (L.N.H.A.) and have excelled in administrative positions within the nursing care field. In most of my jobs, I have taken on a wide range of problems and have developed and implemented solutions that improved the census, boosted morale, improved staff skills, and resolved a wide range of problems which had resulted in deficiencies.

In my current position, I have decreased deficiencies from eight to one while increasing the census from 87% to 99%. In my previous position, I increased the census from 90% to 97% while decreasing deficiencies from 14 to five. I am skilled at planning, organizing, and directing administrative functions and monitoring conformance to regulatory guidelines. In one job, I took over the management of an organization experiencing a variety of staffing problems and I restored confidence in the staff while improving public relations and profits.

I am well aware of the many significant contributions your organization makes to the long-term care industry. As an administrator, I have utilized the services you provide in inservice training as well as in mediation and problem solving. Based on my understanding of your role within the nursing home and long-term care industry, I feel I could make valuable contributions through my ability to establish and maintain outstanding relationships as well as through my highly professional approach to solving problems within our very unique industry.

I hope you will give me the opportunity to talk with you in person about my interest in this position. I can provide outstanding personal and professional references at the appropriate time, and I can assure you in advance that I am a loyal and hardworking professional who would be a valuable addition to your team.

Yours sincerely,

Maureen Spears, L.N.H.A.

Nursing Home Administrator
Notice paragraph four. She is commenting on the strengths of the organization to which she is writing this letter applying for a specific position. With minor changes, this special cover letter could become a versatile all-purpose letter.

Date

Exact Name of Person
Title or Position
Name of Company
Address (number and street)
Address (city, state, and zip)

Dear Exact Name of Person: (or Sir or Madam if answering a blind ad)

Clinical Research Assistant
This cover letter was written specifically to apply for a clinical research position. Ms. Haege offers a diversified background in laboratory processing and clinical studies.

With the enclosed resume, I would like to make you aware of my interest in applying for the position of Clinical Research Assistant. I offer knowledge of psychology and human services, well-developed communication and motivational skills, as well as prior experience in laboratory processing, telephone screening for clinical studies, and data entry.

As you will see from my enclosed resume, I have earned a Bachelor of Arts in Psychology from the University of Kentucky at Louisville. I supplemented this rigorous degree program with a 57-hour crisis intervention course through the Carter County Rape Crisis Center and a 40-hour insurance course leading to the designation of Life and Health Agent from the Kentucky Department of Insurance.

In my current position as a Call Center Representative for Nelson Clinical Recruitment, I am excelling in interviewing physicians and potential study subjects to secure their participation in clinical studies. Previously, as Member Services Representative at Wellness 65, I responded to telephone and walk-in inquiries from members and care providers in order to resolve problems and complaints, achieving and maintaining a 99% effectiveness rate to stated service goals.

I have previously served as a Processing Assistant for Bowling Green Hospital, a position that required great attention to detail, as I was performing laboratory procedures and entering the resulting data into a computer. My communication skills, both written and oral, are excellent, and I am familiar with Microsoft Word, WordPerfect, and Microsoft Excel.

I feel certain I could make significant contributions as a Clinical Research Assistant, and I hope you will give me the opportunity to interview with you so that I can show you in person that I am an ideal match with your requirements. I can provide outstanding references and I offer a reputation as a highly motivated young professional with unlimited personal initiative, knowledge of clinical research methodology, excellent planning and organizing skills, and adaptability. Thank you in advance for your time.

Yours sincerely,

Rhonda Haege

Date

Exact Name of Person
Title or Position
Name of Company
Address (number and street)
Address (city, state, and zip)

Dear Exact Name of Person: (or Dear Sir or Madam if answering a blind ad)

HUMAN RESOURCES

Human Resources Manager
A human resources manager now working within the human services field is trying to move up to greater responsibilities and become Human Resources Director for a city.

With the enclosed resume, I would like to make you aware of my interest in the position of Human Resources Director for the City of Anchorage. In my current position as Human Resources Director of the Macedonia County Mental Health Center overseeing 395 people in 20 locations, I have earned widespread respect for my skill in all aspects of human resources management, and I have earned a reputation as a skilled problem solver in personnel matters as well as an insightful administrator and strategic planner.

A lifelong resident of Anchorage, I offer a broad base of contacts in and knowledge of the people and the resources available in this city. I have been very effective in managing all functional areas of the human resources activities of the Macedonia County Mental Health Center through my excellent communication and leadership skills. This organization has allowed me opportunities to establish goals and policies, solve problems, and develop time- and money-saving improvements in a variety of areas. Examples of my accomplishments include the creation of an annual training program for new supervisors, automation of all position and personnel files, development of guidelines adopted by the area mental health authority, and creation of a new department for staff development.

I am confident that I possess the human relations management expertise, education, and communication skills you expect in a candidate for such an important role. I hope you will contact me to suggest a time when I might meet with you in person to discuss my strong qualifications for this position. I take great pride in the many milestones and achievements which have been accomplished at the Macedonia County Mental Health Center under my leadership, and it would be a great pleasure to serve the City of Anchorage.

Sincerely,

Dana T. Deloy

Date

Exact Name of Person
Title or Position
Name of Company
Address (no., street)
Address (city, state, and zip)

Dear Exact Name of Person: (or Dear Sir or Madam if answering a blind ad)

I would appreciate an opportunity to talk with you about how my background related to personnel administration could benefit your organization.

As you will see from my resume, I offer a proven ability to strengthen the human resources area of any size organization. In one job with a Fortune 500 Company, I managed a $600 million project which involved setting up new offices in London, Bangkok, Tel Aviv, and New York. In another job with a 20-year-old company with 500 employees, I designed formal personnel policies and initiated programs related to safety, security, and training. Most recently, I have developed the strategic plans related to closing two plants and downsizing the work force at three other facilities.

My prior work in finance complements my background in the human resources area. In a job with Mony Financial Services as a financial planner and sales manager, I transformed one of the company's worst-performing offices into one of the company's top sales producers among its 112 offices. While motivating and leading a sales team, I also prepared financial profiles for individuals, planned savings and retirement packages, designed corporate pension/profit-sharing plans, and developed health and disability programs.

You would find me to be an energetic and hardworking professional who thrives on solving problems in our fast-changing economy.

I hope you will welcome my call soon to arrange a brief meeting at your convenience to discuss your current and future needs and how I might serve them. Thank you in advance for your time.

Sincerely yours,

Christopher D. McKinney

Alternate last paragraph:
I hope you will call or write me soon to suggest a time convenient for us to meet and discuss your current and future needs and how I might serve them. Thank you in advance for your time.

Date

Exact Name of Person
Title or Position
Name of Company
Address (number and street)
Address (city, state, and zip)

Dear Exact Name of Person: (or Dear Sir or Madam if answering a blind ad)

HUMAN RESOURCES

Human Resources Manager
A human resources manager now working in a unique research-and-development facility is exploring opportunities in scientific and technical environments.

I would appreciate an opportunity to talk with you soon about how I could contribute to your organization through the application of my experience in human relations management and personnel administration.

With a reputation as an articulate, intelligent, and adaptable professional, I am currently excelling in a position as a Personnel Manager for a unique self-contained research-and-development organization. I have been credited with totally revitalizing the evaluation and personnel management process in an organization which recruits, interviews, assesses, tests, and selects its members based on more than 100 factors which include technical skills and personality characteristics.

In earlier assignments I became known as an individual who could be counted on to find creative ways to increase productivity, efficiency, team spirit, and the level of customer service. I have revitalized and transformed poorly functioning offices into model facilities while managing multimillion-dollar budgets, developing operating procedures which were adopted for widespread use, and ensuring that thousands of people were assigned to jobs where their particular skills and training were maximized.

I offer a unique blend of skills, experience, and education which would make me a valuable asset to an organization in need of an enthusiastic, positive thinker.

I hope you will contact me to suggest a time when we might meet to discuss your needs and how I might help you. Thank you in advance for your time.

Sincerely,

Myron B. Detweiler

Alternate last paragraph:
I hope you will call or write me soon to suggest a time convenient for us to meet to discuss your current and future needs and how I might serve them. Thank you in advance for your time.

Date

Exact Name of Person
Title or Position
Name of Company
Address (number and street)
Address (city, state, and zip)

Dear Exact Name of Person: (or Dear Sir or Madam if answering a blind ad)

Personnel Manager
With this all-purpose
cover letter, this qualified
individual is exploring
opportunities in both large
and small companies.

With the enclosed resume, I would like to make you aware of my experience in the management of services related to human resources and personnel administration.

As you will see from my resume, I have been promoted ahead of my peers because of my strong personal initiative, analytical skills, and problem-solving ability. In my most recent job, I was selected to manage personnel and administrative support in a plant with 1,200 hourly workers and more than 100 salaried staff. On my own initiative, I developed a performance feedback tracking log which boosted morale and I was selected to write a pamphlet for the entire base. On another occasion, I authored a Continuity Book which translated corporate personnel programs and benefits into layman's language; this booklet was so popular that it became a model for other plants in the company.

In all of my jobs I have expertly utilized a computer with numerous software applications in order to maintain databases, write reports, compile statistics, and track data. I am highly computer literate and offer an ability to rapidly master new programs.

In my most recent performance evaluation, I was described as "the most motivated personnel administrator I have met in 8 years" by my immediate supervisor. I pride myself on my strong customer service orientation and believe my professional customer service attitude is inspired by my sincere desire to help others. I have discovered that my attention to detail and organizational skills have helped me be of service to numerous people on many occasions. For example, I once created a New Employee's Welcome Package, and I also took the initiative to validate and then correct personnel locator information which I found was 90% in error.

I would like to become a part of an organization that can use a hardworking and disciplined professional who aims for excellence in all things. If you can use my considerable skills and talents, please contact me to suggest a time when we might meet to discuss your needs and how I might serve them. Thank you in advance for your time.

Yours sincerely,

Andrea L. DeYoung

Exact Name of Person
Title or Position
Name of Company
Address (number and street)
Address (city, state, and zip)

Dear Exact Name of Person: (or Dear Sir or Madam if answering a blind ad)

HUMAN RESOURCES

Personnel Manager
A personnel manager for a prominent retailer describes her track record of promotion to increasing responsibilities as well as her dedication in earning her college degree while working full time.

Can you use a hardworking and energetic young professional who offers a background in personnel administration along with outstanding management skills?

As you will see from my enclosed resume, I most recently have worked in the personnel administration field in the administrative offices of the Target Store location in Raleigh, NC. As the Assistant Personnel Manager, I played a role in setting up procedures for and organizing the personnel department. I oversaw the management of personnel records, time cards, and scheduling for 150 employees while directly supervising six people. While excelling in my full-time job, I used my spare time to complete my college degree in Human Resources.

In earlier jobs, I was cited for my customer service and managerial abilities and placed in positions of responsibility usually reserved for older, more experienced managers. For instance, at the Peachtree Plaza Hotel in downtown Atlanta, GA, I directed a staff of 18 people at one of the hotel's popular restaurants.

With exceptional organizational, motivational, and communication skills and a reputation as a fast learner, I am proficient in utilizing a variety of popular software programs.

I hope you will welcome my call soon to arrange a brief meeting at your convenience to discuss your current and future needs and how I might serve them. Thank you in advance for your time.

Sincerely yours,

Gail Davies

Alternate last paragraph:
I hope you will call or write me soon to suggest a time convenient for us to meet and discuss your current and future needs and how I might serve them. Thank you in advance for your time.

Date

Exact Name of Person
Title or Position
Name of Company
Address (number and street)
Address (city, state, and zip)

Dear Exact Name of Person: (or Sir or Madam if answering a blind ad)

Newspaper Writer
Almost by definition, journalists and writers don't write like other people, even when they write cover letters. This award-winning journalist seeks a specialized reporter position at a major metropolitan newspaper.

I have been working for the same newspaper–*The Savannah Enterprise*–for 14 years. I'm an award-winning journalist who is ready to tackle journalism on the next level. *The Los Angeles Times* offers just that, and I am interested in the Radio/TV Reporter position at your paper.

For the past two years, I have been covering American life and culture for the daily newspaper here in Savannah. For the past year, I have also written a column that focuses on local and regional radio and TV. That column now runs on Sundays on the Arts and Leisure front, giving readers news and information on hirings and firings, industry trends, station takeovers, programming and market ratings. At the same time, I have carved out a niche with the radio/TV beat. This area went largely unreported before I was given the beat and treated it as news.

I am appreciative of how *The Savannah Enterprise* has given me the opportunity to break news with this beat. I would relish the thought of pursuing radio/TV reporting full-time at a large metropolitan paper.

I was born and raised in the Los Angeles area, and I like Los Angeles. I also like what you do at *The Los Angeles Times*. I want to be part of it. I am thorough. I am fair. I meet deadlines and my copy is clean. I'm a low-maintenance employee and a positive force in the newsroom.

I'll follow up with a telephone call to make sure you received this package. In the meantime, if you need anything from me, please call me at (910) 483-6611, home, or (910) 483-2439, work.

Thanks for your time and consideration.

Sincerely,

Mitch Schultz

Date

Exact Name of Person
Title or Position
Name of Company
Address (number and street)
Address (city, state, and zip)

Dear Exact Name of Person: (or Sir or Madam if answering a blind ad)

   With the enclosed resume, I would like to make you aware of my interest in working for your organization as a freelance reporter or news stringer.

   As you will see from my resume, I have worked as a reporter for the Delaney Publishing Company and as a stringer and journalist for nationally distributed magazines and weekly newspapers. While serving as a consultant and reporter for the national news magazine *20/20*, I developed a story which resulted in an Emmy-nominated news-feature broadcast. I have also served as a stringer for the *Washington Post* and *Los Angeles Times*. My work as a stringer covering the Bradley Triple Murder Trial resulted in a *Washington Post* front page story.

   I can provide excellent references which will attest to my total reliability and ability to meet the tightest deadlines. I have earned respect for my investigative skills and for my ability to develop news and feature stories that illuminate and entertain. I have reported news and developed features internationally while traveling and living worldwide.

   If you can use a solid performer who could become a valuable freelance resource, I hope you will contact me to suggest a time when we might meet to discuss your needs and how I might meet them. Thank you in advance for your consideration.

                              Yours sincerely,

                              Allie LaGuardia

Exact Name of Person
Title or Position
Name of Company
Address (number and street)
Address (city, state, and zip)

LEGAL & PARALEGAL

Dear Exact Name of Person: (or Sir or Madam if answering a blind ad)

Paralegal

This recently graduated paralegal is relocating and will use this cover letter to send to law firms in the town where he and his family will be settling. He's not sure what kind of opportunities are available, so he wants the cover letter to "blow doors open" so that he can have as many interviews as possible.

With the enclosed resume, I would like to initiate the process of being considered for employment within your organization. I am in the process of permanently relocating to the Maine area where both my wife and I have family. We will be permanently settling in the Brunswick area around May 18, immediately after my college graduation on May 12.

As you will see from my resume, I have recently earned my Associate of Applied Science in Paralegal Technology in an ABA-approved program in Utah. With a 4.0 GPA, I am graduating as the #1 student in my class. While excelling academically, I have also been selected as Honorary Legal Research Assistant at my college because of my academic standing and personal reputation. In that capacity I tutor students and assist faculty in projects that involve legal writing and research. I also have worked 15 hours a week in a paid job as an Assistant Manager while earning my degree.

Prior to enrolling in my current degree program, I excelled as a Legal Specialist in the U.S. Army, and I received 15 medals, awards, and certificates in recognition of outstanding performance. I worked with numerous attorneys and was entrusted with the responsibility for supervising legal work at numerous organizations.

Recently I have worked as a Paralegal for five months in an internship with one of Salt Lake City's most respected law firms. This has given me exposure to real estate, corporate law, civil litigation, personal injury, and criminal defense.

You would find me in person to be a congenial individual, and I can assure you that my legal research and legal writing skills are top-notch. If you can use a hardworking, resourceful, and thorough Paralegal in your firm, I hope you will contact me to suggest a time when we might meet after I arrive in the Brunswick area on May 18. Feel free to call my current number to suggest a time for us to meet, or you may also call the number on my resume, which is my sister's residence.

Thank you in advance for your time.

Sincerely,

Bentley Venable

Date

Exact Name of Person
Title or Position
Name of Company
Address (no., street)
Address (city, state, and zip)

Dear Exact Name of Person: (or Dear Sir or Madam if answering a blind ad)

LEGAL & PARALEGAL

Attorney
This versatile young attorney gained his first work experience as an Army officer. Now he is ready to explore opportunities in private practice. This all-purpose cover letter will allow him to explore opportunities at firms in the town where he and his wife wish to relocate.

I would appreciate an opportunity to talk with you soon about how I could contribute to your organization through my proven abilities as a trial attorney and my experience related to criminal, insurance, consumer, contract, and international law.

After receiving my J.D. degree, I entered the U.S. Army and became chief of a legal assistance office serving more than 15,000 military professionals and their families. In that job I became skilled in techniques related to mediation and arbitration as I resolved many cases without litigation. Promoted ahead of schedule to captain, I was commended for exceptional management skills and was cited as the driving force behind this legal office's being singled out as the best by the Army Chief of Staff.

In a special consulting assignment providing expert legal advice to military executives, I prepared a briefing regarding Rules of Engagement and the Posse Comitatus Act related to drug interdiction.

Most recently as a Trial Defense Attorney, I have handled a heavy and varied work load as one of four defense attorneys serving a 15,000-person military population. Because of our small legal staff, I have conducted all legal research for my cases and drafted all requests, responses, agreements, briefs, and motions while gaining experience with cases that involved issues ranging from domestic violence and rape, to armed robbery and fraud, to personnel matters. I recently received a prestigious medal for extraordinary accomplishments as a trial attorney.

I can provide excellent personal and professional references which would attest to my reputation for integrity, congenial personality, and dedication to excellence. I am certain I could add value to your organization as I have to my other employers.

I hope you will welcome my call soon to arrange a brief meeting at your convenience to discuss your needs and goals and how I might serve them. Thank you in advance for your time.

Sincerely yours,

Jonathan West

Date

Exact Name of Person
Exact Title of Person
Exact Name of Organization
Address
City, State Zip

This linguist offers English,
Polish, Ukranian, Russian,
Czech, Slovak, and Byelorussian
capabilities.

Dear Exact Name:

With the enclosed resume, I would like to make you aware of my expertise in the intelligence field, my skills as an interrogator and debriefer, as well as my extensive experience as a linguist, analyst, instructor, and interpreter.

As you will see, I possess a Top Secret security clearance, a talent for languages, and a wide-ranging education which has emphasized government, politics, and criminal justice. Throughout my career in the U.S. Army, I have been selected to attend technical and leadership training programs with a concentration in interrogation and languages. I offer linguistic abilities in languages which include, in addition to English, Ukranian, Polish, Russian, Czech, Slovak, and Byelorussian.

Recently promoted to Sergeant First Class, I manage 18 Intelligence Operations Specialists as an Intelligence Operations Supervisor with the Army's only airborne interrogation company. In my prior position as an Instructor, I conducted Russian language instruction while planning and organizing several major events, coordinating with Russian journalists and correspondents and acting as an interpreter for high-ranking international VIPs. On my own initiative I wrote and published a Russian-language "crisis survival packet" which was distributed for use throughout the Army's quick response community.

The recipient of numerous medals and awards for exceptional initiative, technical expertise, and leadership, I have consistently been credited with bringing about improvements which have boosted scores in all measurable areas of performance.

If you can use an experienced interrogator and debriefer who possesses a keen analytical mind, excellent communication skills, and high levels of dedication and integrity, I hope you will contact me to suggest a time when we might meet to discuss your needs. I can assure you in advance that I could rapidly become an asset to your organization.

Sincerely,

Mikhail Olatokun

Date

Exact Name of Person
Title or Position
Name of Company
Address (number and street)
Address (city, state, and zip)

Dear Exact Name of Person: (or Sir or Madam if answering a blind ad)

With the enclosed resume, I would like to formally express my desire to become a member of the United Nations team of linguists and interpreters.

A French teacher and subject matter expert on Sub-Sahara Africa is seeking a position as a linguist and interpreter with the United Nations.

Currently a French Instructor, I am teaching the French language to Special Forces and Psychological Operations soldiers. I have become known for my creativity in helping nonlinguists acquire excellent speaking and writing skills in a foreign language, and my students have excelled in their results on the Defense Language Proficiency Test (DLPT). I am fluent in English and French and in some African languages including Mandingo and Sarakole.

I am now a citizen of the U.S., but I was formerly a citizen of the Ivory Coast, and I am a subject matter expert on Sub-Sahara Africa. With expert knowledge of the Ivory Coast, I am knowledgeable of Sub-Sahara African countries including their customs, culture, history, geography, politics, religion, and distinguishing features and philosophical characteristics.

While earning my Bachelor of Science and my Master of Science degrees in Economics from the University of the Ivory Coast, I facilitated the adaptation of foreign exchange students from different English-speaking countries to the university and to the Sub-Sahara African environment. While in that role, I gained an excellent understanding of the process through which English-speaking foreigners can best gain an understanding of the Sub-Sahara African countries.

Currently completing my Master of Science in International Relations from Ohio State University, it would be a great honor to be associated with the United Nations as a linguist and interpreter.

Thank you in advance for your professional courtesies. I can provide outstanding personal and professional references at the appropriate time.

Yours sincerely,

Abramy Sofassi

Date

Exact Name of Person
Title or Position
Name of Company
Address (number and street)
Address (city, state, and zip)

Dear Exact Name of Person: (or Dear Sir or Madam if answering a blind ad)

With the enclosed resume, I would like to make you aware of my experience in supply, logistics, and warehouse management including my ability to account for all types of materials in large quantities as well as my strong computer skills and budgetary knowledge.

As you will see from my resume, I offer knowledge of numerous software programs which include the Microsoft Office Suite as well as programs for inventory control and supply management. In my current job as Logistics Management Supervisor in charge of two employees, I have become recognized as the "internal expert" on all logistics matters within my organization while flawlessly accounting for property valued at more than $35 million and managing a budget of more than $100,000. On my own initiative, I have provided the leadership required to establish new automated systems which have boosted productivity and efficiency. I have also served as Instructor for the Unit Level Logistics System S4 (ULLS-S4). I have earned a reputation as a skilled problem solver.

While gaining expertise in logistics and supply management, I have been selected for difficult assignments which required an astute problem solver and strategic thinker who could accurately forecast future needs. I have established highly effective logistics systems in field and headquarters environments, and I once supervised the closure of a government installation and the geographical relocation of the unit with no loss of accountability.

In my previous position, I worked in human resources administration and managed five employees while supervising a Customer Service Desk. I offer excellent communication and negotiating skills.

If you can use a highly motivated self-starter known for unlimited personal initiative, I hope you will contact me to suggest a time when we might meet to discuss your needs. I can assure you in advance that I could rapidly become an asset to your organization.

Sincerely,

Wendell Blickendorf

Date

Exact Name of Person
Title or Position
Name of Company
Address (number and street)
Address (city, state, and zip)

Dear Exact Name of Person: (or Sir or Madam if answering a blind ad)

Operations Manager

With the enclosed resume, I would like to make you aware of my interest in utilizing my considerable experience in logistics, supply, and financial management within your organization.

As you will see from my enclosed resume, I rose to the rank of Chief Warrant Officer 3 (CW3) while receiving nearly 50 medals including the Legion of Merit and Bronze Star. In my most recent job in Bosnia-Herzegovina, I managed more than 320,000 pieces of equipment valued at $3.2 billion while supervising 39 personnel, managing automated systems, and monitoring equipment in 215 companies. On my own initiative, I vastly improved the organization's computer hardware and software architecture. During that time, I also managed supply functions for personnel in Sarajevo.

In my previous job, I was handpicked by the famed "Golden Wings" as Supply and Budget Officer, and I was in charge of a $2.7 million budget and its related 200-plus contracts for goods and services. When I took over the position, the "Golden Wings" —the Army's famous performing parachute team—was crippled by supply problems, accountability issues, and bureaucratic roadblocks which were preventing numerous international performances by the team. I brought all contracts under control, managed the budget with no overages, introduced new safety devices, and cut through frustrating red tape in order to permit the team to perform in Cuba and other countries. In my previous job, I masterminded logistics plans during the war in the Middle East.

During formal performance evaluations, I have consistently been described by my supervisors as "the best" Warrant Officer they ever served with, and I was offered a promotion to CW4 recently, which I declined. I thoroughly enjoyed serving my country, but I am eager to apply my logistics and supply expertise in the private sector. I am extremely knowledgeable of government contracting procedures and am experienced with virtually all of the Army's automated logistics and supply systems. Known for my resourcefulness, I have always found creative ways to save money, including in the area of making warranty claims for goods and services.

If you feel that my considerable talents could be of benefit to you, I hope you will contact me to suggest a time when we might meet to discuss your needs.

Sincerely,

Craig J. Kooienga, Jr.

In addition to specialized expertise in automated systems, this talented logistics and supply expert possesses a proven ability to troubleshoot complex supply and logistics problems. More cover letters like this one are in the Distribution and Warehousing Section.

Date

Exact Name of Person
Title or Position
Name of Company
Address (number and street)
Address (city, state, and zip)

Supply Manager

In this cover letter, a talented leader is emphasizing his team-building skills in addition to his distinguished career in government service. He is selectively exploring opportunities in private industry and has given much thought to embarking on a second career in the private sector.

Dear Exact Name of Person: (or Sir or Madam if answering a blind ad)

With the enclosed resume, I would like to make you aware of my background as an experienced supply operations manager who offers a reputation as a knowledgeable professional with a talent for team building and initiative.

As you will see, throughout my career in the Department of Defense I was placed in leadership roles where I continually excelled through my ability to guide, lead, and motivate others. I consistently led my units to accomplishments which resulted in high scores in inspections of supply operations and in recognition as top-notch supply support facilities.

In my most recent position in Arizona, I was evaluated by a senior executive as "the best of 65" managers and supervisors under his leadership. I was credited with transforming a substandard, poorly functioning supply center into the best of its kind in the parent organization within my first nine months in the unit. One example of my efforts in this job was when I took the initiative to identify excess and underutilized property. A total of more than 1,900 items valued in excess of $4.5 million were identified and reallocated. As a result of my efforts, I led the unit to recognition with a Defense Department "Supply Excellence Award."

In my prior job as Supervisory Information Analyst for a national training center, I operated a unique multimillion-dollar data collection computer facility. Promoted to this leadership role after only eight months as a Supply Observer/Controller, I was evaluated as a multifunctional and knowledgeable logistician who was familiar with all aspects of supply, transportation, and maintenance.

The recipient of numerous awards in recognition of my professionalism and accomplishments, I applied my time management and organizational skills while completing a Bachelor's degree in Logistics Management and simultaneously meeting the demands of a career which required frequent relocations.

If you can use an experienced supply operations manager, I hope you will contact me to suggest a time when we might meet to discuss your needs.

Sincerely,

Charles Rydzinski

Date

Exact Name of Person
Title or Position
Name of Company
Address (number and street)
Address (city, state, and zip)

Dear Exact Name of Person: (or Dear Sir or Madam if answering a blind ad)

Auto Mechanic

With the enclosed resume, I would like to make you aware of my interest in exploring employment opportunities within your company in which my strong mechanical skills could be put to work for your benefit.

As you will see from my resume, I received a diploma in Auto Mechanics from a vocational school and worked as an Auto Mechanic prior to joining the U.S. Army. Even as a basic trainee, my leadership abilities were recognized as I was named Squad Leader and placed in charge of 10 employees. I graduated as Honor Graduate from Helicopter Repair School and was promoted ahead of my peers into management positions which placed me in charge of managing up to four individuals. The recipient of numerous medals and awards recognizing my technical skills and management abilities, I am known for my ability to train employees to perform complex troubleshooting while continuously emphasizing the importance of a drug-free, safety-conscious, and clean work environment.

This auto mechanic is attempting to return to the field in which he worked prior to serving his country as a helicopter mechanic. Notice that the first paragraph stresses his mechanical skills. This choice of words allows him to use the letter in an all-purpose way in case he decides to approach industrial companies and production facilities.

I am skilled at operating and repairing numerous types of equipment as well as in operating backhoes, bulldozers, and dump trucks.

I hope you will contact me to suggest a time when we might meet to discuss your needs and how I might help you. I can provide outstanding personal and professional references, and I thank you in advance for your time.

Sincerely,

Clay Bauman

Date

Exact Name of Person
Title or Position
Name of Company
Address (number and street)
Address (city, state, and zip)

Dear Exact Name of Person: (or Sir or Madam if answering a blind ad)

Technical Inspector

After a distinguished first career with the Federal Aviation Administration, this knowledgeable executive seeks to transfer his quality assurance background and technical inspection skills to private industry. Although he loved his job with FAA, he traveled extensively and he would like to find a job which will allow him to be at home most evenings.

With the enclosed resume, I would like to make you aware of my interest in discussing the possibility of joining your organization in some capacity in which you could utilize my management and communication skills. After a distinguished 20-year career with the federal government, I have recently resigned and my wife and I have resettled permanently in the Santa Fe area so that we can live near my wife's family.

In jobs with the Federal Aviation Administration, I have advanced to critical supervisory positions in the maintenance inspection and quality assurance field. In my most recent assignment, I inspected critical maintenance performed on a multi-million-dollar fleet of the highest-priority equipment at one of the nation's busiest airlift centers. The recipient of numerous honors for exceptional performance, I have learned to operate and manage in environments in which there is "no room for error." On numerous occasions I have saved taxpayers thousands of dollars through my resourceful problem-solving ability as well as my ability to train, motivate, and manage others.

When you look at my resume, you will see that I have demonstrated an ability to excel in any challenge I take on. I believe my communication skills have been the key to success in all my jobs. Although I have not worked in a professional position in a profit-making organization, I offer a strong bottom-line orientation and I am confident of my ability to maximize results in any functional area, from sales, to production operations, to management.

If you can use a dedicated and hardworking professional with highly refined time-management skills, I hope you will contact me to suggest a time when we might meet to discuss your needs. I can assure you in advance that I could rapidly become an asset to your organization.

Sincerely,

Merle G. Wilcox

Date

Exact Name of Person
Exact Name of Company
Address
City, State Zip

Dear Sir or Madam:

Maintenance Supervisor
As rumors circulate that his company is preparing to downsize and eliminate thousands of employees, this maintenance supervisor has decided to explore opportunities in other companies that can use his customer service and quality assurance background.

Can you use a highly skilled professional who offers extensive experience in the area of electronics and electrical repair, safety management, quality assurance, and production control?

As you will see from my resume, I have excelled as an Electronics Maintenance Supervisor and Team Chief while working for the Bannington Corporation. While training and supervising electronics personnel, I have been involved in all the functions related to delivering a quality repair product to the customer—inventory control, customer relations, supply management, as well as budgeting and financial administration.

In most of my supervisory positions, the electronics specialists I managed were performing work for more than 100 customer facilities, and it was my job to make sure that customers were satisfied, turnaround time was appropriate, and that employees were always concerned with "doing it right the first time." I pride myself on my excellent supervisory skills, and I am skilled in motivating employees to perform productively and take pride in their work. From my experience in working at locations all over the world, including in Korea and Germany, I am accustomed to working with multiracial and multicultural work forces.

Especially during the past five years, I have been extensively involved in Quality Assurance functions as a Quality Inspector. In my most recent job, I expertly prepared my team for a rigorous quality assurance inspection after making numerous internal changes which reduced the shop's backlog of repair jobs, decreased turnaround time, and improved customer relations.

You would find me in person to be an amiable individual who prides myself on my ability to rapidly become a valuable asset to any organization which can use a hard worker with a strong bottom-line orientation. I have become known as a skillful cost cutter and always try to instill a philosophy of "waste not, want not" in the employees I manage. Please contact me if you can use my considerable skills in the area of mechanical, electrical, and electronics repair.

Yours sincerely,

Sam Shepherd

Date

Exact Name of Person
Title or Position
Name of Company
Address (number and street)
Address (city, state, and zip)

Dear Exact Name of Person: (or Sir or Madam if answering a blind ad)

Plumber and Pipefitter

The purpose of this cover letter is to sell the potential of Edmond Means to do something he has never done before: work as a Chemical Plant Technician. In his cover letter, he presents himself as a hardworking and intelligent technical expert with numerous skills relevant to the advertised job.

Please accept the enclosed resume as an indication of my interest in being considered for the position of Chemical Plant Technician which you recently advertised in the New York *Daily Post*.

In addition to being a high school graduate with mechanical aptitude who is willing to work rotating shifts and overtime, I have completed the one-year Plumbing and Pipefitting course at Buffalo Technical Community College, one year of studies in Electronics, and am licensed as a Plumbing Contractor by the State of New York. I have supplemented my college programs with additional courses such as the Reliance, Inc., Workshop, Davis School of Plumbing Mechanical Seal Course, Leak and Spill Control School, and Hazardous Communications/Confined Space Safety Program.

For the past two years I have been employed by Williams, Inc., in Brooklyn, NY, where I have earned promotion to Master Mechanic–Utilities after advancing from Utilities Mechanic to Preventive Maintenance Coordinator.

Earlier with Sara Lee, Inc., in Niagara Falls, NY, I advanced quickly and worked as a Quality Control Inspector before earning promotion to Filter Plant Operator. Through the years I have attended numerous seminars to develop knowledge of areas such as quality improvement, HVAC, and steam trap operations.

I am confident that I offer the type of dedication to quality you seek. I hope you will contact me to suggest a time when we might meet to discuss your needs and how I could contribute to your organization as a Chemical Plant Technician.

Sincerely,

Edmond R. Means

Date

Mabel Kennedy
Human Resource Assistant
Bell Atlantic Mobile
20 Alexander Drive
Wallingford, CT 06492

Dear Ms. Kennedy:

MAINTENANCE & PRODUCTION

Security Systems Mechanic
This mechanic offers specialized knowledge related to security systems and metal fabrication. You will find more cover letters of this type in the Electronics Section of this book.

I would appreciate an opportunity to talk with you soon about how I could contribute to Bell Atlantic Mobile through my excellent technical electronics and mechanical skills. I have a reputation as a fast learner and I am sure I would be a valuable member of your team.

As you will see from my resume, my technical skills include installing, repairing, and maintaining security systems and experience with metal fabrication machinery. My additional experience includes time spent as a cellular phone, VCR, mobile radio, and CNC equipment technician. During approximately three years with Southeast Security Systems, I routinely worked with blueprints, schematics, plans, and electrical drawings while performing maintenance on all types of mechanical equipment.

I feel that my "track record" of promotion and selection for special training are indications of my talents. I have often been singled out by customers and employers to receive their thanks for "a job well done" while earning their trust and confidence for my professionalism and emphasis on customer service.

I genuinely hope you will call or write me soon to suggest a time convenient for us to meet to discuss how I might best serve your current and future needs. Thank you in advance for your time.

Sincerely yours,

Avery Jordan

Date

Exact Name of Person
Title or Position
Name of Company
Address (number and street)
Address (city, state, and zip)

Dear Exact Name of Person: (or Sir or Madam if answering a blind ad)

Shop Foreman

After traveling the world with defense industry companies, this professional is ready to grow some roots and offer his expertise related to environmental issues and petroleum waste handling.

I would appreciate an opportunity to talk with you soon about how I could contribute to your organization through my mechanical aptitude and proven ability to motivate, lead, and train others to achieve outstanding results and reach high levels of productivity and efficiency. I have recently returned to the Green Bay area where I grew up and where my family lives.

As you will see from my enclosed resume, in addition to my experience as a Shop Foreman and Fleet Supervisor, I offer specialized training and experience with environmental issues. While working all over the world for companies in the defense industry, I was selected ahead of my peers for leadership roles and special projects. I excelled in special consulting assignments worldwide including projects in Puerto Rico, Korea, Turkey, Haiti, and Vietnam as well as in Hawaii and Kansas.

During my most recent assignment as a Shop Foreman in Alaska, I took the initiative to bring a poorly functioning environmental program up to standard and saw it improve enough to pass numerous inspections. In addition to establishing the prescribed parts inventory to support the program, I conducted informational meetings which allowed all unit personnel to become aware of how to handle petroleum waste safely in order to comply with government regulations and rules.

If you can use an experienced supervisor with excellent mechanical aptitude who has been singled out for numerous awards for professionalism and dedication, I hope you will contact me to suggest a time when we might meet to discuss your needs. I can assure you in advance that I could rapidly become an asset to your organization.

Sincerely,

Jon Schoonveld

Date

Exact Name of Person
Title or Position
Name of Company
Address (number and street)
Address (city, state, and zip)

Dear Exact Name of Person: (or Sir or Madam if answering a blind ad)

With the enclosed resume, I would like to make you aware of my background as an experienced shop foreman with outstanding mechanical skills and a strong background in the supervision of maintenance, repair, and troubleshooting activities.

As you will see, I have been employed by the Coca Cola Bottling Company and have earned advancement to Shop Foreman after originally being hired as a Diesel Mechanic. In this job I oversee the day-to-day operations of a shop which maintains and repairs a fleet of 125 vehicles. My responsibilities include inventory control and ordering parts, scheduling work to ensure timely completion, and dealing with outside contractors. I have been credited with bringing about significant cost reductions through my ability to manage time and human resources for the highest levels of productivity.

In previous jobs, I advanced in supervisory roles and held assignments as a Shop Foreman, Assistant Shop Foreman, and Assistant Maintenance Manager/Training Supervisor. In every job I earned the respect of my superiors for my dedication as a teacher and mentor for my subordinates as well as for my knowledge of shop procedures. I have controlled multimillion-dollar parts and equipment inventories, developed procedures which increased employee job performance, and implemented changes which increased productivity and reduced expenses.

If you can use an experienced shop foreman with the ability to get the most out of all available resources while handling pressure and deadlines, I hope you will contact me to suggest a time when we might meet to discuss your needs. I can assure you in advance that I could rapidly become an asset to your organization.

Sincerely,

Darnell Curtis

Date

Exact Name of Person
Title or Position
Name of Company
Address (number and street)
Address (city, state, and zip)

Dear Exact Name of Person: (or Sir or Madam if answering a blind ad)

With the enclosed resume, I would like to make you aware of my background as an experienced professional with exceptional supervisory, communication, and analytical skills as well as a strong bottom-line orientation and a proven ability to maximize profits and sales.

I was recruited by Boise Auto World for my present position as Business Manager, and my rapid success in that position resulted in my being entrusted with the responsibility for overseeing the finance departments at both of their locations. I supervise three finance managers as well as a sales force of 15 automotive sales representatives. Through my efforts in promoting finance and warranty products, the dealership's average aftermarket profit has increased from $300 per vehicle to $500 per vehicle.

In my previous position with Wachovia Bank, I was promoted rapidly, achieving a position as Assistant Vice President after only 33 months. I began with the company as a Credit Analyst and was promoted to Commercial Relationship Manager at the end of seven months of service. In this position, I actively recruited new commercial accounts and serviced existing accounts. During my tenure, my commercial accounts portfolio grew from $15 million to $25 million, and I doubled non-interest (fee-based) income from $20,000 per year to $40,000 per year.

I have earned Master of Business Administration and Bachelor of Science in Business Administration degrees from Idaho State University.

If you can use a hardworking young manager with proven business savvy, I would enjoy an opportunity to meet with you in person to discuss your needs. Although I can provide outstanding references at the appropriate time, I would appreciate your holding my interest in your company in confidence at this point. I can assure you in advance that I have an exceptional reputation and could become a valuable asset to your company.

Sincerely,

Martin L. Jameson

Date

Exact Name of Person
Title or Position
Name of Company
Address (number and street)
Address (city, state, and zip)

Dear Sir or Madam:

MANAGERS

Retail Manager
Although he has spent an impressive first career in retailing, this individual is interested in shopping his resume around to companies outside the retail industry. Like most talented and versatile professionals, he is attempting to locate a job which he will enjoy.

With the enclosed resume, I would like to make you aware of my interest in your organization. I would appreciate the opportunity to talk with you in person about my considerable background in training, team building, and customer service as well as my track record of achievement in retail operations.

As you will see from my resume, I am known for my team building, time management, and organizational abilities. For the past two years, I have been employed as a District Manager with Family Dollar Stores, Inc. I am responsible for 14 locations producing in excess of $15 million in annual sales volume while handling the responsibility for total merchandising and operations functions for all units. While controlling shrinkage to an average of 1.11 percent, I have significantly refined the skills and knowledge of our management staff through aggressive recruitment, training, and development.

In prior positions with Marshall's Family Clothing and earlier with Wal-Mart Stores, Inc., I was singled out to manage complex projects related to overseeing store openings including hiring and staffing locations and providing operational oversight. I have also been involved in managing projects to remodel multiple stores and as well as in corporate strategic planning.

I have gained experience in all operational environments in retail settings: human resources and personnel management, purchasing and inventory control, customer service, public relations, merchandising, office operations, and loss prevention. Having been in management for approximately 17 years, I offer expertise in numerous areas and am confident that I am a professional capable of contributing successfully to your organization's "bottom line."

If my considerable talents and skills interest you, I hope you will call or write me soon to suggest a time convenient for us to meet to discuss your needs and how I might serve them. I can provide outstanding personal and professional references at the appropriate time. Thank you in advance for your time.

Sincerely,

Shandal Franklin

Date

Exact Name of Person
Title or Position
Name of Company
Address (number and street)
Address (city, state, and zip)

Dear Exact Name of Person: (or Sir or Madam if answering a blind ad)

Restaurant Manager

This restaurant manager is not going to wait for an advertisement in the newspaper describing his ideal job. He is aggressively going after his ideal job by using the direct approach in job hunting. That means he will send this cover letter to companies he considers attractive in order to signal his availability and his interest in the role of General Manager or Director of Operations. Letters like this enable you to manage your career and get to the next level of advancement you deserve!

With the enclosed resume, I would like to make you aware of an experienced food service professional with exceptional motivational, communication, and organizational skills. I offer a background as a General Manager and Director of Operations who has demonstrated the ability to produce extraordinary "bottom-line" results.

With Jake's Grille, I was aggressively recruited and hired to design, coordinate the construction of, and manage the kitchen for the opening of this location. My exemplary management skills were quickly recognized, and I was promoted to Director of Operations, with final accountability for all aspects of the operation of a busy restaurant with annual sales of $1.5 million. I train and supervise the Kitchen Manager, Bar Manager, and Front End Manager as well as the kitchen, wait and bar staff, totaling 65 employees. I prepare and manage the monthly operations budget, evaluating all expenses to maximize profits and ensure budget compliance.

In previous positions with Foster's Seafood, I first coordinated the construction and development of this family seafood restaurant, and then was actively sought out by the owners to "turn around" the operation, taking over at a time when it was on the verge of bankruptcy. Using the same innovative, cost-cutting inventory control procedures I had implemented when I first worked for the company, I quickly transformed the restaurant into a popular and profitable organization with a $200,000 increase in sales.

If you can use an experienced General Manager and Director of Operations whose supervisory and leadership skills have been tested in a variety of restaurant environments, I hope you will contact me to suggest a time when we could meet in person to discuss your needs. I can assure you in advance that I have an excellent reputation and could quickly become a valuable asset to your company.

Sincerely,

Bruce Pollicino

Date

Exact Name of Person
Title or Position
Name of Company
Address (number and street)
Address (city, state, and zip)

Dear Exact Name of Person: (or Sir or Madam if answering a blind ad)

With the enclosed resume, I would like to make you aware of my background as an experienced manager with excellent communication, organizational, and motivational skills as well as my background in operations management, staff development, and customer service.

I started with Harris Teeter as a meat cutter and advanced to Assistant Manager positions after being selected for the Store Manager Training Program, which is normally reserved for employees who have held a Department Manager position. In my present position as Store Manager for the Charlotte location, I am responsible for all aspects of the operation of a $9.5 million store. I supervise up to 52 employees, including six department managers while directing the implementation of company programs, policies, and procedures. Through my initiative, the store's product levels and cleanliness have increased by 10%, and net contribution for the Charlotte location has risen by 2.3%.

As you will see, I have earned a Bachelor of Arts in Education from the University of Tennessee. In addition, I have completed the Harris Teeter Store Manager Training Program and quickly mastered the proprietary computer system utilized by the company. I feel that my strong combination of education, initiative, and management experience would make me a worthy addition to your company.

If you can use a positive, results-oriented manager with a strong background in customer service, operations management, and staff development, I hope you will contact me to suggest a time when we might meet in person to discuss your needs. I can provide excellent references.

Sincerely,

Harold C. Mohrmann

Store Manager
The grass is not always greener in another company or industry, but it certainly can look greener. This store manager thinks there might be greener pastures than grocery store management, so he is using this all-purpose letter to explore management and customer service positions in other organizations.

Date

Exact Name of Person
Title or Position
Name of Company
Address (number and street)
Address (city, state, and zip)

Dear Exact Name of Person: (or Sir or Madam if answering a blind ad)

Bookseller

Sometimes a change is as good as a rest, they say, and this bookseller was delighted to read that a high-volume, large-format bookstore is moving to his hometown. If he can secure a management position with the company, he will eliminate a 45-minute commute to work each way, every day. He can improve the quality of his life by changing employers and yet still remain in an industry which he loves.

With the enclosed resume, I would like to make you aware of my background as an energetic, self-motivated, and highly experienced retail bookstore manager whose proven communication, organizational, and leadership skills have been tested in a high-volume, large-format environment.

As you will see from my resume, I have been with Books A Million for ten years and have served in a managerial capacity in the Rochester store for most of that period. Supervising an average of 18 employees in a store that averages $2.5 million dollars a year, I have consistently received high marks on all employee evaluations. Since my promotion to Manager, I am solely responsible for all aspects of personnel recruitment, staff development, and scheduling.

As Manager, I perform the role of an operations manager, directing the day-to-day functions of the store and prioritizing and assigning tasks to employees. In addition to administering payroll, benefit and personnel programs, I handle the hiring process and am proud of the low turnover I have achieved in a job market with a very high transient rate. I attribute this success to my ability to select highly motivated employees.

Although I am highly regarded by my present employer and can provide excellent references at the appropriate time, I would like to take on the new challenge of a larger store. I am confident that my enthusiasm, high energy level, and "can-do" attitude, as well as my strong management, staff development, and organizational skills would benefit Borders Books and Music as they enter the Rochester market.

If you can use an Operations or Merchandising manager with a strong commitment to providing the highest possible levels of customer service and the proven ability to motivate employees to achieve excellence, I hope you will contact me soon. I can assure you that I have an excellent reputation within the community and would quickly become a valuable addition to your organization.

Sincerely,

David Delancy

Date

Exact Name of Person
Title or Position
Name of Company
Address (number and street)
Address (city, state, and zip)

Dear Exact Name of Person: (or Sir or Madam if answering a blind ad)

MANUFACTURING

Electrician
Skilled in wiring, maintenance, troubleshooting, and repair, this electrician is seeking new challenges in industrial and commercial environments.

With the enclosed resume, I would like to acquaint you with my skills as an experienced commercial and industrial electrician with a solid background in the wiring, maintenance, troubleshooting, and repair of electrical systems.

As you will see from my enclosed resume, I have extensive training in various types of wiring and electrical systems. In my most recent position at Purolator, I assembled, wired, and performed troubleshooting on motor control units for industrial and commercial grade air compressors and chillers. Through our efforts, the department was awarded ISO 9000 certification while achieving the company's goal of "zero defects" in on-time shipping.

At Amarillo Electric I acquired valuable experience in new construction wiring and installation as I refined my knowledge in reading blueprints and schematics while working on the new Gruber Army Medical Center building.

During my years of experience, I have learned to troubleshoot and repair high-tension systems and electrical substations while working with the wiring and electrical systems of a wide variety of ships and power equipment. In addition to the Electrical Wireman Journeyman's Course, I have completed supplementary training courses at El Paso University and Austin Technical Community College. I feel that my extensive industrial experience and education would be strong assets to your organization.

If you can benefit from the services of a highly experienced electrician whose skills have been tested in a wide variety of industrial and commercial environments, please contact me to suggest a time when we might meet to discuss your needs and how I might meet them. Thank you in advance for your time and consideration.

Sincerely,

Nick Klosinski

Date

Exact Name of Person
Title or Position
Name of Company
Address (number and street)
Address (city, state, and zip)

Dear Exact Name of Person: (or Sir or Madam if answering a blind ad)

Department Manager
Experience in producing I.S.O.
documentation is what many
companies are looking for,
and this job hunter offers
experience in helping a
corporation's first plant gain
I.S.O. compliance. You will
find more cover letters like
this one in the Electronics
and Engineering Sections
of this book.

With the enclosed resume, I would like to make you aware of my background as an experienced management professional with a strong manufacturing emphasis. I offer proven leadership ability and strong communication skills along with the ability to develop and implement new programs and procedures that increase efficiency and lower production costs.

As you will see, I am currently excelling as a Department Manager for Sunflower Industries at its Cedar Rapids facility. In this position, I manage seven supervisors and a production team of 140 employees producing 250,000 pounds of finished product per week. I manage and develop supply and project budgets totaling more than $800,000 and am responsible for the maintenance and accountability of over $7 million worth of manufacturing equipment. I started with the corporation as a Product Manager, where I quickly distinguished myself by producing two-thirds of the written documentation for implementing I.S.O. procedures. Due in large part to my efforts, the Shenandoah facility was the first corporate plant to achieve I.S.O. 9002 certification.

Prior to joining Sunflower Industries, I proudly served as a Captain in the United States Marine Corps, where I excelled as a HAWK missile Firing Platoon Commander during the Persian Gulf War. I managed 70 personnel and was responsible for the maintenance, security, and accountability of more than $45 million worth of advanced equipment. I received a number of prestigious awards and medals for my exemplary service to my country.

I have earned a Bachelor of Arts degree from Kentucky State University at Bowling Green, which I have supplemented with military training as well as with professional development courses related to manufacturing, leadership, and management.

If you can use an experienced management professional whose strong supervisory and communication skills have been tested in a variety of challenging environments, then I look forward to hearing from you to suggest a time when we might meet to discuss your needs. I can provide excellent references.

Sincerely,

Pierre Dufrene

Date

Exact Name of Person
Title or Position
Name of Company
Address (number and street)
Address (city, state, and zip)

Dear Exact Name of Person: (or Sir or Madam if answering a blind ad)

MANUFACTURING

Production Supervisor
Mr. Canzoneri has reached a plateau in his company, so he is using this all-purpose cover letter to apply for positions within production and manufacturing environments. He feels that his strong background in production supervision will help him locate a more challenging management position, and he is confident that his quality control background is transferable to numerous industries.

With the enclosed resume, I would like to make you aware of my excellent communication and organizational skills as well as my background in production management and quality control.

In my most recent position with the Goodyear Tire Company, I supervise five sorters in the operation of nine force variation machines. I assure the security and proper functioning of more than $9 million worth of manufacturing equipment, reporting any maintenance problems or malfunctions to minimize the effect on production. On numerous occasions, I have had the highest production in my department, and I was a member of the team that implemented procedural changes for correction factors, enabling the plant to achieve QS-9000 certification.

In earlier positions at Purolator, Inc., and Cutler-Hammer, Inc., I further honed my skills in manufacturing and quality control. At Purolator, I mixed rubber, fed materials to extruders, and conducted viscosity testing of rubber butylene products. While working for Cutler-Hammer, I ensured that wire manufactured for use in automotive wiring harnesses met engineering specifications, pull-testing for rated strength and inspecting the number of copper strands in each wire. In addition, I improved the pull-testing process by recommending a shield on the pull tester to prevent buildup of debris.

I have completed a degree in Mechanical Engineering at Sarasota Christian College. Course work included numerous classes in which I utilized AutoCAD version 12 and 13 as well as other courses with application to a manufacturing environment.

If you can use a motivated, experienced manufacturing professional, I would appreciate your contacting me to suggest a time when we might meet. I can assure you in advance that I have an excellent reputation and would quickly become an asset to your organization.

Sincerely,

Hank Canzoneri

Date

Exact Name of Person
Title or Position
Name of Company
Address (number and street)
Address (city, state, and zip)

Dear Exact Name of Person: (or Sir or Madam if answering a blind ad)

Industrial Engineer
This well-educated and highly
credentialed engineer has many
accomplishments to write
about in his cover letter. When
writing your own cover letter,
make sure you identify three
main achievements or facts
about yourself which you
would like to communicate
to an employer.

With the enclosed resume, I would like to acquaint you with my exceptional skills and years of experience as an industrial and quality engineer with a solid background in manufacturing, quality assurance, and project management.

As you will see from my resume, I have worked at the same facility since before Watson-Bennett Corporation took over the operation from Monroe, Inc. In my years at this plant, my loyalty to the company as well as my outstanding problem-solving skills, strong personal initiative, and extensive knowledge of all phases of industrial, manufacturing, and quality engineering have allowed me to progress into positions of increasing responsibility.

Most recently as Senior Quality Engineer, I have been responsible for increasing first-pass yield of a complex manual assembly from 3% to 56%, exceeding the company objective six months before the projected deadline to meet that goal. I served on the Certification Committee that achieved ISO 9001 certification for the facility and have worked hard to ensure increased productivity by increasing awareness of initial quality, reducing rework and warranty cost by more than 50%.

I have earned a Master's of Business Administration degree from Kentucky State University, possess a Bachelor of Science in Electrical Engineering, and supplemented my degree programs with graduate-level courses on planning, scheduling, and inventory control.

If your organization could benefit from the services of a talented and self-motivated engineer, I would enjoy talking with you in person about your needs. I can assure you that I have an excellent reputation and can provide outstanding references at the appropriate time.

Sincerely,

Gilmore Lacy

Date

Exact Name of Person
Exact Title
Exact Name of Organization
Address
City, State Zip

Dear Sir or Madam:

MANUFACTURING

Machine Operator

With the enclosed resume, I would like to express my interest in seeking employment with your organization and make you aware of my skills and experience related to your needs.

As you will see from my resume, I have gained experience in both manufacturing and retail environments. In my current job with the Champion Company, I am a machine operator in charge of a shift of 15 people. Previously employed by Russ Knitwear, the Champion Company hired me immediately upon the strong recommendation of my supervisor when Russ closed its plant and moved its manufacturing operations to Mexico.

Prior to working in manufacturing companies as a machine operator and service technician, I worked as a manager and assistant manager in the convenience store business. I began as a Cashier and was promoted into management to handle responsibility for training and developing other employees, controlling inventory, preparing daily report and operating summaries, making deposits, and coordinating with vendors. I earned a reputation as a dependable hard worker known for honesty and attention to detail in handling finances.

If you can use a loyal and dedicated employee, I hope you will call or write me soon to suggest a time when we might meet to discuss your needs. I can provide excellent references and could make myself available for a personal meeting at your convenience. Thank you in advance for your time.

Sincerely,

Jimmie Nowland

Sometimes people bounce back and forth between two industries they enjoy. In the case of Mr. Nowland, he has worked in both retail and manufacturing environments. This cover letter is intended to help him find suitable jobs in manufacturing firms as a machine operator. If he wanted to look for suitable jobs in retail, he would have to modify this cover letter slightly.

Date

Exact Name of Person
Title or Position
Name of Company
Address (number and street)
Address (city, state, and zip)

Dear Exact Name of Person: (or Sir or Madam if answering a blind ad)

**Distribution Assistant
Supervisor**

A cover letter can be very helpful in taking your best shot at an opening within your company. Even when you have worked for a company for a while, the people involved in the hiring process may not be fully aware of your background or accomplishments. Therefore, approach internal openings in a rather formal manner and prepare cover letters that sell you to your current employer, just as you would to prospective employers whom you don't know.

With the enclosed resume, I would like to request that I be considered for the position of Distribution Assistant Supervisor. I am a flexible and adaptable individual and am willing to work any shift including second shift. I have worked with oil, filter, and rubber products of Kelly-Springfield.

As you will see from my resume, I am extremely proficient with the CIM system. I began working for Kelly-Springfield as a temporary worker through Man Hours, Inc., and I am now employed as a permanent employee as a Cycle Counter for Kelly-Springfield. I have become known for my strong attention to detail, and I am regarded as an internal expert on the CIM system, on which I originally gained experience while working for the Kmart Distribution Center.

A licensed forklift operator, I also offer proven supervisory skills and an extensive management background. While serving my country in the U.S. Army, I was promoted ahead of my peers to supervisory jobs in the supply management field, and I trained and developed many junior associates who became excellent supply managers. While managing dozens of individuals, I managed the procurement, supply, inventory control, and distribution of items including weapons, vehicles, military equipment, laundry, night vision goggles, as well as many other types of supplies including food and field rations. I also gained some experience with hazardous materials and became acquainted with the special safety concerns related to HAZMAT materials.

I am certain that I could make a valuable contribution to the distribution operations of the Kelly-Springfield Corporation, and I hope you will permit me to formally interview for the position.

Yours sincerely,

Gabriel Hendrickson

Date

Exact Name of Person
Title or Position
Name of Company
Address (number and street)
Address (city, state, and zip)

Dear Exact Name of Person: (or Sir or Madam if answering a blind ad)

With the enclosed resume, I would like to make you aware of a motivated, experienced professional with strong communication, organizational, and supervisory skills.

As Area Manager in the shipping department of B.F. Goodrich, I oversee all aspects of the shipping operation for a facility with an inventory of more than $1 million dollars, supervising up to 26 associates. I prioritize daily tasks and assign personnel to ensure that all tasks are completed while controlling hours to minimize overtime. In previous positions as a Tire Classifier and Tire Inspector, I was responsible for identifying defects in tires coming off the production line and for determining whether the product was salvageable or would have to be scrapped.

In addition to a year of college coursework at South Carolina State University, I have completed numerous courses related to leadership, personnel development, manufacturing, and communications through B.F. Goodrich.

Although I am highly regarded by my present employer and can provide excellent personal and professional references at the appropriate time, I am interested in exploring other career opportunities where I can utilize my strong communication skills in a service environment.

If you can use an experienced professional with excellent communication skills and a desire to work with the public, I hope you will contact me soon to suggest a time when we might meet to discuss your needs. I can assure you in advance that I have an excellent reputation and would quickly become a valuable asset to your company.

Sincerely,

Rachel M. Thiessen

Date

Exact Name of Person
Title or Position
Name of Company
Address (number and street)
Address (city, state, and zip)

MANUFACTURING

Wiring Technician

A wiring technician with ISO 9000 experience is seeking a position with a defense industry contractor. She would like to find a job wiring the equipment of manufacturers whose equipment she worked on while she was in military service.

Dear Exact Name of Person: (or Sir or Madam if answering a blind ad)

I would appreciate an opportunity to talk with you soon about how I could contribute to your organization through my technical electronics skills as well as through my experience in office operations, computer applications, and customer service.

As you will see from my enclosed resume, I am a versatile and adaptable professional who offers experience in manufacturing and military aircraft service environments as well as in the office and customer service setting of a major super-market. Most recently employed as a Wiring Technician with Chesebrough-Ponds in Terre Haute, IN, I made important contributions in the areas of reaching on-time shipping goals for the company's products and qualifying for ISO 9000 certification.

While serving in the U.S. Air Force as a Journeyman Avionics Technician, I translated my knowledge into a money-saving idea which was adopted and resulted in changes to technical orders used worldwide. My suggested modification to the IFF (Identification Friend or Foe) system resulted in multimillion-dollar savings.

Through my initiative, attention to detail, and dedication to bottom-line results, I am confident I could become a valuable asset in helping you achieve your goals for productivity, safety, and quality. I hope you will contact me to suggest a time when we could meet to discuss your goals and needs.

Sincerely,

Evangeline K. Pickering

Date

Exact Name of Person
Title or Position
Name of Company
Address (number and street)
Address (city, state, and zip)

Dear Exact Name of Person: (or Sir or Madam if answering a blind ad)

With the enclosed resume, I would like to make you aware of the considerable marketing skills and sales abilities I could put to work for you in the position as Pharmaceutical Sales Consultant which you recently advertised.

As you will see from my resume, I am currently excelling in a job which requires a dynamic recruiter, manager, and motivator. As Area Executive Director for the American Diabetes Association (A.D.A.), I manage more than 170 volunteers in seven counties. Since taking over the position, I have nearly tripled the number of volunteers while increasing income by 170%. I have developed a strong network of contacts throughout those seven counties while working with hospitals, health departments, and other health agencies to communicate the mission of ADA.

In a part-time job for two years while earning my college degree in Marketing at Philadelphia University (where I was on scholarship and a member of the Honors Program), I excelled in my first sales job while working as a Sales Associate at Bass Shoe Outlet.

You would find me in person to be a poised individual with outstanding leadership ability and a high level of personal initiative. Known for creativity and resourcefulness, I am respected for my attention to detail and follow-through. I would welcome the opportunity to work with a fine company that challenges its employees to adopt an attitude of "what if?"

Thanks for your time and consideration.

Sincerely,

Queen P. James

Date

Exact Name of Person
Exact Title of Person
Exact Name of Company
Exact Address
City, State Zip

Dear Exact Name:

Retail Executive
This successful retailer used
this cover letter to explore
opportunities in numerous
industries when he moved to
Duluth. For more cover letters
like this, see the sections on
Sales and Management.

With the enclosed resume, I would like to make you aware of my strong skills in marketing with a view to exploring employment opportunities within your organization. Although I have been working in Maryville, I own a home in Duluth and am seeking to relocate to the Duluth area.

As you will see from my resume, I have excelled in roles as a Sales Manager, Operations Manager, Store Manager, and Project Manager as well as Warehouse Manager. In one job as a Store Manager and Project Manager for Family Dollar Stores, I completed numerous assignments which involved solving profitability, merchandising, and operations problems in stores throughout South Carolina.

A few years ago Circuit City recruited me and I earned rapid promotion because of my strong operations management skills. After managing operations for an $18 million store in Atlanta, I was promoted to manage operations for a $24 million store in Augusta which grew to $35 million in annual sales volume during my three years as Operations Manager. I have routinely managed between 30 to 80 people while scheduling up to 130 employees for maximum efficiency.

In 1996 Best Buy aggressively recruited me, and I have recently excelled in jobs as Sales Manager and Operations Manager in Maryville. I offer proven abilities related to P & L management and can provide outstanding personal and professional references at the appropriate time.

If you can use my extensive management skills and operational problem-solving experience, I hope you will contact me to suggest a time when we might meet to discuss your needs and goals and how I might serve them. Thank you in advance for your time.

Yours sincerely,

James C. Fairchild

Date

Performance Recruiters
Attention: Lawrence Murphy
BY FAX TO: (205) 956-3845

Dear Mr. Murphy:

MARKETING

**Medical Marketing
Representative**
A top-performing Medical Sales
Representative used this letter
to indicate her interest in a job
which she had already
discussed by phone with the
prospective employer.
Although the letter is directed
specifically to a company, Ms.
Shaw could make the cover
letter all-purpose by making
minor changes in the first
paragraph and last paragraph.

With the enclosed resume, I would like to formally apply for the position with Parke-Davis Pharmaceuticals, which you and I discussed yesterday.

As you will see from my resume, I am excelling in my current position as a Medical Sales Representative with Jones Pharma, Inc. While developing this territory "from scratch," I have successfully launched new products and have opened and stocked pharmacies from West Virginia to Georgia. I was inducted into the President's Club, won two sales contests with monetary awards, and was one of the company's three top producers while being ranked #1 in my district. I have consistently won sales awards and contests since I began with the company and am proud of the excellent relationships I have established within the medical community.

I can provide outstanding personal and professional references at the appropriate time, but I would appreciate your not contacting my employer until after we have a chance to talk more about the position which we discussed earlier yesterday. I am single, will relocate according to the company's needs, and would cheerfully welcome overnight travel.

If Parke-Davis can use a dynamic sales professional with a proven ability to "make it happen," I hope you will call or write me to suggest a time when we might meet to discuss how I might help Parke-Davis achieve its goals. While working with Jones Pharma, I have become acquainted with some of the Parke-Davis sales representatives who work in my territory. Through them, I have learned about Parke-Davis and have gained an appreciation of their products and reputation, and I feel that I could rapidly become a valuable addition to the Parke-Davis team.

Yours sincerely,

Faison Shaw

Date

Exact Name of Person
Title or Position
Name of Company
Address (number and street)
Address (city, state, and zip)

Dear Exact Name of Person: (or Sir or Madam if answering a blind ad)

Photographer

This cover letter helped a young professional apply for a non-editorial photography position at a newspaper. Notice that she sent the cover letter to her current employer in an attempt to move from a part-time position to full time. If you are applying for an internal position or promotion, behave just as formally as you would with an outside employer and send a cover letter and resume expressing your interest in the job.

With the enclosed resume, I would like to express my interest in the Non-Editorial Photography position. When you review my portfolio which accompanies the resume, I believe you will see that I am the ideal candidate for the position. There are several points to which I would like to draw your attention.

As a B.A. graduate of New York School of the Arts with a strong background in Fine Arts and Photography, I believe I could draw upon my knowledge and skills to benefit the department. While earning my B.A. degree, I worked as a Free-Lance Photographer and was involved in commercial work as well as with weddings, portraits, and lab work.

As a current Part-Time Editorial Photographer with the *Seattle News And Record's* Photography Department, I am already familiar with the systems, procedures, and staff of the *Seattle News And Record*.

In summary, I am a hard working and positive individual with excellent interpersonal skills along with the high degree of creativity necessary for success in Commercial Photography. I am confident that I would be an asset in this position. I look forward to a personal interview at your earliest convenience.

Thank you for your time and consideration.

With sincere best wishes,

Melanie Bequette

Date

Ms. Patty McCorkle
Promotions Sales Manager
CBS-TV
Post Office Box 5000
New York, NY 10020

Dear Ms. McCorkle:

MEDIA & PUBLIC RELATIONS

News Photographer and Editor
This Emmy-nominated journalist has seen a job posted on the Web which he wishes to learn more about. For more cover letters like this, also see the section on Journalism.

I am writing to express my strong interest in the position of Online Account Executive, which was posted on the CBS employee Web page. With the enclosed resume, I would like to make you aware of my background as an articulate young professional whose proven communication skills, natural salesmanship, and strong leadership ability have been tested in versatile and challenging positions in sales, management, and broadcast journalism.

Most recently, I have been excelling in a number of broadcast journalism positions with CBS, NBC, and Fox affiliates on the east coast. Currently with KXYZ-TV in Minneapolis, MN, I shoot and edit a wide variety of feature stories and photoessays while serving as editor and photographer for general assignment and sports. In a similar job with WEZT-TV in Los Angeles, CA, my exceptional efforts in these areas earned me an Emmy nomination in the News/Public Affairs/Community Issues category from the National Academy of Television Arts and Sciences. In these and other positions with various network affiliates, I have demonstrated my outstanding communication skills while preparing scripts for news anchors and providing editing and photography support. I am expert at setting up, troubleshooting, and operating the ENG live broadcast truck.

In earlier positions, I refined my natural sales ability. As Sales Representative for Blue Chip Rent-A-Car, I prospected for new accounts and boosted the profitability of existing accounts. While serving as a Route Salesman for a distributing company during college, I serviced existing accounts and maximized market share by employing creative and effective marketing strategies.

Although I am highly regarded by my present employer and can provide outstanding personal and professional references at the appropriate time, I am interested in exploring other career opportunities. I feel that my extroverted personality, strong communication skills, and natural salesmanship would make me a valuable addition to your sales or management team. If you can use an outgoing, articulate young professional with natural sales and leadership skills, I hope you will contact me to suggest a time when we might meet to discuss your needs.

Sincerely,

Fallon James

Date

Exact Name of Person
Title or Position
Name of Company
Address (number and street)
Address (city, state, and zip)

Dear Exact Name of Person: (or Sir or Madam if answering a blind ad)

With the enclosed resume, I would like to make you aware of my qualifications for the position of Radiology Staff Nurse. I offer an extensive background as a radiology nurse with more than nine years of service to New Orleans Medical Center, and I hold an extensive list of certifications and credentials.

Currently excelling as a Staff Registered Nurse in the Emergency Department, I serve as Triage Nurse. I interview presenting patients, assigning a triage category and prioritizing the placement of patients into the appropriate treatment areas based on the nature and severity of the patient's condition.

Although I am highly regarded within the Emergency Department and can provide excellent references at the appropriate time, it is my desire to return to Radiology, where I previously served with distinction. As you will see, I hold certifications in ACLS, BCLS, and PALS, in addition to credentials which qualify me to administer a wide range of medications specific to radiology procedures, including nuclear medicines and special procedures.

My knowledge, my skills, and my personal loyalty made me a strong asset to the Radiology Department in the past and would continue to do so in the future. I was proud to be a part of the growth and development of the radiology team during the nine years I served, and I would relish the opportunity to rejoin that team. I have a deep respect for the expertise and reputation of the radiology team headed by Dr. Smith, and it is my strong desire to be of service to Dr. Smith and the other team members.

Sincerely,

Michele Blanchard

Date

Exact Name of Person
Title or Position
Name of Company
Address (number and street)
Address (city, state, and zip)

Dear Exact Name of Person: (or Sir or Madam if answering a blind ad)

With the enclosed resume, I would like to make you aware of my reputation as an experienced management and accounting professional with excellent communication, organizational, and motivational skills.

With First Health of Hot Springs, in Arkansas, my loyalty and dedication have been rewarded by advancement into positions of increasing responsibility. I started with the company as a registration clerk in the Emergency Room and quickly advanced to Assistant Supervisor, overseeing the activities of as many as 30 clerks, providing administrative, patient registration, and accounting services. In this position, I prepared weekly schedules for three rotating shifts of 30 employees while counseling marginal performers and conducting employee evaluations. I attended seminars on ICD-9 coding and coded emergency room charts daily, entering data into the computer for billing.

You will also notice from my resume that I am experienced in the full range of accounting activities. Prior to my employment with First Health of Hot Springs, I handled the accounting function for a furniture retailer, and in that capacity I was involved in accounts payable, cost accounting, shipping and freight reports, and inventory control.

Of course all of my jobs have involved customer service, and I offer strong customer service and public relations skills. I have frequently been commended for my gracious manner of dealing with the public and for my skill in troubleshooting difficult problems so that customer satisfaction is retained while safeguarding the company's bottom line goals.

I can provide outstanding references at the appropriate time, and I would appreciate an opportunity to talk with you in person about how my versatile skills and background could make a difference to your organization. I hope you will call and suggest a time when we might meet in person to discuss your needs and how I might serve them.

Sincerely,

Nelda Lavern Bird

Date

Exact Name
Exact Title
Exact Name of Company
Address
City, State Zip

Dear Exact Name:

Gerontology Background

It is not uncommon for someone to get a college degree or even a master's degree in an area in which they subsequently do not work. This creative and resourceful individual worked for banks and profit-making organizations after receiving her M.A. in Gerontology, and now, years later, she wishes to utilize some of that scientific and medical training as a Pharmaceutical Sales Representative.

With the enclosed resume, I would like to make you aware of my strong interest in the job of Pharmaceutical Sales Representative which may be available with the departure of Mrs. Anne Jones. I believe she has mentioned me to you, but I wanted to more formally approach you and make you aware of my outstanding qualifications for the job.

With an M.A. in Gerontology which I earned from Temple University, I have completed numerous courses related to pharmacology and medicine. Indeed, as the daughter of a respected surgeon who practiced in Nantucket, I feel I have actually been "in medicine" all my life. I am a respected member of the Nantucket community and belong to numerous professional organizations and women's groups in addition to McPherson Downs Country Club.

As you will see from my resume, I offer proven skills as a sales professional. Most recently as an entrepreneur, I established and sold a computer training business which I developed from scratch. In a previous job as a Sales Rep with Massachusetts Power and Light, I developed and implemented a sales system to market computer software and hardware to computer resellers nationwide. While working for National Bank in Plymouth, I won numerous sales contests and achieved the "Top Gun" Award while selling life, health, annuity, and home owner's insurance policies in seven states.

Throughout my years of achievement in sales, I have become aware of the fact that the selling process is unique within specific environments. I would like you to know that I thrive on learning new systems and approaches, and I can assure you that I would be a flexible and adaptable personality whom you could train and mold as you feel appropriate.

I hope you will contact me to suggest a time when we might meet to discuss your needs and goals and how I might help you achieve them. I can provide excellent references and I thank you in advance for your time.

Yours sincerely,

Laurel Ivaska Swan

Date

Exact Name of Person
Title or Position
Name of Company
Address (number and street)
Address (city, state, and zip)

Dear Exact Name of Person: (or Sir or Madam if answering a blind ad)

MEDICAL

CAP/CBI Technician
If you read this letter carefully, you will see that it is actually a very versatile and all-purpose presentation. He could use this letter to approach social services, medical, and law enforcement organizations, and he could also use the letter to explore opportunities outside his field. If you are looking for more letters like this one, consult the Social Work and Human Services Section.

I would appreciate an opportunity to talk with you soon about how I could contribute to your organization through my experience in criminal justice, sociology, and human services as well as through my superior analytical, communication, and management skills. I hold a B.S. degree which I earned magna cum laude.

In my current position with Topeka Residential Services, I am working as a CAP/CBI Technician and Habilitation Technician and am involved in teaching consumers independent living habits. In a previous position I was recruited as a social worker for an 80-bed long-term care facility offering skilled nursing beds, intermediate care beds, and domiciliary beds. I have also served as a correctional officer.

As you will see from my resume, I have skills and abilities that could make me a valuable part of your team. In addition, I feel certain that you would find me to be a hardworking and reliable professional who prides myself on doing any job to the best of my ability. I can provide excellent personal and professional references if you request them.

I hope you will call or write me soon to suggest a time convenient for us to meet and discuss your current and future needs and how I might serve them. Thank you in advance for your time.

Sincerely yours,

Tyrone L. Cooper

Alternate last paragraph:
I hope you will welcome my call soon to arrange a brief meeting at your convenience to discuss your current and future needs and how I might serve them. Thank you in advance for your time.

Date

Exact Name of Person
Title or Position
Name of Company
Address (number and street)
Address (city, state, and zip)

MEDICAL

Dear Exact Name of Person: (or Sir or Madam if answering a blind ad)

Licensed Practical Nurse
This Licensed Practical Nurse (LPN) offers specialized experience in respiratory patient care along with a background in obstetrics and gynecology. This all-purpose cover letter is designed to blow doors open at hospitals and private practices. See the Health Care Section for more cover letters like this one.

With the enclosed resume, I would like to make you aware of an experienced licensed practical nurse with exceptional time management and communication skills as well as a background in obstetrics and gynecology, respiratory care of ventilator patients, and general patient care.

In my most recent position with the Veteran's Administration Medical Center, I specialized in providing nursing care to respiratory patients, many of whom were totally dependent on ventilators and other life support equipment. I closely monitored the operation of this equipment to ensure that it was functioning properly. I also provided care to a number of physically challenged patients in addition to those for whom I cared for in my area of specialty.

At Wilmington Medical Center, I served as an Obstetrics and Gynecology Nurse, where my primary responsibilities were caring for new and expectant mothers, transporting patients in labor to the delivery room, and providing nursing care in the obstetrics recovery room and newborn nursery.

I earned a certificate from the Licensed Practical Nursing Program at Dover Technical Community College and am licensed in the state of Delaware. I have supplemented my degree program with numerous continuing education courses designed to keep my medical skills up to date.

If you can use a motivated, caring licensed practical nurse, I hope you will contact me to suggest a time when we might meet to discuss your needs and goals. I have an excellent reputation and would quickly become a valuable asset to your company.

Sincerely,

Altressa Theobald

Date

Exact Name of Person
Exact Title
Exact Name of Organization
Address
City, State Zip

Dear Sir or Madam:

With the enclosed resume, I would like to make you aware of my background as a licensed practical nurse with exceptional organizational, communication, and patient relations skills who has excelled in obstetrics/gynecology, medical/surgical, and geriatric nursing in challenging environments worldwide.

Licensed Practical Nurse
Here is a cover letter for an LPN with diversified experience in gynecology and obstetrics, medical/surgical environments, and geriatric nursing. The Health Care Section contains more cover letters like this one.

As you will see, I completed the Practical Nurse and Medical Specialist course from the Academy of Health Sciences. I have excelled in numerous additional military training programs including the Medical Proficiency Training Program, Algorithm-Directed Troop Medical Care Course, Deployable Medical Systems New Equipment Training, Medical Management of Chemical Casualties, and Hazard Communication Program.

I am currently working part-time weekends as Night Shift Supervisor for a local long-term care facility. Prior to this position I served as a Licensed Practical Nurse, providing medical-surgical care on a 20-bed Intermediate Care Ward at a busy 296-bed DEPMEDS-equipped Combat Support Hospital. I supervised and trained 13 personnel in a Medical Inprocessing Center in Virginia which handled more than 1,200 personnel per month while overseeing $300,000 worth of medical equipment, immunization medicines, and expendable supplies. On my own initiative, I organized and developed a Breast Health Awareness Program for women inprocessing to Fort Eustis, and I served as a phlebotomist for the Operation Life Gift Bone Marrow Drive.

My earlier nursing experience was focused in obstetrics and gynecology. In Germany, I served on a 42-bed mixed ward comprising a 17-bed newborn nursery, a six-bed labor and delivery unit, and a 19-bed obstetrics and gynecology unit. In that position, I supervised a staff of three, acted as Preceptor to newly assigned personnel, and took on additional responsibilities as Infection Control Officer.

If you can use an experienced nursing professional with a strong background in obstetrics and gynecology and exceptional patient relations skills, I hope you will contact me to suggest a time when we might meet to discuss your needs. I can provide outstanding references.

Sincerely,

Cena Marie Alvarez

Date

Exact Name of Person
Title or Position
Name of Company
Address (number and street)
Address (city, state, and zip)

MEDICAL

Dear Exact Name of Person: (or Sir or Madam if answering a blind ad)

Medical Doctor

This cover letter expresses the desire of a medical doctor to change from private practice to an academic setting. Notice that he refers to his enclosed curriculum vitae. For your information, a curriculum vitae is essentially the same as a resume and is used by academic and medical professionals.

I am writing this letter to follow up on a telephone conversation we had earlier, which I hope you will recall, in which I mentioned that Dr. Janet Stephanolos had referred me to you. An M.D., I am currently employed as a primary care provider at Tulsa Medical Care. My office is in Tulsa, OK, where I share an office with an Internist.

Presently I am pursuing a position which will allow me to continue to be a primary care provider in an academic setting where I can be on the forefront of current pediatric practices. I would like to become more involved with teaching.

My future goals are directed toward being in a position wherein I can positively affect trends in pediatric health care. I would like to address current social and economics issues which affect the pediatric population (including adolescent health care). This will be of importance in the present era of cost cutting trends and growing managed health care systems.

Enclosed is my curriculum vitae. Please call if I can assist you with any other information. Thank you for your time and attention.

Sincerely,

Gene Willoughby, M.D.

Date

Exact Name of Person
Exact Title
Exact Name of Company, Hospital, or Organization
Exact Address
City, State Zip

Dear Exact Person: (Or Dear Sir or Madam if answering a blind ad):

With the enclosed resume, I would like to make you aware of my interest in your organization and acquaint you with the considerable experience and skills I could offer you.

As an RN licensed in NC and PA, I offer five years of experience in critical care nursing, primarily in emergency rooms, along with five years of experience as an Operating Room RN and two years of experience on a medical/surgical ward. I have also excelled in private nursing assignments and have been involved in the medical management of injured workers. Most recently, I have managed the medical care of severely neurologically impaired patients and have made major medical management decisions which improved the quality of their lives. An experienced and versatile professional, I have floated among ER, ICCU, CCU, PACU, and OR.

Known for my caring and empathetic nature, I pride myself on my ability to assess patient needs and develop sound long-term and short-term care plans. To me, there is no greater satisfaction in life than seeing a patient thrive under medical plans I have helped to develop and administer. I believe I am a professional care-giver "through and through." I have raised five children to adulthood and have found time to volunteer in Guardian Ad Litem and Hospice Programs. I especially enjoy opportunities to administer quality care to the elderly, poor, and very young.

Although I have excelled in my nursing career even while raising five children, I am at a point in my life when my child-raising years are behind me and I am able to devote all of my energies to my career. I am certain that I could make a valuable contribution to an organization that could make use of an experienced professional with excellent analytical, decision-making, and communication skills as well as expert clinical nursing know-how.

You would find me in person to be a congenial individual who has found the nursing profession to be a natural outlet for my caring nature. I can provide excellent references from all previous employers. I hope you will contact me soon to suggest a time when we could meet to discuss your needs and how I might be of service to you.

Yours sincerely,

Anna P. Gaskins

Date

Exact Name of Person
Title or Position
Name of Company
Address (number and street)
Address (city, state, and zip)

Dear Exact Name of Person: (or Sir or Madam if answering a blind ad)

Nurse

This nurse gained experience in pediatric, medical-surgical, orthopedic, and geriatric nursing in home health, hospital, and long-term care situations. This cover letter is designed to help her discover the best jobs at the best facilities.

With the enclosed resume, I would like to make you aware of my background as an accomplished nursing professional who offers experience in pediatrics, medical-surgical, orthopedic, and geriatric care in home health, hospital, and long-term care environments.

As you will see, I have recently completed my Associate's degree program in Nursing from Redondo Beach Community College in California. I had previously completed the Licensed Practical Nurse program at Boca Raton Community College in Florida and practiced as an LPN.

In my present job with Obstetrics and Pediatrics of California, I provide private duty pediatric home health care to critically ill children, most of whom are referred to OPC by the University of California at Berkeley Medical Center. To enhance my abilities in this area, I attended a ventilator care seminar through OPC, as many of my patients require respirators or ventilators. I implement occupational, physical, and speech therapy programs and educate patients and family members on care-related issues.

While completing my Associate's degree in Nursing, I worked in a number of units at Peace Haven Nursing Center, a long-term care facility in Redondo Beach, CA. Prior to that, I served as a Licensed Practical Nurse on a 32-bed orthopedic and adolescent unit at Children's Hospital, a 175-bed pediatric teaching hospital in Palm Harbor, FL. In this challenging environment, I gained valuable knowledge related to the care and treatment of orthopedic disorders resulting from birth injuries or genetic diseases.

In an earlier position at Whispering Pines Nursing Center, I further developed my time management skills while supervising four nursing aides providing total patient care for 60 chronically ill patients in this long-term care facility.

If you can use a motivated, experienced nursing professional whose abilities have been tested in a wide range of challenging environments, I hope you will contact me to suggest a time when we might meet to discuss your needs. I can provide outstanding references.

Sincerely,

Annette Van Houten

Date

Vencor, Inc.
Recruiting Services Department
3300 Providian Center
400 West Market Street
Louisville, KY 40202

Dear Sir or Madam:

With the enclosed resume, I would like to make you aware of my interest in the position as Vencor's Regional Rehabilitation Director. As I believe you will see from my resume, I meet all your criteria and would welcome the opportunity to show you in person that I am the candidate you are seeking.

Occupational Therapist
This cover letter is designed to express the interest of an experienced Occupational Therapist in the job as Regional Rehabilitation Director. Notice in the third paragraph how she explains her track record of "job hopping" by explaining that her spouse was an airline executive and was frequently relocated. In a cover letter, you can go ahead and explain facts about your past that you think might cause a negative reaction.

With more than 16 years experience as an Occupational Therapist, I have excelled in hospital corporate management for 13 of those years and most recently I have been involved in long-term care/SNF. Clinically my expertise is in orthopedics, orthotics, hand therapy, and contracture management. My experience in Rehab Services Management has afforded me the opportunity to oversee large departments, programs, volumes, and revenues with large fiscal responsibility related to budgeting, productivity analysis, cost accounting, and marketing. I am experienced in supervising Rehab Managers, product lines, and staff clinicians and offer extensive experience in program development, quality assurance, teaching, and training in all disciplines and with all types of rehab services and programs. I am very familiar with Medicare, Medicaid, and third party regulations and requirements.

You may notice from my resume that I held a couple of my jobs for rather short durations. This was due to the fact that my husband was an airline executive and we relocated frequently. I am proud of the fact, however, that I made significant contributions to all organizations which employed me; I can provide outstanding references from all of them. My husband is retiring and we are relocating permanently to Colorado.

My management skills are extensive. At St. Michael's Medical Center, I was Director of Occupational Therapy for four years and supervised a staff of 25 while overseeing departmental gross revenue of $2 million. I was cited as a major program developer as I initiated a new Cancer Rehabilitation Program, a new Hand/Upper Extremity Clinic, and numerous other programs.

I hope I will have an opportunity to meet with you in person, as I would very much enjoy having the opportunity to see your facility and meet your staff. I am aware of your fine reputation, and I am certain I could become a valuable asset to you.

Yours sincerely,

Annie Rose

Date

Exact Name of Person
Title or Position
Name of Company
Address (number and street)
Address (city, state, and zip)

Dear Exact Name of Person: (or Sir or Madam if answering a blind ad)

Physical Therapist
In the fourth paragraph, this Physical Therapist reveals that she and her husband are permanently relocating to the Ocean City area. She emphasizes that she can provide outstanding personal and professional references at the appropriate time.

With the enclosed resume, I would like to make you aware of my background as an experienced Licensed Physical Therapy Assistant and supervisor with a background of excellence in hand therapy, general orthopedics, wound care, and all aspects of direct patient care.

As you will see, I graduated with honors from the Associate degree program in Physical Therapy at New Haven Technical Community College. I have supplemented my college education with numerous continuing education courses.

At ProFit Therapy's busy clinic in New Haven, I have played a key role through my expertise in hand therapy, and my contributions to their success have been rewarded with promotion to positions of increased responsibility. In my most recent position as Assistant Director, I supervised the clinic staff of 15 employees, including Licensed Physical Therapy Assistants, Physical Therapy Technicians, office staff, and Staff Therapist. Previously as Senior Licensed Physical Therapy Assistant, I served as clinical preceptor for the Physical Therapy Assistant program at New Haven Technical Community College and mentored Medical Sciences students from local high schools.

Although I was highly regarded by this employer and can provide outstanding references at the appropriate time, my husband and I have permanently relocated to the Ocean City area.

If you can use a highly experienced Licensed Physical Therapy Assistant with a proven background in hand therapy, wound care, general orthopedics, and supervision, I hope you will contact me to suggest a time when we might meet to discuss your needs. Thank you in advance for your time.

Sincerely,

Leslie Rhea

Date

Exact Name of Person
Title or Position
Name of Company
Address (number and street)
Address (city, state, and zip)

Dear Exact Name of Person: (or Dear Sir or Madam if answering a blind ad)

MEDICAL

Public Health Nurse
This Public Health Nurse has decided to move from public health to private practice. You will find more cover letters like this in the Health Care Section.

I would appreciate an opportunity to talk with you soon about how I could contribute to your organization through my nursing skills along with a reputation for possessing high levels of initiative, compassion, and the ability to educate others.

Presently working as a Public Health Nurse for the Hartsfield County Health Department, I provide care for 1,500 county employees who receive quarterly wellness examinations. I complete procedures ranging from venipuncture and urinalysis, to taking blood pressure readings, to conducting hearing and vision tests, to maintaining up-to-date immunizations. One aspect of this job which I have really enjoyed has been the opportunity to work with people to educate them on health issues.

Earlier at Metro Atlanta Medical Center, I was one of a small group of only 15 nurses who were trained and qualified in peritoneal dialysis. Working with these clients with chronic renal failure was rewarding and allowed for direct client care which included changing sterile dressings, maintaining IVs, and administering blood products and medications.

As you will see from my resume, I earned my Associate's degree in Nursing from Kennesaw Technical Community College where I was recognized for my academic achievements with membership in two honor societies. I am confident that through my knowledge and experience as well as my strong desire to contribute to others through my skills as a Registered Nurse, I would be a valuable asset to a medical facility which could benefit from my positive attitude and concern for others.

I hope you will welcome my call soon when I try to arrange a meeting to discuss your needs and how I might help you. Thank you in advance for your time.

Sincerely,

LeDora V. Henry

Alternate last paragraph:
I hope you will call or write me soon to suggest a time convenient for us to meet and discuss your current and future needs and how I might serve them. Thank you in advance for your time.

Date

Exact Name of Person
Title or Position
Name of Company
Address (number and street)
Address (city, state, and zip)

MEDICAL

Dear Exact Name of Person: (or Sir or Madam if answering a blind ad)

Registered Nurse

This Registered Nurse with critical care experience decided she wanted a change from hospital nursing, so this all-purpose cover letter helped her explore administrative positions which could utilize her technical knowledge as well as her management abilities. You will notice the subtle emphasis on office skills if you read the cover letter carefully.

I would appreciate an opportunity to talk with you soon about how I could contribute to your organization through my strong combination of nursing experience, organizational and supervisory skills, and attention to detail.

In my six years as a Registered Nurse in the state of South Carolina, I have excelled in assessing and serving the needs of critical care patients in several major hospitals, most recently at Greenville Medical Center. Prior to this job, I worked in the intensive care and cardiac care units at Mercy General Hospital and also at Florence Hospital, where I was a Charge Nurse for four years. In these positions, I was able to refine my skills in direct patient care and patient assessment as well as in problem-solving and staff supervision while becoming known as a dedicated, compassionate nurse with a strong commitment to patient and guest relations.

With an Associate's degree in Nursing Education Options from Florence Community College, I offer general office skills in addition to my nursing skills and previous sales background.

If you can use my considerable skills as an R.N., I hope you will contact me to suggest a time when we might meet to discuss your needs and goals and how my background might serve them. Thank you in advance for your time.

Yours sincerely,

Jeannette Gianato

Date

Exact Name of Person
Title or Position
Name of Company
Address (number and street)
Address (city, state, and zip)

Dear Exact Name of Person: (or Sir or Madam if answering a blind ad)

With the enclosed resume, I would like to acquaint you with my strong administrative, organizational, and problem-solving skills as well as my extensive background in nursing supervision and administration.

With a Bachelor of Science in Nursing from Midwestern University, I also hold an Associate's degree in Registered Nursing and Licensed Practical Nurse programs. I have been certified as an instructor in Basic Cardiac Life Support (BCLS) and have received my ANCC Gerontological Nurse Certification.

At Leisure Living Homes of Annapolis, I was hired as an R.N. Supervisor and was quickly promoted to Assistant Director of Nursing/Staff Development. In this position, I support the Director of Nursing, supervising 75 Registered Nurses, Licensed Practical Nurses, and Certified Medical Assistants while coordinating and directing day-to-day operations of the nursing department to insure that appropriate levels of direct care are provided to the residents. I am responsible for assessing, selecting, and implementing training programs for the nursing staff and developing other programs to meet the needs of the facility's employees.

As you will see from my resume, I have worked at this level of responsibility for most of my nursing administration career. In previous positions at Village Community Center and Shady Oaks Center of Baltimore, my leadership and management skills were recognized, and I was either hired at the Assistant Director of Nursing level, or quickly advanced to that level and beyond.

If you can use a highly educated, articulate professional with a strong background in nursing administration and long-term care environments, I hope you will contact me soon to suggest a time when we might meet to discuss your needs. I can provide excellent references at the appropriate time.

Sincerely,

Marci Ragozine-Goodson

Date

Exact Name of Person
Title or Position
Name of Company
Address (number and street)
Address (city, state, and zip)

MEDICAL

Dear Exact Name of Person: (or Sir or Madam if answering a blind ad)

Registered Nurse

Although this cover letter
presents the background of a
Registered Nurse, she is
working in a part-time job for
approximately 30 hours a week
as a Pharmaceutical Sales Rep.
The cover letter is designed to
help her respond to a phone
call made by a recruiter who
made her aware of a full-time
job with a competitor.
Although she enjoys her
current job, she is interested in
a full-time job with benefits.

Thank you for your recent expression of interest in my background, and I am faxing with this cover letter an updated resume which describes my current job as a Pharmaceutical Sales Representative for Pfizer. In my current job servicing chain drug stores and doctors' offices in 30 cities, I am consistently ranked among the company's top producers in my efforts to increase market share, develop new accounts, and boost sales of Vancenase and Provental F.A. I believe my rapid success as a Pharmaceutical Sales Representative has been due in large part to my background as an R.N., and I have come to be regarded by all the doctors and pharmacists with whom I work as a trusted advisor and Marketing Consultant.

As you will see, I have lived in Portland all my life, except for a few years after high school when I worked as a model in New York. After my stint in modeling, I earned my Bachelor's degree in Business Administration and then graduated from nursing school as an R.N. In a job with Urgent Care prior to my current position, I traveled to surrounding counties handling a patient case load and training new nurses. In a previous job, I worked for Hood River Medical Center, where I advanced to increasing responsibilities as a Staff Nurse in the Medical Intensive Care Unit, Emergency Department, and Coronary Care Unit.

Although I am excelling in my current job and am highly regarded by the company, I would enjoy learning how your company could make use of my considerable marketing and sales abilities. I am sure my extensive contacts and outstanding reputation within the medical community could be of value to you. You would find me in person to be a congenial individual who interacts with others with poise and professionalism. I hope you will contact me soon to suggest a time when we could meet to discuss your needs and how I might be of service to you.

Yours sincerely,

Laurie Ward Schoepke

Date

Exact Name of Person
Title or Position
Name of Company
Address (number and street)
Address (city, state, and zip)

Dear Exact Name of Person: (or Sir or Madam if answering a blind ad)

MEDICAL

**Assistant Director
of Nursing**
The purpose of this cover letter
is to apply for an Assistant
Director of Nursing position.
She offers experience in long-
term care environments.

     I would like to make you aware of my interest in the Assistant Director of Nursing Services position at the Veterans Administration Nursing Facility in Washington, D.C. As you will see from my enclosed resume, I am an experienced RN Supervisor and Registered Nurse whose communication, motivational, and time management skills have been proven in long-term care and hospice environments.

     At Highmount House of Alexandria, VA, I started as a Unit Supervisor and Staff RN, supervising two nursing assistants while providing quality patient care for a 30-bed skilled care unit. My leadership and initiative quickly earned me a promotion to my present position, managing all night shift activities for a 159-bed long-term care facility. I currently direct 25 employees, including nine licensed nurses and 16 nursing assistants. Responsible for training and orientation of new employees, I prepare weekly schedules and shift assignments for staff members while coordinating activities of the nursing staff with other departments, including the Therapy and Dietary Departments.

     In a previous position with Complete Home Health Care and Hospice, I managed a case load of 36 home health patients, providing comfort, care, and support for dying patients. Earlier as a Charge Nurse at Annapolis Memorial Hospital and Staff Nurse at Kennedy Memorial, I worked in cardiac and medical surgical/telemetry units. At Annapolis Memorial, I supervised a staff of 12, including monitor technicians, nursing assistants, and licensed nurses.

     With an Associate's degree in Nursing from Appomattox Technical Community College, I am a licensed Registered Nurse for the state of Virginia.

     If you can use an Assistant Director of Nursing who offers excellent motivational and time management skills as well as supervisory experience in long-term care environments, I hope you will contact me to suggest a time when we might meet in person to discuss your needs. I can provide excellent references.

Sincerely,

Gwen R. Berthiaume

Date

Exact Name of Person
Exact Title of Person
Exact Name of Organization
Address
City, State Zip

Dear Sir or Madam:

Veterinary Technician

After a move to Peoria, this young Veterinary Technician is ready for her job hunt, and she acquaints prospective employers in the Peoria area with the fact that she has experience in internal medicine, emergency care, and pharmacy.

With the enclosed resume, I would like to make you aware of a dedicated, experienced Veterinary Technician with exceptional communication and organizational skills as well as a background in internal medicine, emergency care, and pharmacy.

I have permanently relocated to Peoria to be near my family. In Florida, I was employed as a Veterinary Technician at The Animal Hospital, Inc. in addition to performing part-time duties as a Veterinary Technician at Florida Veterinary Specialists. I have assisted veterinarians in all phases of treatment, taking vital signs, performing venipunctures, administering medications, and communicating with pet owners.

In a previous job in an emergency care environment as a Veterinary Technician, I learned to deal with stressful situations while caring for sick or injured animals, interacting with distressed pet owners, and assisting veterinarians with emergency procedures.

With an Associate in Science degree in Veterinary Technology from Florida State University, I am a Registered Veterinary Technician.

If you can use a compassionate Veterinary Technician with strong diagnostic skills, I hope you will contact me to suggest a time when we might meet to discuss your needs. I can provide outstanding references.

Sincerely,

Ellen Woehrmann

Date

Exact Name of Person
Title or Position
Name of Company
Address (number and street)
Address (city, state, and zip)

Dear Exact Name of Person: (or Sir or Madam if answering a blind ad)

I would appreciate an opportunity to talk with you soon about how I could contribute to your organization through my experience as a military officer who has advanced to the rank of captain in the U.S. Army.

As you will see from my enclosed resume, I have built a reputation as an exceptional performer who can be counted on to exceed standards while excelling in high-visibility jobs vital to national security operations. Presently the Chief of Current Operations and Flight Management in a selectively manned special operations organization, I have provided my expertise while significantly improving the quality of training, solving long-standing problems, and earning recognition as an "exceptional manager and leader."

Throughout my military career I have been handpicked ahead of my peers and placed in positions where my ability to direct multifunctional operations, respond quickly to pressure and rapid change, and lead others have been demonstrated. In every job I have developed innovative solutions which increased productivity, reduced costs, and improved strategic effectiveness.

Holding a B.S. in Criminal Justice, I will be receiving my M.A. in Security Management shortly. I have been entrusted with a Top Secret security clearance with SCI and have qualified with weapons which include the Beretta M-9 and Colt M-16.

If you can use an experienced management professional with a reputation for handling pressure and rapid change with control, a positive attitude, and an aptitude for innovation, I would appreciate the opportunity to meet with you to discuss your needs. I can provide excellent references at the appropriate time.

Sincerely,

Clyde Grady

Often people leaving military service don't know what they want to do next. This U.S. Army captain is different. He is aggressively pursuing a career in the law enforcement field with the ultimate long-range goal of becoming a chief of police in a major metropolitan area.

Date

Exact Name of Person
Title or Position
Name of Company
Address (number and street)
Address (city, state, and zip)

Dear Exact Name of Person: (or Sir or Madam if answering a blind ad)

Military Officer

This senior executive who
retired from the military as a
colonel began his enlisted
service as an equipment
technician. Now that he has
been all over the world and
has excelled in both line and
staff positions, he has decided
that he wishes to represent a
company involved in the
international import/export
business. Like most senior
military officers, he must make
sure civilian employers
understand what he did as a
military professional.

With the enclosed resume, I would like to make you aware of my background as an experienced professional in the security field and military officer with demonstrated expertise in high-level international environments.

As you will see, I was handpicked to serve for four years as a Missile Inspector for United Nations Security Council-mandated monitoring, verification, and inspection of Iraqi weapons sites. In this highly visible position vital to international peace and security, I represented the U.S. and the United Nations in a volatile and hazardous environment. Consistently cited by senior officials for my assertive yet diplomatic manner, I was successful in negotiating sensitive issues and ensuring the safe and diplomatic completion of missions conducted by international teams of specialists.

I began military service as a repairman and rapidly distinguished myself through strong management and communication skills, which led to my subsequent success as an officer. Prior to my assignment with the United Nations, I held successively more responsible roles at the Air Force's training center for ICBM systems, where I managed multimillion-dollar training facilities and brought about improvements in numerous functional areas in facilities which trained the nation's future weapons systems managers and technical specialists.

If you can use an experienced security expert who has built a reputation as an exceptionally talented and masterful leader, I hope you will contact me to suggest a time when we might meet to discuss your needs. I can assure you in advance that I could rapidly become an asset to your organization.

Sincerely,

Ross Burks

Date

Exact Name of Person
Title or Position
Name of Company
Address (number and street)
Address (city, state, and zip)

Dear Exact Name of Person: (or Sir or Madam if answering a blind ad)

MILITARY TRANSITION

Electronics Technician
A job hunt is usually easier and less stressful if you know what you want to do. This individual knows that he is an electronics technician and he is seeking a position in avionics.

I would appreciate an opportunity to talk with you soon about how I could contribute to your organization through my troubleshooting and technical electronics skills as well as through my motivational and supervisory abilities.

You will see from my enclosed resume that I served my country in the U.S. Air Force where I built a reputation as an adaptable quick learner who could be counted on to motivate others and set an example of dedication to excellence. While meeting the demands of a military career with its frequent temporary assignments, I completed an A.A.S. degree in Avionics Systems Technology from the Community College of the Air Force.

Upon my retirement from military service, I will be offering my strong background in troubleshooting and functional testing of analog and digital circuits to the system, subassembly, and component level to other organizations. I am confident that the expertise and knowledge I have acquired will allow me to easily adapt to any situation where personal integrity and technical precision are valued.

If you can use a positive, results-oriented professional, I hope you will contact me to suggest a time when we might meet to discuss your needs. I can provide excellent references at the appropriate time.

Sincerely,

Cephus James Simmons

Date

Exact Name of Person
Title or Position
Name of Company
Address (number and street)
Address (city, state, and zip)

MILITARY TRANSITION

Dear Exact Name of Person: (or Sir or Madam if answering a blind ad)

Junior Military Officer

There are lots of companies that appreciate the disciplined nature of the military professional, and this junior officer is using the cover letter to explore opportunities with Fortune 500 companies. He offers experience in both line and staff positions.

With the enclosed resume, I would like to make you aware of my interest in utilizing my leadership experience and management skills within your organization.

As you will see from my enclosed resume, I have served my country as a junior military officer while advancing to the rank of Captain. Because of my accomplishments, I am considered to be on the "fast track" and was recently selected as one of six captains out of 160 to be scheduled for promotion ahead of schedule. Although I am being groomed for further rapid promotion and received the highest evaluations of my performance in every job I held, I have decided to resign my commission as a military officer.

While serving my country, I have excelled in both line management and staff consulting positions. In one job as a Company Commander managing 188 personnel, I was evaluated as the best of 26 commanders in the Group, and I gained valuable experience in distribution management. For example, I provided leadership in managing the supply/distribution of all sources of supply for 500 soldiers which involved managing a food storage and distribution site for perishables and nonperishables, storage and distribution sites for ammunition and petroleum (bulk and packaged), as well as the supply of housekeeping supplies and other equipment.

Because of my outstanding performance evaluations and reputation as a top-notch performer, I was handpicked for my current position which involves developing strategic plans for personnel systems. With a reputation as a creative and hardworking leader, I offer a strong bottom-line orientation. I have excelled in managing budgets of up to $750,000 and have been personally accountable for multimillion-dollar assets.

If you can use a proven leader with the ability to take a concept and transform it into an operating reality, I hope you will contact me to suggest a time when we might meet to discuss your needs and how I might serve them. I can assure you in advance that I am a creative problem solver and enthusiastic self-starter with unlimited personal initiative. On numerous occasions, senior executives have chosen me for the toughest assignments because they were confident of my ability to manage and persevere in the most difficult conditions. It would be a pleasure to speak with you about complex and challenging opportunities within your organization.

Sincerely,

Linville Gaines

Date

Exact Name of Person
Title or Position
Name of Company
Address (number and street)
Address (city, state, and zip)

Dear Exact Name of Person: (or Sir or Madam if answering a blind ad)

MILITARY TRANSITION

Lieutenant Colonel
If you feel you have a gift for teaching and training others, go ahead and say so in your cover letter. This distinguished professional is attempting to transition into a second career as an instructor, training program manager, or counselor.

With the enclosed resume describing my exceptional track record as a leader and communicator, I would like to express my interest in applying my extensive experience in training management and in providing instruction and guidance to others for the benefit of your organization.

As you will see, I have advanced to the rank of lieutenant colonel while serving my country in the U.S. Army. Although I have excelled in "line management" jobs, for a great deal of my military career I have been heavily involved in jobs in training management as well as in instructing and developing educational programs. I am presently the Chairman of the Military Science Department and Professor of Military Science at Texas A & M University.

Now that I have served my country with distinction, upon my retirement I believe that the most productive application of my expertise would be in positions as an instructor, training program manager, or counselor/mentor. You would find me to be a congenial person who offers an innate ability to work with people and inspire them to peak performance. I sincerely believe I have a gift for teaching and training people and for "translating" abstract concepts into understandable language.

I hope you will contact me to suggest a time when we might meet to discuss your needs. I can assure you in advance that I could rapidly become an asset to your organization.

Sincerely,

Paul Delph

Date

Exact Name of Person
Title or Position
Name of Company
Address (number and street)
Address (city, state, and zip)

MILITARY TRANSITION   Dear Exact Name of Person: (or Sir or Madam if answering a blind ad)

Junior Officer

All employers are looking for people whom other employers want to hire, so if you are on the "fast track" but have decided to resign from military service, say so. Notice that this young officer points out that he has been placed in positions usually reserved for someone of higher rank.

With the enclosed resume, I would like to make you aware of my background as an experienced manager who is excelling as a junior military officer through the application of excellent human relations and motivational skills as well as a talent for finding a way to maximize all available resources.

As you will see, I am an exceptionally well-organized and detail-oriented individual who has earned promotion ahead of my peers to leadership roles while serving in the U.S. Army. Handpicked as a first lieutenant for my current job, a position usually reserved for a captain, I am controlling logistics support for the 18,000-person 18th Airborne Corps. Prior to this assignment, I earned respect for my achievements as "second-in-command" of a 134-person company where my responsibilities included overseeing maintenance, operations, and training. In every military assignment, I have been effective in leading and motivating personnel to exceed expected standards in all areas and have managed maintenance and logistics support for millions of dollars in equipment and supplies. I am accustomed to performing in environments which demand the ability to handle high levels of stress and pressure while operating under life-and-death conditions where any error or misjudgment could quickly lead to disaster.

While I am earning the highest performance evaluations and being groomed for advanced managerial roles, I have decided to resign my commission as a military officer. I feel that one of my greatest strengths is in working with people. With my degree in Sociology, work history, and background, I could apply my strong interest in working with juveniles in the criminal justice system.

If you can use an intelligent, articulate, and assertive management professional, I hope you will contact me to suggest a time when we might meet to discuss your needs. I can assure you in advance that I could rapidly become an asset to your organization.

Sincerely,

Jason Demeyer

Date

Exact Name of Person
Title or Position
Name of Company
Address (number and street)
Address (city, state, and zip)

Dear Exact Name of Person: (or Sir or Madam if answering a blind ad)

With the enclosed resume, I would like to make you aware of my interest in utilizing my considerable experience in logistics, safety, and management for the benefit of your organization.

As you will see from my enclosed resume, I served my country as an officer in the U.S. Army and I worked in management positions which permitted me to gain specialized training and experience related to logistics and safety. In one job, I managed 15 individuals while accounting for more than $1 million in weapons and vehicles. In another job, I managed a specialized 36-person team and led employees through challenging and rugged training projects in field environments.

In my most recent job as a Logistics Officer, I played a key role in planning and implementing logistics operations for a 750-person organization which had to remain continuously ready to relocate worldwide for international projects. While managing 30 people, I also assisted in administering a $405,000 budget. I have become very familiar with OSHA, Department of Defense, and Department of the Army safety regulations, and I am knowledgeable of OSHA regulations pertaining to the use, storage, and disposal of hazardous materials.

While earning my B.A. degree with honors from Stanford University, I received numerous awards and honors for outstanding leadership and achievements.

If you can use a versatile young professional with a dedicated and hardworking attitude, I hope you will contact me to suggest a time when we might talk in person. I can provide outstanding references at the appropriate time.

Sincerely,

Oliver M. Goff

U.S. Army Officer
This military officer has gained extensive experience in logistics and safety which will enable him to transition into a job in the environmental field. He points out that he is knowledgeable of OSHA and other regulations related to hazardous material disposal.

Date

Exact Name of Person
Title or Position
Name of Company
Address (number and street)
Address (city, state, and zip)

Dear Exact Name of Person: (or Sir or Madam if answering a blind ad)

After extensive military service which refined his teaching and training skills, this military professional is ready to embark on a career in the civilian world using the same skills.

With the enclosed resume, I would like to make you aware of my background as an experienced and versatile technical instructor/course developer, manager of human and material resources, and supervisor.

As you will see, I have served with distinction in the U.S. Army where I earned a reputation as an adaptable, articulate, and well-rounded professional. My most recent assignment was as an instructor for officer candidates for international and American military students at the U.S. Army's Special Warfare Training School at Ft. Jackson, SC.

I was consistently selected for jobs which required the ability to think and react quickly, develop workable solutions, apply sound judgment, and set an example of dedication and professionalism. I have screened and assessed candidates for specialized training programs, controlled thousands of dollars worth of weapons and equipment, counseled and evaluated students, and developed detailed operations plans and realistic training exercises.

A seasoned manager and supervisor, I am confident that I offer a broad range of knowledge and experience that would make me a valuable asset to an organization in need of mature results-oriented professionals. I hope you will call me soon to suggest a time we might meet to discuss your needs. I can assure you in advance that I could rapidly become an asset to your organization.

Sincerely,

Jorge Finizza

Date

Exact Name of Person
Title or Position
Name of Company
Address (number and street)
Address (city, state, and zip)

Dear Exact Name of Person: (or Sir or Madam if answering a blind ad)

With the enclosed resume, I would like to make you aware of my background as an experienced manager and supervisor who offers a reputation for possessing, and continually demonstrating, high levels of initiative and perseverance along with a positive and enthusiastic approach.

As you will see, I advanced to the rank of Sergeant Major and recently retired from the U.S. Army. Throughout my military career, I was promoted ahead of my peers and earned respect for my versatile abilities, superior organizational and management skills, as well as my ability to apply my versatile knowledge in creative ways that solved real-world problems. In addition to positions which emphasized personnel management, administrative operations, and training, I have also supervised vehicle maintenance activities, prepared and controlled budgets, provided logistics support, and developed plans for large-scale worldwide missions. I hold a current Top Secret security clearance with SCI.

With a degree in Business and a talent for working with automated systems, I offer a track record of accomplishments in every facet of my work history. In addition to my success in the military, I have been involved since 1998 in managing a wide range of operations for an area small business. While overseeing job costing and bidding, budgeting, and payroll processing, I designed spreadsheets and a database which significantly aided the company as it experienced growth in annual gross income from $3.5 million in 1999 to its current annual level of more than $3.9 million. With a strong bottom-line orientation, I offer the proven ability to transform an idea into an operating reality.

If you can use an experienced manager who has received numerous awards for meritorious accomplishments and who offers resourceful leadership and managerial abilities, please contact me to suggest a time when we might meet to discuss your needs. I can assure you in advance that I could rapidly become an asset to your organization, and I can provide outstanding references at the appropriate time.

Sincerely,

Kareem Mealey

Date

Exact Name of Person
Title or Position
Name of Company
Address (number and street)
Address (city, state, and zip)

MILITARY TRANSITION

Marine Corps Veteran
After 20 years of service in the U.S. Marine Corps, this hardworking leader is ready for a new challenge. This all-purpose cover letter will allow him to approach employers in numerous industries.

Dear Exact Name of Person: (or Sir or Madam if answering a blind ad)

I would appreciate an opportunity to talk with you soon about how I could contribute to your organization through my diversified experience in functional areas including supply and logistics management, sales and marketing, and personnel counseling and training.

You will see from my enclosed resume that I have served my country in the U.S. Marine Corps for nearly 20 years. I am proud of my accomplishments as a Marine and feel a great deal of pride in having earned A.A. and B.A. degrees while fulfilling the obligations of a demanding military career. My extensive training has included computer operations as well as courses designed to develop my personnel recruiting and leadership development skills.

The recipient of many awards and recognition for my professional knowledge and accomplishments, I have excelled in every job I have held. Whether I have been involved in sales and recruiting, supervising supply operations, or ensuring smooth transportation of large quantities of people, supplies, and equipment, I have always performed to the highest standards.

If you are searching for a hardworking leader, I am an enthusiastic self-starter with an eye for detail and a proven ability to maximize available resources in order to get the job done.

I hope you will welcome my call soon to arrange a brief meeting to discuss your current and future needs and how I might serve them. Thank you in advance for your time.

Sincerely,

Angelo Perrotta

Alternate last paragraph:
I hope you will call or write me soon to suggest a time convenient for us to meet and discuss your current and future needs and how I might serve them. Thank you in advance for your time.

Date

Exact Name of Person
Title of Position
Company Name
Address (street and number)
Address (city, state, and zip)

Dear Exact Name of Person: (or Dear Sir or Madam if answering a blind ad)

MILITARY TRANSITION

Marine Corps Veteran
The confusing thing to most people leaving military service is figuring out what they can do in the civilian world. This experienced professional most enjoyed the personnel administration field, and with this cover letter he is hoping to find jobs in the personnel field.

Can you use a creative thinker and versatile problem solver who has compiled a track record of achievement based on my success in developing and conducting training programs, supervising and counseling personnel, as well as managing administrative support?

While serving my country in the U.S. Marine Corps, I advanced in rank ahead of my peers because of my organizational, supervisory, and administrative abilities. I was selected for demanding roles in the personnel administration field, and I became known for my ability to maximize organizational efficiency and inspire teamwork. I have managed personnel testing, developed and administered training programs all over the world, and directed course registration and scheduling at a training academy. My critical-thinking skills and problem-solving ability have been tested and refined in both line management and consulting positions which required an astute strategic thinker who could formulate plans for future needs while resourcefully responding to quickly changing daily priorities.

While excelling in demanding roles as a Marine Corps leader, I used my spare time to further my education and complete my B.S. degree in Psychology. I have completed numerous executive development training programs sponsored by the U.S. Marine Corps.

You would find me in person to be an enthusiastic and self-motivated professional with versatile abilities which could be valuable to you. If my considerable talents and strong bottom-line orientation are of interest to you, I hope you will contact me to suggest a time when we might meet to discuss your current and future needs and how I might serve them. I can provide outstanding personal and professional references at the appropriate time. Thank you in advance for your time.

Sincerely,

Jack Myshka

Date

Exact Name of Person
Exact Title
Exact Name of Company
Address
City, State Zip

Dear Exact Name of Person (or Dear Sir or Madam if answering a blind ad)

I would appreciate an opportunity to talk with you soon about how I could contribute to your organization through my marketing and communication skills as well as my experience in solving problems and supervising personnel in highly technical environments. My wife and I are permanently resettling in the Orlando area, and I am seeking to aggressively contribute to the bottom line of a company that can use a versatile professional with extensive technical knowledge and proven management abilities.

As you will see from my resume, I recently completed my B.S. degree with dual majors of Business Management and Marketing from Texas University. I am highly proficient with many software programs including Microsoft, and I can program in C++.

Prior to college, I served my country in the U.S. Navy, which gave me an opportunity to become involved in numerous projects which required an astute problem solver known for attention to detail. As a Navy diver, I was promoted to supervise complex diving operations which included salvage operations such as recovering the remains of the Space Shuttle Challenger. In my final position in the Navy as a Division Officer, I coordinated diving operations at an elite Research and Development facility in Florida where I supervised 15 specialists including electricians, mechanics, and other technical specialists. As a Quality Assurance Inspector in my previous job, I managed complex repair and overhaul projects and was recognized for my exemplary leadership ability and technical skills. I have managed budgets of up to $1 million and have coordinated all aspects of complex maintenance management projects.

After leaving the Navy, I devoted myself full time to completing my college degree and, in that process, I have refined my natural sales and marketing skills. I am confident that I offer a strong combination of technical knowledge, management experience, and sales ability that could benefit an organization.

If you can use an experienced professional with my unique and versatile talents, I hope you will contact me to suggest a time when we might meet to discuss your needs. I can assure you that I could rapidly become an asset to your organization.

Sincerely,

Mason Jenkins

Date

Exact Name of Person
Exact Title
Exact Name of Company
Address
City, State Zip

Dear Exact Name of Person (or Dear Sir or Madam if answering a blind ad)

With the enclosed resume, I would like to make you aware of my desire to become a Mathematics Teacher as part of your teaching staff. As you will see from my resume, I am completing a B.S. in Secondary Education in order to transfer my skills into the academic sector as a Mathematics Teacher. A West Point graduate with a B.S. degree in Mechanical Engineering, I also hold an M.S. degree in Business Administration.

In my student teaching experience, I taught Geometry and Algebra I to tenth graders in the fall, and I am assigned to teach Algebra I and Geometry to high school students in grades 9-12 at Bethune High School in the spring.

As a military officer, I served my country with distinction and was involved throughout my career in training individuals and providing training management expertise to organizations. In my most recent position as a Division Chief, I provided leadership in the area of training management to thousands of individuals in 418 different organizations located in 21 states while directly managing 38 people and a budget of $175,000. In another job I managed the placement of 2,100 different people in 119 career paths. In every job I have held, I earned a reputation as an inspirational leader who subscribes to the concept of "leadership by example." Through my positive leadership style, I have always been able to develop a top-notch staff dedicated to quality results. Where leadership is concerned, I believe leadership is not leadership without initiative, and I have demonstrated initiative while inspiring initiative in others. I am confident these personal qualities will transfer into a classroom.

Although I was encouraged to remain in military service and receive a promotion to lieutenant colonel with an excellent possibility of becoming a general one day, I made the decision to resign my commission as an officer and make a career change into secondary school teaching. I am certain that my strong leadership and excellent teaching skills could become a worthy addition to the teaching staff of a quality institution, and I am positive that I would thrive on the challenge of training young minds.

If you can use a well-educated and enthusiastic Mathematics Teacher, please contact me to suggest a time when we might talk in person. I can assure you that I can provide outstanding references at the appropriate time.

Yours sincerely,

Jason Murphy

West Point Graduate
This talented officer could have remained in military service for the next certain promotion and then for possible promotion to general, but he decided to resign his commission and embark on a second career as a Mathematics Teacher in high school. Notice that he emphasizes his considerable background in training and developing personnel in this cover letter, rather than his extensive management experience. (If he were writing to a Fortune 500 company seeking a management position, he would use a different cover letter focusing on his management abilities.)

Date

Exact Name of Person
Title or Position
Name of Company
Address (number and street)
Address (city, state, and zip)

Dear Exact Name of Person: (or Sir or Madam if answering a blind ad)

Program Manager

Applying for internal
promotion is the motivation
behind this cover letter. As you
can see, a cover letter designed
to apply for an internal
opening is no different from a
cover letter to a prospective
employer in another
organization.

    With the enclosed resume, I would like to formally indicate my interest in the position of **Regional Development Director** and make you aware of my strong qualifications for the job. I hold a B.S. in Marketing which I earned with a 3.7 GPA while on a four-year scholarship based on my high school performance and exceptional SAT/ACT scores.

    As Area Executive Director for the American Diabetes Foundation in Southeastern Florida, I have vigorously breathed new life into ADF's activities in seven counties. With a reputation as an aggressive fund raiser with expert knowledge of all ADF programs, I have become skilled at consistently raising the dollars needed to meet or exceed income goals. Under my strong leadership, income increased 179% in the fiscal year 1998-99 and posted a 69% increase in the past fiscal year. I have become skilled at training and motivating volunteers for both fund raising and patient services, and my enthusiastic approach to income generation and program development is well known. I am proud of the accomplishments we have made through the 190 volunteers I have recruited, trained, managed, and motivated.

    It is my desire to work on an even higher level of responsibility for ADF while applying my expertise in fund raising, strategic planning, community organization, volunteer management, and program development. I am confident that I could play a key role in helping the Southeast Division Income Team realize new heights of net income generation while resourcefully identifying new sources of income and potential. In addition, my expert knowledge of ADF programs would enable me to expertly coordinate communication and assessment programs and work effectively with field personnel to gain their commitment of strategic goals. I offer demonstrated business planning experience as well as an exceptional ability to plan strategically, solve problems resourcefully, and negotiate complex issues with tact and diplomacy.

    I am truly eager to be of service to the Southeast Division of the American Diabetes Foundation in the role of Regional Development Director. As an experienced Area Executive Director, I am certain I could make a valuable contribution as Regional Development Director, and I hope you will contact me to suggest the next step in the process of being considered for this key role.

Sincerely,

Alexandra Rios

Date

Exact Name of Person
Title or Position
Name of Company
Address (number and street)
Address (city, state, and zip)

Dear Exact Name of Person: (or Sir or Madam if answering a blind ad)

NONPROFIT MANAGEMENT

Arts Council Director
A talented director of an arts organization moving to another state is seeking a position similar to her most recent job with this cover letter. She emphasizes her effectiveness in the main areas that nonprofit executives focus on—fundraising, volunteer recruiting and management, and public education as well as board liaison and financial administration.

With the enclosed resume, I would like to make you aware of my background as an arts management professional with exceptional communication, organizational, and motivational skills. I offer the proven ability to recruit, train, and manage volunteers, direct grant writing and fundraising activities, and increase public awareness of and involvement in the arts.

In my most recent position, I served as Program Director for the second largest arts council in California, which has an annual operating budget of nearly $800,000. With the San Francisco Arts Council, I developed and implemented a number of new programs, including a comprehensive dance program that generated more than $10,000 annually in class fees and a drama troupe for teenagers funded by an annual grant that I secured. In addition to events planning and coordination, I excelled in marketing and public relations designed to raise community awareness of the Arts Council's programs.

In an earlier job as Executive Director for the Anaheim Arts Council, I oversaw all operational aspects of the organization, from managing an annual budget of $100,000 to acting as liaison between the arts council and local schools, arts organizations, and the local government. I created and implemented the first-ever Special Arts Festival for mentally handicapped children and adults in Anaheim County.

As you will see, I have earned my Bachelor of Science in Theatre Arts and have supplemented my degree program with additional courses in Arts Management from Salem University. I am completing the Certificate in Nonprofit Management program at Stanford University.

If you can use a motivated and experienced arts management professional whose dedication to the arts and skills in volunteer management, fundraising, and program development have been proven in challenging positions statewide, I hope you will contact me to suggest a time when we might meet. I can provide excellent references at the appropriate time.

Sincerely,

Lucia Russo

Date

Exact Name of Person
Title or Position
Name of Company
Address (number and street)
Address (city, state, and zip)

NONPROFIT MANAGEMENT

Executive Director
A cover letter is often called a
"letter of interest," and it is
actually a letter of
introduction to you and to
your resume. In this case, an
accomplished nonprofit
executive is relocating back to
the Atlanta area and is seeking
a position in nonprofit
management. She has
identified numerous nonprofit
organizations with which she
would like to be associated,
and she is using the "direct
approach" and mailing this
"letter of interest" to
organizations that interest her.
By using the "direct approach,"
you can choose your next
employer.

Dear Exact Name of Person: (or Sir or Madam if answering a blind ad)

With the enclosed resume, I would like to introduce myself and my desire to explore suitable positions within your organization which can utilize my experience in providing leadership to nonprofit organizations. I am relocating back to the Atlanta area where I own a townhouse, and I believe my extensive background in nonprofit management may be of interest to you.

As you will see from my resume, I have most recently served as Executive Director of an organization in Maryland, where I have managed recruitment and training of a 65-person volunteer staff while also supervising three professional staff personnel. I have developed effective collaborative efforts among numerous community organizations while simultaneously identifying gaps in community services and developing programs to fill those needs.

In my previous position in Washington, D.C., I was promoted from Community Services Coordinator to Assistant Director and then to Director of a community shelter with a staff of 30 human services professionals and paraprofessionals. In addition to developing and maintaining the $800,000 budget, I was active in grant writing and in numerous community activities which raised the shelter's profile.

The recipient of numerous awards and honors for my contributions and service, I have enjoyed the respect of my colleagues in being elected to leadership positions in professional organizations and high-profile committees. I am widely respected for my ability to develop and maintain effective working relationships, organizational partnerships, and collaborative efforts.

If you can use my considerable leadership abilities and team building skills, I hope you will contact me to suggest a time when we might meet to discuss your needs and goals and how I might meet them. Thank you in advance for your time.

Sincerely,

Bernice Kunkel

Date

Exact Name of Person
Title or Position
Name of Company
Address (number and street)
Address (city, state, and zip)

Dear Exact Name of Person: (or Sir or Madam if answering a blind ad)

NONPROFIT MANAGEMENT

Nonprofit Executive
This versatile manager of
human and physical resources
could move in several
directions in his job hunt. He
has spent some time in
economic planning in
municipalities, and he has
managed human services
activities, which is his real love.
This all-purpose cover letter is
designed to introduce his
considerable talents to
numerous organizations.

With the enclosed resume, I would like to make you aware of my interest in becoming employed by your organization in some capacity in which you can utilize my exceptional communication, organizational, management, and human resources skills.

Nonprofit Management Experience
In my most recent position as Director for the Red Cross Homeless Shelter, I managed an annual budget of $183,000 while overseeing operations of a 44-bed nonprofit organization. This included interviewing and hiring of salaried personnel as well as recruiting volunteers for a program providing lunches to 120 people daily. I routinely performed case management and client counseling, providing referrals to other agencies including state and local mental health and social services, churches, as well as philanthropic and charitable organizations.

Economic Development Background
In my previous job as Associate Director of the Shreveport Area Economic Development Corporation, I played a key role in efforts to attract new industry to the area. In that capacity, I performed liaison with representatives of companies interested in locating in Shreveport while also coordinating with local contractors, public works, colleges and universities, and government agencies at the state and local level. On my own initiative I compiled, developed, and updated a database of industry contacts in conjunction with other economic development agencies in Louisiana, and I provided aggressive leadership in submitting business proposals and applications for financial assistance to appropriate state agencies on behalf of corporations.

Educational Credentials
I hold a Master of Arts in Marketing/Geography and Land Use Analysis from Louisiana State University and a Bachelor of Arts in Geography (with a minor in Psychology) from Lafayette College.

If you can use an astute manager and planner whose decision-making and problem-solving skills have been proven in a variety of challenging situations, then I hope you will contact me soon. I can assure you in advance that I have an outstanding reputation and can provide excellent references.

Sincerely,

Sidney J. Le Blanc

Date

Exact Name of Person
Title or Position
Name of Company
Address (number and street)
Address (city, state, and zip)

NONPROFIT MANAGEMENT

Dear Sir or Madam:

Nonprofit Executive

This Girl Scout executive has had extensive experience in program management. In her working career, this nonprofit executive has spent the past 10 years in manufacturing environments but physical problems prevent her from continuing to work in such a physically rugged setting. Therefore, the purpose of this cover letter is to resurrect a nonprofit career that she left a decade ago. She probably won't return to the Girl Scouts as an organization, but she might find a suitable position in social services or youth services.

With the enclosed resume, I would like to express my interest in your organization and acquaint you with my skills and experience related to your needs.

As you will see from my resume, I hold a B.A. in Human Relations degree which I put to good use immediately after college when I served for 11 years as a District Executive with the Girl Scouts of America. In that capacity, I managed districts in Washington, Maryland, and Virginia and was responsible for recruiting, training, financial administration, program planning and management, and community liaison. Since Girl Scouts of America is an organization devoted to shaping youth in moral, ethical, and spiritual ways while teaching leadership ability as well as a variety of skills useful throughout life, I was continually involved in training and counseling young people. I acted as Director of Summer Camp operations during the summers, which involved planning and managing summer camp experiences for thousands of girls trying to earn Merit Badges and acquire skills in areas ranging from carpentry to first aid. I am a skilled counselor and program manager.

As a result of my involvement with the Girl Scouts, I gained numerous technical and mechanical skills which I subsequently put to use in production and manufacturing environments.

If you can use a dependable and experienced individual who offers a proven ability to adapt easily to new situations and rapidly master new tasks, I hope you will contact me. I enjoy being in a position in which I can help others, and I offer highly refined skills in dealing with the public. I can provide excellent personal and professional references at the appropriate time, and I hope I will have the pleasure of talking with you soon in person.

Yours sincerely,

Rosemary Digiovanni

Date

TO: Search Committee
FROM: Michael Knight
RE: Position of Executive Vice President, National Association of Health Underwriters

In response to the urging of someone familiar with your search for the Executive Vice President for the National Association of Health Underwriters, I am sending you a resume which summarizes my background. I offer a unique combination of knowledge, experience, and abilities which I believe would ideally fit the requirements of the National Association of Health Underwriters.

Health industry expertise

You will see from my resume that I offer expertise related to health insurance and underwriting. In my current job I have sought out and negotiated contracts with major insurance companies to provide insurance for the organization. On a $1 million budget, I have developed insurance programs which generated $2 million in net income based on $32 million in premium. These highly regarded programs which I developed have brought 6,000 new members into the organization.

Proven executive ability

I offer proven executive ability. I have earned a reputation as someone who has not only strategic vision and imagination but also the tenacity and persistence to follow through on the "nitty-gritty" details of implementing new projects, programs, and concepts. I know how to delegate, and I know how to "micro manage," and I am skilled at tailoring my management style to particular circumstances while always shouldering full responsibility and accountability for results. My current job has involved the responsibility of recruiting, training, and continuously developing a national sales force of brokers throughout the U.S. which broke with the tradition of passive mail solicitation and led to dramatic growth in sales and profitability. With a strong "bottom-line" orientation, I have streamlined headquarters staff and reduced central office expenses to save at least half a million dollars while continuously supervising the association's five regional offices in the recruitment and training of more than 1,200 insurance agents nationally.

Extensive association experience

You will also see from my resume that I am accustomed to "getting things done" within the unique environment of a trade/membership association. I am well known for my ability to attract and retain a cohesive and productive staff, and I am also respected for my exceptional skills in relating to, inspiring, and supporting key volunteer members. A skilled communicator, I have made countless speeches.

I am aware of the requirements defined by the search committee, and I would enjoy the opportunity to discuss this position further with the Executive Committee. I feel certain I could contribute significantly to the growth and financial health of the National Association of Health Underwriters as its Executive Vice President. Thank you for your time and consideration.

Date

Exact Name of Person
Title or Position
Name of Company
Address (number and street)
Address (city, state, and zip)

Dear Exact Name of Person: (or Sir or Madam if answering a blind ad)

With the enclosed resume, I would like to make you aware of my interest in working for the Central Intelligence Agency.

You will see that I have served my country with distinction while achieving the rank of Captain in the U.S. Army. I hold a Top Secret security clearance, possess extensive skills in utilizing software that includes the Microsoft Office Suite, and hold a BA degree in History from the University of Missouri where I was named ROTC Outstanding Military Graduate.

You will also see from my resume that I offer skills and knowledge related to firearms. I am qualified on the M9 pistol and M16A2, and am familiar with the M60 machine gun.

While serving my country as a military officer, I have received the highest possible evaluations of my performance in every job I have held. In my current job as a Captain with a Military Intelligence organization, I am in charge of training military professionals in 38 specialized areas with eight foreign languages. In my previous job, I was Officer in Charge in a Military Intelligence Company where I supervised 39 people while overseeing the utilization of tactical cryptological program assets within the U.S. Eastern Command. In that job I was responsible for the closure of a Sensitive Compartmented Information Facility on Langley Air Force Base and its relocation to Ft. Myer with flawless accountability and no security violations. In my prior job as Executive Officer, I managed all administrative and logistical support for a Human Intelligence Company performing missions in Europe. As a First Lieutenant with a Military Police organization in Berlin, I oversaw the collection of intelligence and performed liaison with numerous federal and foreign agencies. As a Second Lieutenant in a job as a Special Security Officer, I managed the MACOM-level Sensitive Compartmented Information (SCI) program and, on my own initiative, I developed numerous enhancements to the program.

I am willing to travel and/or relocate worldwide as your needs require, and my salary is negotiable. If my considerable skills and talents interest you, I hope you will contact me to suggest a time when we might meet to discuss suitable positions which could utilize my versatile management ability and technical knowledge.

Yours sincerely,

Ernie I. Novak

Central Intelligence Agency

Gaining employment with the CIA is the motivation behind this cover letter. The background of this individual is well suited to the Central Intelligence Agency—former military with one of the nation's highest security clearances. If employment with the CIA doesn't work out, he can use this cover letter to explore opportunities with police departments and other law enforcement organizations.

Date

Exact Name of Person
Title or Position
Name of Company
Address (number and street)
Address (city, state, and zip)

Dear Exact Name of Person: (or Sir or Madam if answering a blind ad)

Police Chief
This seasoned manager is
seeking a top job in a law
enforcement organization after
military service. In the military
he served in a position which
was the equivalent of "police
chief." He has traveled the
world and is an antiterrorism
and counterterrorism expert.

   With the enclosed resume, I would like to make you aware of the background in security and police operations management which I could put to work for your organization.

   While rising to the rank of Lieutenant Colonel, I have excelled in both line management and staff consulting positions worldwide. I was handpicked for my current job in charge of executive training programs at the U.S. Army's most prestigious graduate-level academic institution. While working with military officers to improve their communication and problem-solving skills, I have rewritten a major course curriculum and have revised materials used by more than 8,000 officers.

   In my previous position as a Police Chief in Europe, I was in charge of all military police units disbursed over 32,000 square kilometers. I also planned and managed the relocation of police assets and personnel to Bosnia-Herzegovina where I functioned as an international police chief in charge of a division with Russian, Nordic-Swedish-Polish, and Turkish brigades. I am very proud of the fact that the police company I managed was named "the best" in the U.S. Army.

   In previous positions all over the world, my strategic thinking abilities and operational management skills have been tested and refined. As a Commander of a detachment in Haiti, I provided leadership related to migrant operations for 46,000 Haitian refugees. In a previous job, I set up camps and developed plans for dislocated civilians in Somalia.

   I have earned a master's degree in International Relations, a BA in Criminology/Criminal Justice, and an AA in Administration of Justice. I have also completed extensive training including the Ranger Course, Airborne School, Antiterrorism and Counterterrorism Courses, as well as training sponsored by the U.S. State Department. I hold a Top Secret/SBI security clearance.

   If you can use a proven professional who is known for an ability to establish and maintain excellent working relationships with people at all levels, I hope you will contact me to suggest a time when we might meet to discuss your needs and how I might serve them. I can provide outstanding personal and professional references.

Sincerely,

Eddie Rimondi

Date

Exact Name of Person
Title or Position
Name of Company
Address (number and street)
Address (city, state, and zip)

Dear Exact Name of Person: (or Sir or Madam if answering a blind ad)

Corrections Officer
This corrections
professional also offers an
extensive background in
automation security.

With the enclosed resume, I would like to make you aware of my exceptional supervisory, communication, and organizational skills as well as my background in corrections, automation security, and personal and property accountability.

As a Corrections Officer for the Las Vegas Correctional Institution, I am responsible for the security and supervision of 400 inmates. I conduct visual, audio, and video surveillance of the facility and search all vehicles entering and leaving the facility to ensure that no personnel, weapons, drugs, or other contraband are smuggled into or out of the institution.

In my previous position as Customer Service Representative for TASCOR (IBM), I handled all drug screenings for IBM personnel worldwide, coordinating with drug screening agencies to schedule testing and verifying that personnel took the prescribed tests. As Postal Operations Manager in Germany, I worked with German customs agents to detect illegal shipments of drugs, weapons, ammunition, and other contraband coming into and out of the country.

While serving at Fort Detrick as Information Systems Operations Supervisor, I completed the rigorous U.S. Army Logistics Security course and established and trained a reaction force to meet the growing threat of terrorism. In addition, I served as Automated Data Processing Systems Security Officer, and I have excelled in numerous military training programs having to do with security procedures, criminal investigation methods, special operations, and other security-related issues.

If you can use an experienced and self-motivated security and corrections professional, then I look forward to hearing from you soon to arrange a time when we might meet to discuss your present and future needs and how I might meet them. I assure you that I have an excellent reputation and would quickly become an asset to your organization.

Sincerely,

Curt Sheldon

Date

Exact Name of Person
Title or Position
Name of Company
Address (number and street)
Address (city, state, and zip)

Dear Exact Name of Person: (or Dear Sir or Madam if answering a blind ad)

Police Officer Applicant
This cover letter is designed to help an accomplished young military professional enter the law enforcement field after military service.

    I would appreciate an opportunity to talk with you soon about how I could contribute to your organization through my leadership experience as well as my skills and experience related to law enforcement.

    As you will see from my resume, I earned a B.S. degree in Criminal Justice with a minor in Business prior to becoming an active duty soldier in the Regular Army. While serving my country in the Airborne Infantry, I have advanced to leadership positions ahead of my peers. As a Squad Leader I have excelled in training, motivating, and managing five people and am responsible for assuring that our team is continuously ready to deploy to any combat situation. I am an expert marksman and have qualified with every personal weapon in the U.S. Army's inventory. In addition to receiving several physical fitness awards and the Army Physical Fitness Badge, I was named Soldier of the Month for my Battalion and my Brigade and was first runner-up in the Division competition.

    I offer a track record of accomplishment in all military training programs which I have completed. I was named to the Commandant's List from the highly competitive Primary Leadership Development Course, was Honor Graduate from the Unit Armorer Course, and was Fast Track Graduate from Advanced Individual Training. A certified SCUBA diver, I am Red Cross CPR and IV Certified.

    It is my strong desire to embark upon a career in law enforcement after leaving military service, and I am confident that my personal initiative, proven leadership ability, and diversified skills could be valuable assets to a law enforcement organization. I hope you will contact me to suggest what you feel is the next step I should take in applying for employment with your organization. I can provide outstanding personal and professional references at the appropriate time.

Sincerely,

Bryan Vivero

Date

Exact Name of Person
Title or Position
Name of Company
Address (number and street)
Address (city, state, and zip)

POLICE, SECURITY, & LAW
ENFORCEMENT

Executive Protection Services
Experience in executive
protection services is what
this law enforcement
professional is offering.

Dear Exact Name of Person: (or Sir or Madam if answering a blind ad)

With the enclosed resume, I would like to introduce myself and the extensive experience I offer in the field of security management and executive protection services.

As a Special Forces professional, I have planned and directed dozens of projects in numerous countries in Central America and South America. I am language qualified in Japanese, Spanish, and Portuguese, and I have taught subjects such as security management and bomb search techniques in Spanish to South and Central American police forces.

Prior to becoming a Special Forces "Green Beret," I excelled as a Combat Engineer and became skilled in construction, destructive demolition, land mine placement and detection, and similar areas.

While managing Special Forces "A" Teams all over the globe, I have been involved in high-profile assignments—such as playing an aggressive role in searching for Manuel Noriega and applying my demolitions expertise to destroy radio stations during the war in Panama. I have also been involved in numerous low-profile protective assignments during which I provided executive protection for VIPs. While my resume is descriptive of my skills, I have usually been involved in assignments of a classified nature and am not at liberty to reveal many details which would give you further insight into my in-depth skills related to security and communications.

A Certified Protection Specialist (CPR), I am completing an Associate of Occupational Studies in Criminal Justice with a major in Executive Protection.

If you can use a skilled security professional known for my vigilant approach to managing security projects and executive protection services, I hope you will contact me to suggest a time when we might meet face-to-face to discuss your needs and how I might serve them. I am confident I could make significant contributions to your security and protective services needs, and I can provide outstanding personal and professional references at the appropriate time. Please be assured that I am ready to travel or relocate anywhere in the world as your needs require.

Sincerely,

Anthony Zenith

Date

Exact Name of Person
Title or Position
Name of Company
Address (number and street)
Address (city, state, and zip)

Dear Exact Name of Person: (or Dear Sir or Madam if answering a blind ad)

Police Officer Applicant
This cover letter is designed to help a young military professional enter the security or law enforcement field after military service.

With the enclosed resume, I would like to make you aware of my interest in working for your organization in some capacity which could utilize my strong background in law enforcement and physical security.

You will see from my enclosed resume that I offer a reputation as a respected professional who has been promoted ahead of my peers to responsible positions which required excellent judgment and problem-solving skills. Entrusted with a Top Secret security clearance, I have excelled in extensive military training including Military Police School, Airborne School, Basic Armor Training, and Defensive Driving.

While serving my country in the U.S. Army, I have had an opportunity to apply my technical skills and management ability in international environments. In Somalia, I excelled in handling pressure and potentially hazardous situations while overseeing American/Indian military police patrols. As a Desk Sergeant and Military Police Team Leader in Korea, I supervised up to nine people and controlled inventories worth hundreds of thousands of dollars.

In my most recent job I have controlled maintenance for more than $120 million in equipment while overseeing physical security. On my own initiative, I recognized the need for changes in the physical fitness program and implemented a new program which transformed high failure rates into high pass rates.

I have been honored with several medals in recognition of my distinguished contributions and achievements, and I can provide outstanding personal and professional references. If my experience, qualifications, skills, and personal attributes interest you, I hope you will call or write me to suggest a time when we could meet to discuss your needs and goals and how I might help you achieve them.

Sincerely,

Waldo Burgess

Alternate last paragraph:
I hope you will welcome my call soon to try to set up a time convenient for us to meet to discuss your current and future needs and how I might serve them. Thank you in advance for your time.

Date

Exact Name of Person
Title or Position
Name of Company
Address (number and street)
Address (city, state, and zip)

POLICE, SECURITY, & LAW ENFORCEMENT

Police Captain

This Police Captain feels that it is time, career-wise, to move up to the job of Chief of Police. Since the Chief of Police in the town where he now works isn't going anywhere any time soon, Mr. Ragozine is selectively exploring opportunities to serve in that role in cities in the state where he lives and in nearby states.

Dear Exact Name of Person: (or Sir or Madam if answering a blind ad)

With the enclosed resume, I would like to formally initiate the process of becoming considered for the job of Chief of Police for the City of Ann Arbor.

As you will see from my resume, I am currently serving the Battle Creek Police Department as a Police Captain in charge of one of the city's three Patrol Divisions. As one of the department's six Captains, I have transformed the city's newest Patrol Division into a highly respected and productive operating unit known for the high morale and productivity of its 62 personnel.

In previous jobs with the City of Battle Creek, I performed with distinction as Lieutenant in charge of both the Major Crimes Investigative Division and Emergency Operations. I began working for the City of Battle Creek as a Patrol Officer after serving my country briefly in the U.S. Army as a Military Policeman. I have enjoyed a track record of promotion because of my hard work and common sense, my outstanding police work in all functional areas, as well as my excellent administrative skills and ability to deal articulately and tactfully with everyone, from employees to citizens' groups.

I can provide outstanding references at the appropriate time, and I can assure you that you would find me to be an individual who is known as a gifted strategic thinker, powerful motivator, and fair supervisor.

Please contact me if you would like me to make myself available for a personal interview at your convenience. Although I am held in high regard within the Battle Creek Police Department, I have a strong interest in exploring ways in which my leadership ability and extensive experience in all aspects of police work could be put to use for Ann Arbor as its Chief of Police.

Sincerely,

Phil Ragozine

Date

Exact Name of Person
Title or Position
Name of Company
Address (number and street)
Address (city, state, and zip)

Dear Exact Name of Person: (or Sir or Madam if answering a blind ad)

POLICE, SECURITY, & LAW
ENFORCEMENT

Police Officer
Salaries are among the lowest
in the nation in the state
where this police officer now
works. Therefore, he is using
this all-purpose cover letter to
explore employment
opportunities for police
officers in other states.

With the enclosed resume, I would like to make you aware of my experience as a law enforcement professional with excellent investigative, communication, and supervisory skills and a strong background in the training of personnel.

As you will see, I have extensive law enforcement experience in a number of diverse metropolitan areas, in addition to the skills that I developed and sharpened during my time in the military. While with the Gulfport Police Department, I have served as a uniformed Police Officer and Police Sergeant. In Jackson, I held similar positions and was also a Major Crimes Investigator. In the military, my exemplary skills as a trainer resulted in assignment as an Instructor to the 82nd Airborne Division NCO Academy, where I further distinguished myself by authoring a "battle book" of training scenarios which was widely praised.

With a Bachelor of Science in Criminal Justice from Mississippi State University, I have a strong educational background to support my years of practical experience. I have also been awarded an Advanced Law Enforcement Certification from the Mississippi Justice Training and Standards Commission.

If you would benefit from the services of a highly experienced and motivated law enforcement professional with a strong background in supervision, training, and investigation, then please contact me to arrange a time when we might meet to discuss your needs. I thank you in advance for your time and consideration.

Sincerely,

Hal Carlson

Date

Exact Name of Person
Title or Position
Name of Company
Address (number and street)
Address (city, state, and zip)

POLICE, SECURITY, & LAW ENFORCEMENT

Special Agent
This Special Agent with extensive experience in fraud investigations could move into retail organizations, insurance companies, or law enforcement organizations, just to name a few of his likely next homes.

Dear Exact Name of Person: (or Sir or Madam if answering a blind ad)

With the enclosed resume, I would like to make you aware of my background related to fraud investigations.

In my current job as a Special Agent with the Criminal Investigation Division (CID), I have specialized in general crimes including auto theft, criminal background checks and information, as well as various fraud investigations. I routinely account for an inventory of equipment which includes burglary kits, visual ID kits, various types of fingerprint kits, body armor, hostage negotiation crisis telephones, cameras, and other devices.

After completing the Army's CID Special Agent Course, I was assigned to Ft. Lee, VA. A successful federally sworn agent with a high level of skill in dealing with people, I have testified before the grand jury and local magistrates in all types of courts martial. I have also obtained arrest and search warrants/authorization before federal magistrates and local authorities. I hold a Top Secret security clearance with SBI.

I was selected for advanced training and career opportunities on the basis of my effectiveness as an investigator and assistant to Army CID Special Agents in Panama. I have qualified "Expert" with the M16 rifle, 9mm pistol, shotgun and am familiar with the processing and protection of crime scene physical evidence.

If you can use a well-trained, thorough, and knowledgeable professional who is highly articulate, cool under pressure, and able to easily adapt to pressure and change, please contact me to suggest a time when we might meet to discuss your needs. I can assure you in advance that I could rapidly become an asset to your organization.

Sincerely,

Gregory A. Remington II

Date

Exact Name of Person
Title or Position
Name of Company
Address (number and street)
Address (city, state, and zip)

Dear Exact Name of Person: (or Sir or Madam if answering a blind ad)

With the enclosed resume, I would like to make you aware of my interest in employment with your organization and acquaint you with the considerable experience and skills I could offer you.

As you will see from my resume, I excelled for 20 years as a member of the Minnesota Highway Patrol and was promoted to the rank of Line Sergeant. My responsibilities included investigating accidents and performing a wide range of administrative duties. In the process of my job, I gained skills in interacting effectively with people at all levels, ranging from public citizens to Police Chiefs, District Attorneys, District and Superior Court Judges, School Administrators, and community leaders.

My management skills are highly refined as I have supervised, led, and coordinated work assignments of a squad of troopers on a daily basis. I am well known for my ability to maintain the highest level of motivation and morale through leading by example while always providing a fair but firm, positive, and consistent presence. On numerous occasions I conducted public education programs at schools and community organizations, and I have earned a reputation as an outstanding public speaker.

Prior to serving with the Highway Patrol, I served with distinction in the U.S. Marine Corps and was promoted ahead of my peers to supervisory positions. I served during combat in Vietnam and was the recipient of numerous medals and awards for exemplary performance.

If you can use a dedicated professional known for absolute integrity as well as common sense, I hope you will contact me to suggest a time when we could meet in person to discuss your needs. I would be delighted to make myself available for personal interviews at your convenience. Although I am highly regarded in my current position with Vacation Bus Tours, Inc., the long absences from my family as I travel cross country are less than ideal for me and my family, and I am seeking a position closer to home. We own a home in St. Paul and are permanent residents. I can provide excellent personal and professional references.

Yours sincerely,

Marvin Zook

Date

Exact Name of Person
Title or Position
Name of Company
Address (number and street)
Address (city, state, and zip)

QUALITY & SAFETY

Dear Exact Name of Person: (or Sir or Madam if answering a blind ad)

Quality Assurance Manager
A quality assurance executive
with extensive experience in a
Fortune 500 company
environment is responding to a
headhunter's request to send
his resume.

I would like to make you aware of my interest in a quality assurance position within a corporation which can utilize my strong executive skills as well as my proven ability to apply my technical expertise in resourceful ways that improve the bottom line while strengthening customer satisfaction.

As you will see from my resume, I have worked for the past 17 years for Kimberly-Clarke, where I have been promoted to increasing levels of responsibility. In my current job, I manage a 19-person QA department in a plant which employs 425 people and manufactures personal care products totaling $250 million. While managing a departmental budget of nearly $1 million, I have transitioned the plant from a regular production assembly line operation into a team-managed operation in which teams of employees are responsible for individual products. This has shifted QA from a "police" role to a consulting and monitoring role. I have also developed, implemented and managed a Cost-of-Quality Program which achieved 1999 cost savings of $150,000 by identifying and eliminating unnecessary processes.

In my previous job as Quality Assurance Manager at the company's Delaware plant, I developed and implemented a Quality Demerit System which the company now uses corporate-wide. The Quality Demerit System transformed the four Kimberly-Clarke manufacturing plants from a quality level of 67% defect-free product to the consumer in 1998, to 98.2% defect-free in 1999. The targeted goal for 2000 is 99.0% defect-free product.

I offer extensive expertise related to blow molding and injection molding. Both in my current job and in my job in Delaware, I managed Quality Assurance related to blow molding and injection molding. In the Delaware plant, we achieved a 10% improvement in lots accepted when using Mil. Std. 105E to determine acceptable quality levels (AQLs).

You would find me in person to be a congenial individual who prides myself on my ability to establish and maintain effective working relationships. I can provide outstanding personal and professional references at the appropriate time. I hope you will contact me to suggest a time when we might meet to discuss your needs.

Sincerely,

Mel Rasmus

Date

Exact Name of Person
Title or Position
Name of Company
Address (number and street)
Address (city, state, and zip)

Dear Exact Name of Person: (or Sir or Madam if answering a blind ad)

Manager
With extensive OSHA knowledge, this safety professional offers specialized HAZMAT knowledge along with impressive management accomplishments.

With the enclosed resume, I would like to introduce myself and the extensive experience I offer in the field of safety management.

As you will see from my resume, I have designed safety standards, codes, and safety requirements for Occupational Safety and Health (OSHA) compliance; DOD safety and health standards; and hazardous waste materials handling and training procedures. I am considered a leading expert in aviation safety including air traffic control, refueling operations, aeromedical evacuations, airport security and antiterrorism, fire prevention, and many other areas. Skilled in implementing Total Quality Management concepts in all aspects of safety program management, I am an experienced auditor of safety programs with the goal of reducing hazards in the workplace.

In my most recent position, I excelled as Safety Officer and senior safety expert. I utilized my knowledge and personal initiative to make changes which reduced accidents, improved risk assessment, and refined hazard awareness plans while authoring numerous procedures, policies, and regulations designed to safeguard lives and property. I have excelled as a Director of Safety supervising a 10-person staff in an organization with 400 employees, 125 vehicles, and 65 aircraft. In prior jobs I managed safety programs for medical organizations, and I have served as a medical evacuation pilot both during combat and in peacetime. I once served as an Aeromedical Evacuation Pilot in an air ambulance company in Korea.

I believe my hands-on experience as a pilot has given me an advantage over my safety counterparts, since I became accustomed early in my career to operating with the attitude that there is "no room for error." As a Safety Director, I have become respected for my enthusiastic and thorough approach to safety management, and I am proud that I have helped every organization in which I have worked achieve new levels of safety accomplishment. Where safety is concerned, there really is no room for error.

If you can use an accomplished safety professional who can provide outstanding personal and professional references, I hope you will contact me to suggest a time when we might meet to discuss your goals and how I might help you achieve them.

Sincerely,

Kevin Clarke McDonnell

Date

Exact Name of Person
Title or Position
Name of Company
Address (number and street)
Address (city, state, and zip)

RESTAURANTS, HOTELS, & FOOD SERVICE

Director of Catering
A Director of Catering is seeking advancement to a position as Manager of Catering. She would also like to explore opportunities as Director of Sales for a prestigious hotel with extensive conference facilities. Her job hunt is geographically focused: she has identified cities where she would like to live and she is sending her resume with this cover letter to General Managers at prominent hotels.

Dear Exact Name of Person: (or Sir or Madam if answering a blind ad)

With the enclosed resume, I would like to make you aware of my background as a detail-oriented sales and hospitality industry professional with exceptional communication, time management, and customer service skills and experience in account management, direct sales, and public relations.

In my current position as a Director of Catering for R.C.H. Hospitality at the Ritz Carlton Hotel in New York, I oversee all aspects of the catering department, including direct sales, planning, and execution of all meetings and conferences for this 6,000 square-foot meeting space. I am responsible for generating projected annual sales of $660,000 for the hotel. In addition to supervising one assistant and a Banquet Manager, I prepare catering forecasts, predicting future sales based on current bookings.

In previous positions with the Hilton in Pittsburgh, PA, I started as a sales assistant and was quickly promoted due to my exemplary job performance and dedication. As Sales and Catering Coordinator, I provided administrative support to two departments. My organizational expertise and detail-oriented approach to problem-solving allowed me to assist the Director of Sales, the Corporate Sales Manager, and the Director of Catering, ensuring that functions were carried out smoothly and to the customer's complete satisfaction. After my promotion to Catering Manager, I assisted the Director of Catering in planning weddings, small meetings, and conferences for this 12,000 square-foot meeting space.

Prior to entering the hospitality industry, I excelled as Legislative Assistant to a member of the Rhode Island House of Representatives, providing clerical and office management services while handling all correspondence from the Representative's constituents.

If you can use a self-motivated, articulate sales and hospitality industry professional with outstanding communication, organizational, and customer service abilities, I look forward to hearing from you soon to arrange a time when we might meet to discuss your needs and how I might meet them. I can provide outstanding references.

Sincerely,

Gail E. McIntosh

Date

Exact Name of Person
Title or Position
Name of Company
Address (number and street)
Address (city, state, and zip)

Dear Sir or Madam:

RESTAURANTS, HOTELS, AND
FOOD SERVICE

Executive Sous Chef
This accomplished hospitality
industry professional is
seeking his next challenge.
Because of family reasons, he is
using the cover letter to
selectively explore
opportunities with prestigious
hotels on the east coast.

With the enclosed resume describing my experience and skills, I would like to formally initiate the process of being considered for a culinary position within your organization.

As you will see from my resume, I have excelled as an Executive Chef and Executive Sous Chef and have been a Certified Executive Chef since 1998. I am a member of numerous professional organizations including the American Culinary Federation of Chefs, the Academy of Chefs, the American Culinary Federation, the Canadian Chef Federation, as well as other clubs for the world's top culinary experts.

In my current job I am an Executive Chef associated with Yankee Stadium. For the Gold Club Membership comprised of 7,000 members, I handle meal preparation and a variety of catered events for VIPs. I also personally cater to the needs of 116 skyboxes which belong to the owners of the Yankees as well as private individuals and corporations. While managing 22 seasonal and part-time chefs, cooks, and others, I have managed a payroll budget with outstanding results. Although payroll costs were projected to be at 26% of our 1998 food and beverage sales of $33.8 million (the largest-ever annual sales), we brought payroll costs in at only 22% of food and beverage sales. This was in a year when we hosted the World Series. I offer a reputation as an outstanding manager of human, financial, and material resources.

In a previous job I was Executive Chef with the Radisson in Melbourne, FL, where I managed an 18-person staff and was extensively involved in the production of banquets and special events ranging from weddings to corporate functions. In previous positions I have excelled as Chef for an athletic club, as Executive Chef for a yacht club, and as Executive Chef for both hotels and businesses.

If you can use a culinary professional, I hope you will call or write me to suggest a time when we could meet in person to discuss your needs and how I might serve them. I have managed budgets, people, and special projects with flair as well as with a bottom-line orientation. I can provide excellent references at the appropriate time.

Yours sincerely,

Adrian G. Dysland, CEC

Date

Exact Name of Person
Title or Position
Name of Company
Address (number and street)
Address (city, state, and zip)

Multiunit Restaurant Manager
A Multiunit Restaurant Manager cites his achievements in new venture start-ups and other areas. This consultant and his wife are ready to relocate anywhere worldwide, and he is open to management or consulting positions.

Dear Exact Name of Person: (or Sir or Madam if answering a blind ad)

With the enclosed resume, I would like to make you aware of my interest in joining your management team in some capacity which could utilize my proven skills in strategic planning, operations management, new venture start-up, and troubled unit turnaround.

As you will see from my enclosed resume, I am currently working as a Multiunit Manager with the Morrison Restaurant Group where I have made dramatic improvements in lowering food costs while increasing unit controllable income, boosting unit net income, and strengthening customer service. In addition to retraining employees and developing three new General Managers who are excelling in their jobs, I have led the company in producing the highest gross profit margin.

In my previous position with J & B Consulting in Asia, I earned a reputation as a creative and resourceful management consultant. (My wife is Asian, and I speak Japanese fluently.) I enjoyed helping business executives make wise investments in the Asian market and I trained numerous area supervisors in effective management techniques. Projects in which I was involved included establishing a 47-unit restaurant facility; developing the strategic plan for an $11 million restaurant; and transforming a downtown bus station into a 32-floor Embassy Suites Hotel with restaurants on nine different floors.

Before I was recruited by J & B Consulting, I excelled in a job as a Multiunit Restaurant Manager where I helped McDonald's establish its first 35 restaurants in the Panamanian market. In that position I oversaw a 450-person work force which was only 5% American.

With a reputation as a dynamic and creative manager with unlimited personal initiative and superior problem-solving skills, I am confident that I could become a valuable addition to your outstanding management team. If you can use a top performer with the proven ability to positively impact the bottom line, I hope you will contact me to suggest a time when we might meet to discuss your goals and how I might help you achieve them. I can provide outstanding personal and professional references.

Sincerely,

Ben M. Wolfe, Jr.

Date

Exact Name of Person
Title or Position
Name of Company
Address (number and street)
Address (city, state, and zip)

Dear Exact Name of Person: (or Sir or Madam if answering a blind ad)

With the enclosed resume, I would like to make you aware of an experienced food service professional with exceptional motivational, communication, and organizational skills. With a background as a restaurant General Manager and Director of Operations, I have demonstrated the ability to produce extraordinary "bottom-line" results.

With Texas Roadhouse, I was aggressively recruited and hired to design, coordinate the construction of, and manage the kitchen for the opening of this location. My exemplary management skills were quickly recognized, and I was promoted to Director of Operations, with final accountability for all aspects of the operation of a busy restaurant with annual sales of $1.5 million. I train and supervise the Kitchen Manager, Bar Manager, and Front End Manager as well as the kitchen, wait, and bar staff totaling 65 employees. I prepare and manage the monthly operations budget, evaluating all expenses to maximize profits and ensure budget compliance.

In previous positions with North Bay Seafood, I coordinated the construction and development of this family seafood restaurant, and then was actively sought out by the owners to "turn around" the operation, taking over at a time when it was on the verge of bankruptcy. Using the same innovative, cost-cutting inventory control procedures I had implemented when I first worked for the company, I quickly transformed the restaurant into a popular and profitable organization with a $200,000 increase in sales.

If you can use an experienced General Manager and Director of Operations whose supervisory and leadership skills have been tested in a variety of restaurant environments, I hope you will contact me to suggest a time when we might meet to discuss your needs. I have an excellent reputation and can provide outstanding references.

Sincerely,

Roy Kuzmic

Restaurant Manager
Notice the third paragraph. A great cover letter often tells a story that will capture the interest of the employer and provides an opportunity, once you're at the interview, for you to describe in more detail some of your accomplishments. Being recruited by a previous employer to "turn around" the restaurant where he had previously worked is something Mr. Kuzmic would want to be asked about at an interview! Here's a tip: what you want to include on your resume and in your cover letter are the things you want to be asked about at an interview!

Date

Exact Name of Person
Title or Position
Name of Company
Address (number and street)
Address (city, state, and zip)

Multiunit Restaurant Manager
A Multiunit Restaurant
Manager cites his achievements
in increasing operating income.
If you can express sales
increases or profit
improvements in dollar
amounts or percentages,
those numbers tend to
establish credibility with
regard to the accomplishments
you are claiming.

Dear Exact Name of Person: (or Sir or Madam if answering a blind ad)

With the enclosed resume, I would like to make you aware of my background as an experienced single and multiunit restaurant manager with excellent communication and problem-solving skills and proven expertise in staff development.

Most recently, I have been excelling as a Restaurant Manager for Applebee's Neighborhood Grill & Bar in Greenville, S.C. This busy branch of the nationwide chain has annual food sales of $2.75 million and retail sales of $900,000. I supervise a staff of 110 employees, scheduling as many as 3,000 labor hours per week in order to fully cover the retail, kitchen, and wait staff. Under my management, the Greenville store has achieved a 10% increase in operating income. This was accomplished through a reduction in turnover, development of sales building programs, and careful monitoring of labor and food expenditures.

At Ruby Tuesday's, I was hired as an Assistant Manager and quickly advanced to Store Manager and then to Area Manager, overseeing the operation of six locations and supervising as many as 25 managers. During my time there, income in my district increased by 10%, sales by 7.5%, and I was named District Manager of the Year in 1998. Several of the managers that I trained went on to become District Managers, and others won Manager of the Year and Store of the Year honors.

Though I am highly regarded by my present employer and can provide outstanding personal and professional references at the appropriate time, I feel that I would be more fully challenged, and my skills and experience better utilized, in a larger volume or multiunit environment.

If you can use a highly experienced restaurant manager with excellent motivational and staff development skills and a strong background in single restaurant and multiunit management, I hope you will contact me soon to suggest a time when we might meet to discuss your needs. I can provide outstanding references.

Sincerely,

Floyd A. Gallagher

Date

Exact Name of Person
Exact Title
Exact Name of Company
Address
City, State Zip

Dear Exact Name of Person (or Dear Sir or Madam if answering a blind ad)

RESTAURANTS, HOTELS, AND
FOOD SERVICE

Bartender
This veteran bartender is
distinguished from other
bartenders by her extensive
management experience,
including experience in
starting up and managing her
own successful club. With this
cover letter she is "fishing" for
a spot on the management
team of a hospitality industry
organization. Notice that she
emphasizes her outstanding
personal and business
reputation, a fact that
prospective employers will like.

With the enclosed resume, I would like to express my strong desire to become associated with your restaurant and make you aware of my background which is ideally suited to your needs.

Throughout my working career, I have excelled in the hospitality industry. In an entry-level position at O'Brien's Restaurant, I was rapidly promoted to Hostess and given the responsibility for training other employees. While living in Canada for two years, I worked as an Airport Rental Agent in Toronto, and I became skilled at serving the busy business traveler as well as the foreigner on holiday.

An expert in mixology, I have also excelled as a Bartender, and I am very proud of the fact that I have trained two bartenders who went on to establish successful businesses in the hospitality industry. As an expert bartender myself, I once founded "from scratch" and managed a respected bar called Janette's Place which attracted a crowd of regulars who enjoyed the atmosphere. I have become an expert at planning and organizing special events for customers including birthday parties, dinners, celebrations of all types, and surprise parties.

Because of my excellent reputation as a respected manager and business person in the community, I was recruited for my current job with a local pub. The owner relies on me to manage the bar and train both bartenders and hostesses while he concentrates on other business areas.

I have become skilled at making excellent decisions in special situations and crises. In one job I was awarded a special Letter of Commendation from the Alcohol Law Enforcement (ALE) Agency because of my professional handling of an out-of-control customer.

I am certain that my professional background and gracious personal style of handling people would be well suited to your needs, and I hope you will welcome my call soon when I try to arrange a brief meeting with you to discuss your needs. I can provide excellent personal and professional references.

Yours sincerely,

Janette Zalenski

Date

Exact Name of Person
Title or Position
Name of Company
Address (number and street)
Address (city, state, and zip)

Dear Exact Name of Person: (or Sir or Madam if answering a blind ad)

General Merchandise Manager
Even when people enjoy their work, sometimes they yearn for a challenge on another level. That's what this senior retailing executive is thinking about. Headhunters call him frequently to discuss industry positions, and he is using this cover letter to identify other opportunities on his own. This cover letter allows him to introduce himself to select retailers in the cities where he and his wife have decided they want to live and retire.

With the enclosed resume, I would like to make you aware of my interest in confidentially exploring the possibility of joining your management structure.

From my enclosed resume you will see that I am excelling as a General Merchandise Manager for Macy's Department Store. I supervise a 20-store operation and manage a staff of buyers and assistant buyers while handling responsibility for sales and gross margin, merchandise mix, and advertising.

In my previous retail management experience, I enjoyed a track record of promotion with Saks Fifth Avenue Department Store, where I began as a Department Manager, was promoted to Assistant Buyer and then to Buyer, directed the company's strategic moves as its Market Research Director, and became Divisional Sales Manager. I was subsequently recruited by Macy's and have been in my current job since 1995.

Although I am held in high regard by the Macy's organization and can provide excellent references at the appropriate time, I am aware of your company's fine reputation and feel that my impeccable retailing credentials could be a valuable addition to your organization. My experience at Saks and Macy's has taught me that doing an average job in retailing will put you out of business, and I have also learned that innovative marketing and aggressive merchandising are the keys to outperforming the competition.

If you can use a successful retailing executive who could bring added strengths and creativity to your strategic initiatives, I hope you will contact me to suggest a time when we could talk about your needs. I would certainly enjoy the opportunity to meet you in person.

Yours sincerely,

Rusty C. Berman

Date

Exact Name of Person
Title or Position
Name of Company
Address (number and street)
Address (city, state, and zip)

Dear Exact Name of Person: (or Sir or Madam if answering a blind ad)

With the enclosed resume, I would like to make you aware of my background as a manager with exceptional recruiting and staff development skills who offers a track record of accomplishment as well as the proven ability to train and motivate personnel and increase the profitability of retail operations.

As you will see, I have excelled in positions of increasing responsibility with The Athlete's Foot. In my present position as Manager Trainer and Market Leader for the Four Seasons Mall location in Martinsburg, WV, I oversee all operational aspects of a retail operation with annual sales of $3 million. In addition, I serve as Market Leader, mentoring five new managers and acting as District Merchandise Coordinator, tracking and redistributing key product for the 23 stores in our district. In 1999, my store had the highest profit percentage in my district, and I received an audit award for reducing inventory shrinkage from the previous audit score, which was an unacceptable .60%, to only .01%, an extraordinarily low shrink figure.

Prior to that, as Manager Trainer and Market Leader at Perimeter Mall, I produced the highest annual profit margin, won the President's Award for my excellence in recruiting and staff development, and was further rewarded for my outstanding performance in human resources management by a promotion to Manager Trainer. Six employees whom I recruited in Augusta moved into the management trainee program as Assistant Managers, and I recruited eight new employees for three different stores in our district.

In an earlier position as Store Manager at Westchester Mall in Austin, TX, I was able to quickly revive an under-producing store, increasing sales by $142,000 and turning a troubled operation into the most profitable store in the district.

If you can use a positive, results-oriented manager with a strong bottom-line orientation and exceptionally strong recruiting and staff development skills, I hope you will contact me to suggest a time when we might meet to discuss your needs. I can provide excellent references.

Sincerely,

Hector Salinas

There is no substitute for networking in a job campaign. A friend in a major consumer products company suggested that this savvy retailing executive send his resume and cover letter for some plum sales management jobs which were opening up. Two weeks after sending this cover letter with his resume, this professional was on an airplane flying to a new job in a new city.

Date

Exact Name of Person
Title or Position
Name of Company
Address (number and street)
Address (city, state, and zip)

Dear Exact Name of Person: (or Sir or Madam if answering a blind ad)

Buyer

One impressive thing about
this individual which will
capture the attention of
prospective employers is that
she has worked for only one
employer. That kind of
dedication and perseverance is
rare in this era of rapid
turnover. The outcome of her
job hunt was that she became
a buyer for a well-known
department store.

With the enclosed resume, I would like to introduce myself and make you aware of the considerable experience in sales, customer service, and retail management which I could put to work for you.

As you will see from my resume, I have spent the past nine years—practically my entire working life since I am only 26 years old—working with Stride Rite Shoe Stores. I began with Stride Rite as a Sales Associate and learned the ropes of retailing at the ground level. During that time, I also worked on my college degree and, in 1997, I completed my B.S. degree in Social Science with a minor in History. Although I earned a teaching degree, my first student teaching experience persuaded me that I was better suited for business management than for classroom teaching.

I became a Manager-in-Training with Stride Rite in 1997 and then excelled in a variety of assignments ranging from managing newly started stores to closing stores in unprofitable locations and transferring inventory and employees to other locations. I am especially proud of the fact that, in a store I managed in Salisbury, MD, I hired and trained three employees who remained with me throughout my tenure at that store. I am grateful to several Stride Rite managers for the many sound principles and techniques they taught me related to managing people and retail operations.

If you can use a reliable hard worker with proven management skills and a solid understanding of retail, I hope you will contact me to suggest a time when we could meet to discuss your needs and how I might serve them. I can provide outstanding personal and professional references. Thank you in advance for your time.

Sincerely,

Greta Anne Kunkel

Date

Exact Name of Person
Exact Title of Person
Company Name
Address
City, State Zip

Dear Sir or Madam:

Merchandising Specialist
This Merchandising Specialist enjoys her job, but she wants to move from part time to full time. Her experience in merchandising the products of major accounts should get her noticed in her job hunt.

With the enclosed resume, I would like to make you aware of my background as an articulate, reliable professional with experience in merchandising, sales, and customer service.

Recently I have been excelling as a Merchandising Specialist for Quality Merchandising Services, Inc. I service large corporate accounts including Hanes, Bali, Playtex, Kodak, and Pepperidge Farms, resetting stock and ensuring that products are effectively displayed. While representing these accounts, I have worked in major retail outlets such as Wal-Mart, Sears, J.C. Penney, Belk, Roses, and Harris Teeter. In earlier positions, I merchandised health and beauty aids and pharmaceutical products for Bayer, Proctor & Gamble, Clairol, Max Factor, and other major companies.

As you will see from my resume, I have completed three years of college course work at the University of Maryland. I have also excelled in extensive training in sales, merchandising, and retailing sponsored by the corporations whose accounts I serviced.

If you can use an enthusiastic, hardworking professional whose highly-developed merchandising, sales, and customer services skills have been tested in fast-paced environments where sound judgement is critical to fast turnover, I hope you will contact me to suggest a time when we might meet in person. I assure you in advance that I have an excellent reputation, and I offer a proven ability to establish effective working relationships with people at all levels.

Yours sincerely,

Mary Edwards

Date

Exact Name of Person
Title or Position
Name of Company
Address (number and street)
Address (city, state, and zip)

SALES

Dear Exact Name of Person: (or Sir or Madam if answering a blind ad)

District Sales Manager

This sales professional cites the increases in profit and in the customer base which he has engineered at the establishments where he has worked. Remember that the main thing you are selling in a job hunt is your track record of results and accomplishments if you are an industry professional remaining in your field.

With the enclosed resume, I would like to make you aware of my abilities as an experienced sales and management professional with exceptional communication and motivational abilities and a background in district-level outside sales, retail and industrial management, and staff development.

In my most recent position, I am excelling as a District Sales Representative for Sunshine Products, the largest broadline food distributor in the Southeast. During my time there, I have raised gross profit dollars by 72%, total sales dollars by 59%, and increased the customer base in my district by 185%. For these and other accomplishments, I was awarded Sunshine Product's President's Club Growth Award.

As Assistant Manager for Target in Hot Springs, AR, I was in charge of all hard lines areas of a $28 million store, supervising 120 people including seven department managers. Areas under my direct supervision contributed nearly $10 million dollars annually in sales, and under my management the hard lines area experienced a sales increase of 20% while reducing inventory shrinkage by 70%. In a previous position as a Manager Trainee with Lexington Furniture Industries, I developed spreadsheets to track productivity and quality in key parts and assemblies, and I maintained databases to analyze the effectiveness of "On Time" processes in assembly areas.

As you will see, I have earned a Bachelor of Science in Economics from University of Florida. I feel that my strong combination of education and experience would make me a valuable addition to your organization.

If you can use an experienced sales or management professional with exceptional communication and motivational skills, I hope you will contact me to suggest a time when we might meet to discuss your needs. I can assure you in advance that I have an outstanding reputation and would rapidly become an asset to your organization.

Sincerely,

Robert ("Buz") White

Date

Exact Name of Person
Title or Position
Name of Company
Address (number and street)
Address (city, state, and zip)

Dear Exact Name of Person: (or Sir or Madam if answering a blind ad)

With the enclosed resume, I would like to make you aware of my versatile background which includes experience in personnel management, human resources, sales, and technical electronics as well as in training situations.

As you will see, I am presently exceeding sales goals as a Personnel Recruiter and Sales Representative. Upon achieving 330% of my goal for fiscal year 1999, I was recognized as a highly effective and visible presence in the community while "selling" an intangible product—the advantages of a military career to qualified young people. You will see that I have held a Top Secret security clearance and have acquired extensive computer skills, including knowledge of Word, Excel, PowerPoint, and Microsoft Access.

Specially selected for positions where the ability to handle pressure and meet strict time restraints was of vital importance, I have consistently found ways to reduce errors, increase productivity, and ensure high levels of customer satisfaction. Special project assignments have included providing personnel service support for 5,000 people during three months with a task force in Haiti, and relocating a maintenance shop 160 miles with no service disruptions in Bosnia.

If you can use an experienced, versatile, and adaptable professional, I hope you will contact me to suggest a time when we might meet to discuss your needs. I can assure you in advance that I could rapidly become an asset to your organization, and I can provide outstanding personal and professional references.

Sincerely,

Jim Tang

Date

Exact Name of Person
Title or Position
Name of Company
Address (number and street)
Address (city, state, and zip)

SALES

Dear Exact Name of Person: (or Sir or Madam if answering a blind ad)

I would appreciate an opportunity to talk with you soon about how I could contribute to your organization through my proven sales skills as well as my ability to train and develop other sales professionals.

As you will see from my resume, I have excelled in a track record of accomplishments based on my results-oriented communication skills including my ability to negotiate deals, resolve critical issues in business situations, create innovate marketing campaigns, and close high-ticket sales. In my current position as a Pharmaceutical Sales Representative with Schering-Plough/Key Pharmaceutical Division, I have been recognized for achieving the highest dollar volume of sales in the Roanoke Division and have been chosen to be the computer trainer because of my superior computer knowledge.

In my previous job as an Account Executive with Brinks, I consistently set new sales records while serving up to 700 commercial and government accounts in cities in Virginia. I was named Top Sales Executive in 1998 and 1999, a distinction I am proud of because I had great respect for my outstanding sales colleagues.

Although I am excelling in my current position and can provide outstanding references at the appropriate time, I have decided to approach your company because I feel you could benefit from my considerable strengths in sales and sales management. I would appreciate your keeping my interest in your company confidential at this time.

If you can use a proven performer with a strong bottom-line orientation along with the ability to relate effectively to people at all levels, I hope you will contact me to suggest a time when we might meet to discuss your needs and how I might serve them. Thank you in advance for your time.

Sincerely,

Jerry Longshore

Date

Exact Name of Person
Title or Position
Name of Company
Address (number and street)
Address (city, state, and zip)

Dear Exact Name of Person: (or Sir or Madam if answering a blind ad)

With the enclosed resume, I would like to make you aware of my background as a self-motivated and persistent sales professional with exceptional communication and time management skills who offers the proven ability to find and develop new accounts while increasing sales of existing accounts.

In my most recent position with WKYZ Country 97.3, I served ably as an Account Executive in the advertising sales department. Within two years on the job, I had nearly quadrupled my monthly sales average, from $15,000 per month when I took the position to nearly $60,000 per month. Due to my exceptional salesmanship, I was able to acquire 60 additional accounts. I quickly built a strong rapport with clients, determining their goals and expectations in order to develop marketing and promotional strategies that would satisfy the needs of each individual customer.

Earlier with Lancôme cosmetics/Macy's stores, I was entrusted with the responsibility of making all purchasing and inventory control decisions for this exclusive product line; I also supervised three Beauty Advisors at the Towne Park Mall location. By planning and implementing innovative and effective marketing strategies, promotions, and other events, I was able to grow sales and increase market share for all products in the line.

If you can use an articulate sales professional with highly-developed account management and prospecting skills as well as the proven ability to increase market share while providing exceptional customer service, I hope you will contact me to suggest a time when we might meet in person. I could rapidly become a valuable asset to your organization, and I can provide outstanding references.

Sincerely,

Pauline A. Burston

Date

Exact Name of Person
Title or Position
Name of Company
Address (number and street)
Address (city, state, and zip)

SALES   Dear Exact Name of Person: (or Sir or Madam if answering a blind ad)

Sales Executive
A track record of
accomplishment with one's
current employer is a big
selling point in a cover letter
and on a resume.

With the enclosed resume, I would like to make you aware of an articulate, results-oriented professional with exceptional communication and supervisory skills, a strong bottom-line orientation, and a track record of success in management, personnel development, and marketing.

I have been excelling with Hertz Rent-A-Car in positions of increasing responsibility. In my most recent position as Regional Manager for the city of Pasadena, CA, I supervised 105 personnel in a region with annual sales of $8.8 million dollars. I also served as Director of Human Resources, conducting final interviews on all potential employees as well as determining labor needs and personnel budgets for the 14 branches in the region. Earlier as Area Manager for the western region of Vancouver, WA, I launched the highly successful start-up of this new region, which quickly grew to six locations employing 49 personnel. By designing and implementing innovative and effective marketing plans, our sales increased 47% per year over a three-year period and the region achieved annual sales of $4.8 million.

As Branch Manager in Raleigh, NC, I was responsible for opening a new office, which became the first location in the Southeast region to reach a monthly net profit of $40,000. Despite being a newly launched branch with a new manager and staff, we were one of the top five branches in the region for total sales. I was promoted to this position after excelling as a Management Trainee in the Asheville, NC, branch where I had the highest inside sales of any management trainee in the region, and I was promoted to Assistant Manager after only six months with Hertz.

I have an A.S. degree in Business from Vancouver Technical Community College and have nearly completed my Bachelor of Science in Business.

If you can use a confident, self-motivated management professional whose exceptional supervisory, communication, and organizational skills have been proven in positions of ever-increasing responsibility, then I look forward to hearing from you soon. I assure you in advance that I have an outstanding reputation and would quickly become a valuable asset to your company.

Sincerely,

Will Borchardt

Date

Exact Name of Person
Exact Title
Exact Name of Company
Address
City, State Zip

Dear Exact Name of Person (or Dear Sir or Madam if answering a blind ad):

SALES

Sales Professional

With the enclosed resume, I would like to make you aware of my strong sales and marketing skills as well as my interest in putting those skills to work for your organization. I am currently in the process of relocating to the Philadelphia area; I am in Philadelphia frequently and could make myself available for an interview at your convenience. I am single and could travel as extensively as your needs require.

As you will see from my resume, I have excelled in positions which required the ability to interact effectively with others while selling concepts, products, and services. Just recently I was involved in a short-term sales-and-marketing consulting project for an Internet company which is making plans to go public in 2001. I am attracted to "start ups" because of my strong entrepreneurial background; in 1996 I established "from scratch" a business which grossed $250,000 in its fourth year.

In prior positions, I utilized my sales ability to accomplish real estate and economic development goals. As a real estate broker in Charlotte, NC, I was consistently in the Top Ten for Mecklenburg County with listings and sales of over $5 million annually. As a Vice President and Broker with an industrial relations firm, I worked with major corporate clients such as Hardee's and First Union Bank in devising plans for large commercial developments. As a business manager and property manager, I negotiated multimillion-dollar sales of prime commercial property and worked effectively within the complex government structure authorizing permits, conducting inspections, and approving infrastructure plans.

Through my varied experience, I have come to appreciate the reality that each day holds numerous opportunities to solve stubborn problems and identify new opportunities. I normally approach each business situation with a view to finding the key problem or opportunity, and I apply my aggressive bottom-line orientation.

If you can use a hardworking and savvy sales professional known for unlimited personal initiative and resourcefulness in business situations, I hope you will contact me to suggest a time when we might meet. I can provide outstanding personal and professional references at the appropriate time, and I can assure you that I could become a valuable asset to your company.

Yours sincerely,

Rebecca Sizemore

Versatile is probably the best word to describe this top producer. Currently in the process of relocating to Philadelphia, she is exploring opportunities at companies that can use a dynamic hard charger with experience in the real estate and industrial fields as well as, more recently, in the Internet industry.

Date

Exact Name of Person
Exact Title
Exact Name of Company
Address
City, State Zip

Dear Exact Name of Person (or Dear Sir or Madam if answering a blind ad)

Sales Professional
Strong negotiating skills set
this individual apart from
other top performers, and with
this cover letter he is
introducing himself to
prospective employers who can
use an experienced sales
professional who is also an
able sales manager.

With the enclosed resume, I would like to make you aware of my interest in discussing the possibility of employment with your organization.

As you will see from my enclosed resume, I have been excelling in a track record of accomplishment while utilizing my skills in communication and customer service.

In my current position, I am in charge of sales and marketing for a small company which is experiencing explosive growth. I began working for the company while finishing my Bachelor's degree and joined the company full-time upon college graduation. My personal contributions have been a significant factor in the company's growth as I have negotiated contracts with military post exchanges (PXs) and military hospitals throughout the United States.

Part of my job involves organizing and supervising the efforts of sales professionals who travel throughout the east coast to participate in computer shows where the company's software and hardware can be demonstrated. Because of my ability to recruit, train, and manage outstanding sales professionals, the small company I work for has been successful in competing with much larger and more established competitors in the computer industry.

Single and willing to travel and relocate as your needs require, I can provide excellent references. I am a highly motivated young professional with a proven ability to produce outstanding bottom-line results.

Please give me every consideration for a position in your company where my superior customer service, sales, and public relations skills could benefit your organization. Thank you in advance for your time.

Yours sincerely,

Ty Gardner

Date

Exact Name of Person
Title or Position
Name of Company
Address (number and street)
Address (city, state, and zip)

Dear Exact Name of Person: (or Sir or Madam if answering a blind ad)

SALES

With the enclosed resume, I would like to express my strong interest in exploring career opportunities with Federal Express and introduce you to my proven customer service, communication, and organizational skills.

As you will see from my resume, I have had a successful sales career with several different companies in Utah, including my current employer, Provo Auto Sales. Through my experience as a Sales Manager with Provo and as an Automotive Sales Representative at Salt Lake Olds-Buick, I have developed the proven ability to quickly build rapport with customers from many different backgrounds while learning to deal amicably with people even in tense and occasionally confrontational situations.

During my tenure as Manager of Roy Pawn & Loan, I utilized my strong organizational and sales abilities to increase profits at the Ogden Road location by an average of $1,500 per month, while insuring the security and accountability of over $200,000 worth of inventory. In addition, I have previous delivery experience, when I was with National Linen Service.

If you can use a highly motivated, detail-oriented individual with strong organizational skills and a commitment to providing the highest possible levels of customer service, I hope you will contact me to suggest a time when we might meet to discuss your needs. Although I have an excellent reputation and can provide outstanding references, I would appreciate your not contacting my current employer until after we speak.

Yours sincerely,

Tony Maneri, Jr.

Sales Manager
This automobile sales manager stresses his strong relationship-building skills in addition to his strong customer service orientation. Here's a tip: If you're looking to change fields, don't use too much lingo from your current field. Focus instead on concepts which are transferable such as customer service, since employers in any field will be able to relate easily to these ideas.

Date

Exact Name of Person
Exact Title
Exact Name of Company
Address
City, State Zip

Dear Exact Name of Person (or Dear Sir or Madam if answering a blind ad):

With the enclosed resume, I would like to make you aware of my background as a seasoned sales professional and sales manager with exceptional communication and negotiation skills.

In my current position with Price Lumber Company, I joined the organization as a Sales Representative, and my strong sales ability, hard work, and loyalty were rewarded with continuous promotions to higher levels of responsibility. I produced double-digit sales increases in ten of my fourteen years with Price, and I finished my tenure with that company as Senior Territory Sales Manager, servicing major building supply, hardware store, and farm supply accounts in a five-state region.

At Brown Corrugating Company, I maximized the profitability of existing accounts and developed new clients in a 33-county area of Alabama, substantially increasing territory sales by consistently adding new accounts. In this position and in earlier posts with Wilson, Inc. and Brown, I earned a reputation as a skillful negotiator and highly effective communicator.

As you will see from my resume, I have an Associate of Applied Science degree from Tennessee Technical Community College. I further supplemented my degree program with numerous courses sponsored by my employers related to sales and marketing, sales management, customer service, techniques for prospecting and closing the sale, and account management.

If you can use a motivated sales professional and experienced sales manager with outstanding communication and negotiation skills and a strong bottom-line orientation, I hope you will contact me to suggest a time when we might meet to discuss your needs. I have an excellent reputation and can provide oustanding references at the appropriate time.

Sincerely,

Drew Criswell

Date

Exact Name of Person
Title or Position
Name of Company
Address (number and street)
Address (city, state, and zip)

Dear Exact Name of Person: (or Sir or Madam if answering a blind ad)

With the enclosed resume, I would like to make you aware of my strong interest in the job of Sales Representative which you recently advertised.

In my current job as Unit Business Manager with The Revlon Company, I am excelling in an outside sales position which involves calling on the buyers for chains and retail stores and military accounts in a territory which covers 35 counties in Georgia and Florida. My territory includes 100 retail stores, 9 indirect headquarters, and three military retail commissaries. Because of my persistence and initiative, I have been responsible for numerous accomplishments including achieving the distribution of **all** new items in **all** stores; increasing the facings for **all** Revlon brands in **all** stores. I have also achieved "gold standard placement" for **all** Revlon brands while achieving the suggested retail price for **all** Revlon brands in **all** accounts.

Most of my success in my current job has been due to my enthusiastic attention to detail as well as my relentless persistence of the highest goals. I have competed against strongly entrenched competitors who had been in the business for more than 20 years. Persistence and relentless marketing paid off, and I have succeeded in obtaining more than my fair share of shelf space for Revlon despite stiff competition.

In my previous job as an Account Representative with Quality Services, I achieved 130% of my sales goal in my first full year while also being honored as "Account Representative of the Year."

I hope you will contact me to suggest a time when we might meet to discuss your needs and goals and how I might help you achieve them. I can provide excellent references and I thank you in advance for your time.

Yours sincerely,

Vinetta Lee Ellis

Account Representative
The most rewarding careers are managed by strategic thinkers who plan ahead, and this individual has been positioning herself for further advancement in her field by her distinguished performance in her current job. "All" is a very strong word, but she uses it effectively in this cover letter to call attention to her impressive results. A great cover letter always reveals someone's personality, too. By reading this cover letter, don't you get the feel of a hard charger who doesn't give up?

Date

Exact Name of Person
Title or Position
Name of Company
Address (number and street)
Address (city, state, and zip)

Dear Exact Name of Person: (or Sir or Madam if answering a blind ad)

Counselor

Most of us end up having at least three different careers during our working lives, and this professional is aiming for a second career in social work with an emphasis on helping the troubled and less fortunate turn their lives around. His background as a Drill Sergeant and military leader has prepared him well for such a field.

I would appreciate an opportunity to talk with you soon to discuss how I could contribute to your organization through the counseling and motivational skills I gained while serving my country in the U.S. Army.

While rising to the rank of Command Sergeant Major, I earned a reputation as an inspiring leader and highly effective manager of human resources. Throughout my career, I transformed marginal performers into motivated and productive individuals. I counseled hundreds of people on family, personal, financial, and career matters, and I helped numerous professionals of all ages learn how to better manage their time, energies, aggressions, and finances. Training and teaching others was a daily responsibility in all of my jobs, and I have developed and implemented training programs in dozens of organizations.

It was during my years in the military that I developed a desire to enter the counseling, social services, or probation services field after I retired. In one job I played a key role in hosting the Special Olympics at Ft. Drum, NY, and that gave me an opportunity to see how important the Special Olympics is to Downs Syndrome individuals. In several jobs I was involved in conducting inspections and investigating complaints. Early in my military career, I excelled as a Drill Sergeant and enjoyed the opportunity to instill in young soldiers an attitude of discipline and skills in teamwork.

In addition to my B.A. in Social Science, I am pursuing completion of an Associate of Science degree in Criminal Justice. As a military professional, I completed numerous courses related to personnel management techniques, drug and alcohol counseling, and other similar areas.

The recipient of numerous awards and medals recognizing my exemplary character and professional contributions, I offer a true desire to help the less fortunate along with a proven ability to motivate others to want to transform their lives. If you can use my considerable counseling and communication skills as well as my management and supervisory experience, I hope you will contact me to suggest a time when we might meet to discuss your needs and how I might serve them. I feel confident I could become a valuable asset to your organization, and I thank you in advance for your time.

Sincerely,

Dwayne Briner

Date

Exact Name of Person
Title or Position
Name of Company
Address (number and street)
Address (city, state, and zip)

Dear Exact Name of Person: (or Sir or Madam if answering a blind ad)

With the enclosed resume, I would like to make you aware of my background as an experienced caseworker with specialized knowledge of the Junior Training Partnership Act. I would like to make you aware of my interest in the job of JTPA Director in Cobb County which has recently been posted.

Case Worker
Case management in the social services field is a high-turnover activity, but some professionals thrive on the work. This social worker offers specialized knowledge of a specific social services program, and it is that program which she now seeks to manage.

In my current position as a Caseworker I for Cobb County DSS in Atlanta, I manage a caseload of 250 clients, interviewing them to determine eligibility for various programs as well as providing counseling and information on community resources and employment opportunities. With regard to the JTPA Program which was launched in Cobb County two years ago, I have played a key role in all phases of the hiring and training process for caseworkers.

As you will see from the enclosed resume, I hold a Bachelor's degree in Human Resources as well as the Master's in Public Administration degree. Highly computer literate, I am proficient with commercial software and systems such as Windows 95, the Microsoft Office suite, WordPerfect, and Lotus 1-2-3, and I also am skilled in utilizing the SUCCESS program used by the Georgia Department of Social Services.

I hope you will give me an opportunity to talk with you in person about the job as the Director of the JTPA Program in Cobb County. I assure you in advance that I have an excellent reputation within the community and could forge the kind of alliances with the business community which will turn this fledgling program into a large-scale success. Since this pilot program is in experimental stages, it would be my great hope that Cobb County could formulate and implement procedures which could be adopted as "models" by other counties throughout America. I am confident I could make great contributions to Cobb County as its JTPA Director.

Sincerely,

Blair S. Wright

Date

Exact Name of Person
Title or Position
Name of Company
Address (number and street)
Address (city, state, and zip)

Dear Exact Name of Person: (or Sir or Madam if answering a blind ad)

Youth Counselor
Offering a proven ability to
work with at-risk juveniles and
in the juvenile corrections field,
this social services professional
has tailored an all-purpose
cover letter to a specific
environment by her language in
the fourth paragraph. That
paragraph focuses her reader
on her desire to work in direct-
service, family-service settings.

With the enclosed resume, I would like to make you aware of my background as a motivated and highly experienced human services professional with a strong background in juvenile corrections and the counseling of at-risk juveniles and their families.

In my most recent job at Detroit Youth Institution, I have proven my dedication and ability, performing a dual role as Juvenile Corrections Officer and Case Manager. I have consistently excelled in these positions, supervising as many as 70 juvenile offenders while reviewing the cases of 6-8 clients to determine possible eligibility for reduction in sentencing or other rewards for good behavior. In previous positions as a Resource Teacher, Rehabilitation Specialist, and volunteer for the Guardian Angel program, I have shown my commitment to protecting and promoting the best interests of at-risk juveniles and insuring that they are provided with the counseling and services they need.

As you will see, I hold an Associate of Applied Science degree in Human Services from Detroit Community College, which I have supplemented with additional training courses. I believe that my strong combination of education and experience will be a great asset to any organization.

Although I am highly regarded by my present employer and can provide excellent references at the appropriate time, I feel that my skills and talents would be better utilized in a direct-service, family-support environment.

If you could use a highly motivated, experienced human services professional with exceptional organizational and problem-solving skills and a background in providing support and services to at-risk juveniles, then I hope you will contact me soon to discuss your needs. I can assure you in advance that I have an excellent reputation within the community and would quickly become a valuable addition to your organization.

Sincerely,

Shirley Hayden

Date

Exact Name of Person
Title or Position
Name of Company
Address (number and street)
Address (city, state, and zip)

Dear Exact Name of Person: (or Sir or Madam if answering a blind ad)

With the enclosed resume, I would like to make you aware of my education and extensive experience related to social work and human services. I offer a reputation as a compassionate, dedicated, and enthusiastic professional with a proven willingness to go the extra mile to help my clients.

For the last six years, I have served as a Juvenile Probation Officer for Dade County Youth Services in Florida. In this position, I managed a caseload of over 100 active probationary juveniles, counseling them and their families and acting as liaison between my clients and local law enforcement, school systems, and other supporting agencies. I reported directly to the Chief Probation Officer, and I was being groomed to take over that position when my father passed away and I decided to return home to Knoxville to be near my mother.

With a Master's degree in Counseling and Psychology and a Bachelor of Science in Social Work, I have a solid educational background in addition to my years of experience. In previous positions, I have utilized my proven ability to coordinate services among agencies as well as my strong skills in youth counseling, patient evaluation and assessment, and substance abuse counseling. Though my main experience has been in providing crisis intervention, rehabilitation, and guidance to at-risk youth, my highly developed organizational, supervisory, and communication skills would be strong assets in any social services environment.

If your organization can use the skills of a highly experienced, motivated counselor or program director, I look forward to hearing from you to arrange a convenient time when we could meet to discuss your present and future needs and how I might serve them.

Sincerely,

Pamela Lawler

Probation Officer
Experienced in youth counseling, this Probation Officer is seeking employment opportunities with organizations that can use a program director with extensive counseling experience.

Date

Exact Name of Person
Title or Position
Name of Company
Address (number and street)
Address (city, state, and zip)

Dear Exact Name of Person: (or Sir or Madam if answering a blind ad)

An experienced Mental Health Technician seeks a School Counselor position with this cover letter. Notice the last paragraph. She is asking the principals to whom she is sending the letter to keep her resume on file in case they have unexpected openings during the summer which they have to fill. Every experienced professional knows this truth: It's easier to get promoted internally once you get inside an organization than it is to get your foot in the door initially. That's why cover letters that blow doors open are so important!

With the enclosed resume, I would like to initiate the process of being considered for employment as a counselor with your school.

As you will see, I am nearing completion of my Master of Education in School Counseling degree which I will receive from Temple University in December, and it is my desire to work full-time as a School Counselor while finishing my four remaining classes in the evenings. I previously earned my B.A. in Psychology and English from Indiana State University, where I completed an internship with "Kids in Education" and provided guidance and motivational development to children up to 10 years of age. While working with "Kids in Education" I conducted in-home visits and assessments and prepared case studies on children. While at Indiana State, I was also a featured undergraduate research assistant and presented my own research design at the 1999 Indiana Psychological Association Regional Conference. During my graduate school program, I have presented in-services including drug abuse, classroom management, counseling in a pluralistic world, and anger management.

My professional training also has included the Prevention Through Intervention Care (PTIC) course sponsored by Community First, and I have completed Red Cross training in CPR and First Aid. In my current job as a Mental Health Technician, I have gained exposure which I feel could be valuable to any School Counselor. I have worked with schizophrenic clients as well as a broad range of mental health problems, and I have played a key role in implementing a new rehabilitation program. As a School Counselor, I would possess many valuable insights related to the mental health field which could be of positive value to at-risk children. I am familiar with the mental health network and would possess the knowledge of resources available outside of what the school can provide.

You would find me in person to be a congenial individual who prides myself on my high personal and professional standards. If you can make use of my strong counseling talents, please contact me to suggest a time when we might talk in person or by phone about your needs. Thank you very much in advance for your consideration, and I hope you will keep this letter on hand throughout the summer even if you do not at this time anticipate an opening in your counseling staff.

Sincerely,

Jill K. Howard

Date

Exact Name of Person
Title or Position
Name of Company
Address (number and street)
Address (city, state, and zip)

Dear Exact Name of Person: (or Sir or Madam if answering a blind ad)

SOCIAL WORK &
HUMAN SERVICES

Case Worker
Experience with the chemically
dependent is what this social
services professional is
marketing in an all-purpose
cover letter which identifies
him as a specialist in addiction
problems. He can use this letter
to open doors in both the
public and private sectors.

I would appreciate an opportunity to talk with you soon about how I could contribute to your organization through my experience, education, and skills which include a background in human services with an emphasis on chemically dependent personalities.

As you will see from my enclosed resume, I am a Case Manager at Total Rehabilitation Center in Eden Prairie, MN, a facility for chemically dependent personnel. While advancing in a track record of promotion and accomplishments in this demanding environment, I have been completing a bachelor's degree. As a Chancellor's List student and member of two scholarship and honors societies, I am scheduled to receive my B.S. in Psychology (with a minor in Criminal Justice) from University of Minnesota.

Initially hired by Total Rehabilitation Center in 1998 as a Security Guard and Corrections Officer, I quickly earned a promotion to Security Operations Supervisor and then to my present job as a Case Manager. I currently maintain a caseload of between 35 and 45 clients and have been effective in developing new programs which improve the quality of life and support for the facility's inmates. For instance, I implemented a Community Volunteer Program and now oversee the five volunteers who provide Bible study classes and take patients off the grounds for leisure and community activities.

I hold professional memberships in Addiction Professionals of Minnesota and in the American Correctional Association.

If you can use an experienced human services professional with an excellent grasp of how to maximize community resources and provide quality social case work management, please call me to suggest a time when we might meet to discuss your needs. As an experienced Case Manager, I can assure you in advance that I could rapidly become an asset to your organization.

Sincerely,

Frederick W. Gushwa

Date

Exact Name of Person
Title or Position
Name of Company
Address (number and street)
Address (city, state, and zip)

Basketball Player
This cover letter was designed
to be sent to the Women's
National Basketball Association
with a copy to each of the
teams listed in the letter. This
top-notch female basketball
player, like anyone else in a job
hunt, must catch the attention
of hiring personnel in order to
blow doors open.

Dear Exact Name of Person: (or Sir or Madam if answering a blind ad)

With the enclosed resume, I would like to formally make you aware of my interest in the WNBA and my desire to play for any expansion teams as well as the following teams in particular:
Charlotte Sting
Cleveland Rockers
Houston Comets
New York Liberty
Los Angeles Sparks
Phoenix Mercury
Sacramento Monarchs
Utah Starzz

As you will see from my enclosed resume, I earned my B.S. degree on a full four-year scholarship and won numerous college honors while excelling as a season leader in scoring, free throws, rebounds, and blocked shots. My style can be described as inside post-up player, rebounder, and shot blocker. I received numerous honors including being named team MVP, All CIAA, Outstanding Sportswoman, Kodak All-American, and College Sports Information Director's Association All-American. I was recruited and received an offer to play professionally in Europe but declined the offer.

Single (never married) with no children, I am available for relocation anywhere and I would welcome the opportunity to talk with you about my desire to discuss my strong qualifications with any appropriate organization that can use a dynamic, crowd-pleasing ball player who is known for my leadership ability, strong personal qualities of reliability and dependability, and character.

Please look over my resume and give me your best advice about how we should proceed in finding suitable opportunities for my exceptional talents and skills.

Sincerely,

Larene Ford

Date

Exact Name of Person
Title or Position
Name of Company
Address (number and street)
Address (city, state, and zip)

Dear Exact Name of Person: (or Sir or Madam if answering a blind ad)

With the enclosed resume, I would like to make you aware, confidentially at this point, of my interest in discussing the position as Golf Course Superintendent for North Coast Country Club.

As a Golf Course Superintendent, I have made significant contributions to every course with which I have been associated. While serving simultaneously as Golf Course Superintendent for the Green Island Golf Course and the Crayfish Country Club, I supervised major projects at these two clubs which are overseeded for winter play.

At Green Island, I supervised the enlargement of the greens along with their conversion from Bermuda greens to Bentgrass, and I provided oversight when the irrigation system around the greens was changed. Also at Green Island, I provided the project management required when the soil mixture was changed to a more favorable Bentgrass environment based on the advice of Dr. Randall Gray of the University of Kentucky. For both Crayfish and Green Island, I managed separate budgets and crews.

With hobbies that include both freshwater and deep-sea fishing, I also am an avid golfer. With a current 1 handicap and index of 1.4, I enjoy competitive golf and have qualified and competed in numerous SC Amateurs, SC Mid Amateurs, and many local tournaments. I am a former individual winner of the Eastern Coastal Community College Conference Championship.

As a great fan of the North Coast area, I am familiar with the reputation as well as the technical composition of your outstanding course, and I believe the work being performed at North Coast Country Club is similar to the work I performed at Green Island.

You would find me in person to be a congenial individual who prides myself on my versatile technical knowledge as well as my management skills. I can provide excellent references at the appropriate time, but I would appreciate your holding my interest in your club in confidence at this point. I hope you will contact me to suggest a time when we might meet to discuss your needs and how I might help you. Thank you in advance for your time.

Sincerely,

Mark Lundy

Golf Course Superintendent
When you're in an industry and you are "fishing" for another situation inside that industry, you can talk the lingo of your industry. Notice how this golf professional talks about types of grass in his cover letter.

Date

Exact Name
Exact Title
Company Name
Address
City, State Zip

Dear Exact Name:

Head Golf Pro

Even people who are happy in their jobs sometimes look around, if only to see if they're missing anything. With this cover letter, a golf professional is approaching the country club which he considers one of the top five in the country to introduce himself and explore the possibility of joining the staff.

With the enclosed resume, I am formally indicating my interest in the Head Golf Professional position at The Master's Country Club of Kentucky.

In my current job as the Head Golf Professional at The Benchley Resort and Country Club in Pine Needle, SC, I have improved every aspect of the golf program at this esteemed country club. Although I am quite happy in my current situation and am appreciated for the significant improvements I have made in every area of the golf program, it has always been my goal to become associated one day with a prestigious club such as The Master's Country Club of Kentucky. I am aware of the high-profile clientele you serve, and I feel certain I could add value to your operation and enhance the superior climate for which you already are known.

At the Benchley Resort and Country Club, I have resourcefully found new ways to save money every year while making sure customers are satisfied with all "the little things" that can drive members crazy if they're not perfect! By those "little things" I include things such as the variety and quality of golf shop inventory, the tournament program, golf instruction, golf cart operation and bag storage, driving range administration, as well as the operation of starters and rangers. I have taken golf instruction to a new level and, while supervising seven employees, I have continually developed the instructional abilities of my assistants.

I have completed PGA Business School I, II, and III, have served on the PGA Oral Interview Committee, and was invited by fellow PGA Professionals to act as instructor for the South Carolina Junior Golf League. I offer extensive experience in organizing an extensive tournament schedule including The Southern Amateur Tournament, National Amputee Tournament, and the U.S. Senior Golf Association Tournament.

You would find me in person to be a congenial individual who prides myself on my ability to relate well to anyone. I believe strongly in the ability of golf to teach and refine virtues including honesty, fairness, courtesy, responsibility, determination, and discipline. I can provide outstanding personal and professional references. I hope you will write or call me to suggest a time when we might meet in confidence to discuss your needs and how I might serve them. Thank you in advance for your time.

Sincerely yours,

Bryce Dawson

Date

Exact Name of Person
Title or Position
Name of Company
Address (number and street)
Address (city, state, and zip)

Dear Exact Name of Person: (or Sir or Madam if answering a blind ad)

I would appreciate an opportunity to talk with you soon about how I could contribute to your organization through my experience as well as through my personal characteristics and reputation as a physically and mentally tough professional who excels in working with others in leadership roles or as a contributor to team success.

As you will see from my enclosed resume, I recently left military service after successfully advancing in supervisory and leadership roles with an emphasis in inventory control, warehousing and distribution, customer service, and quality control/quality assurance operations. Since January I have been a member of the new semiprofessional football team, the Baton Rouge Prowlers. As a Linebacker/Tight End I will be contributing a positive attitude and leadership skills as well as my talents as an athlete.

While serving in the U.S. Army, I was the recipient of numerous honors and several medals for my professionalism and leadership abilities. I was also selected to attend an advanced professional leadership development course to help sharpen and refine my skills. During my last assignment, I supervised eight people while ensuring the quality and reliability of parachutes and related equipment used by specialists from Ft. Benning, GA, one of the largest military posts worldwide.

I am confident that through my versatile experience and training, I am able to offer a track record of accomplishments and abilities which would allow me to rapidly become an asset to your organization. I hope you will contact me soon to suggest a time when we might meet to discuss your needs and how I might contribute. Thank you in advance for your time.

Sincerely,

Mitch Bragg

Date

Exact Name of Person
Title or Position
Name of Company
Address (no., street)
Address (city, state, zip)

Dear Exact Name of Person: (or Dear Sir or Madam if answering a blind ad)

Tennis Pro

A tennis professional is selectively exploring situations available at the top clubs on the east coast. It's okay to throw some of your personal philosophy into your cover letters. Notice the fourth paragraph: This paragraph is designed to make the cover letter a personal experience for the reader instead of a "canned" and impersonal standard cover letter.

I would appreciate an opportunity to talk with you soon about how I could contribute to your organization through my outstanding personal reputation and technical expertise as a Director/Head Tennis Pro.

Although I am highly regarded in my current job as Head Pro for the New World Country Club, I am attracted to your organization because of its fine reputation and feel I have much to offer you. As you will see from my resume, I have excelled as a Tennis Pro at Van Der Meer Tennis University, Tennis Coach at a tennis academy, and Head Pro at a sports center and country club before coming to New World Country Club as Head Pro. Two years ago I became one of only four people in North Carolina certified as a USPTR National Tester, and I have conducted USPTR coaches' workshops for persons wanting to be certified or to upgrade their certification.

So much of what I could offer an already-outstanding program such as yours is my creativity, I believe, since I know you have an excellent staff. I believe that the main way to keep the membership involved and the tennis professionals motivated is by developing new programs, and I have combined my tennis skills and creativity in developing highly successful programs for adults and juniors while also utilizing my public relations and media skills to develop new community awareness of and involvement in tennis.

I would appreciate your keeping my interest in your club confidential at this point, but if you have any idea that you could use a talented tennis pro who could take your program to new levels of excellence, I would appreciate your contacting me.

Sincerely yours,

Clifton Newman

Alternate last paragraph:
I hope you will welcome my call soon to arrange a brief meeting at your convenience to discuss your current and future needs and how I might serve them. Thank you in advance for your time.

Date

Exact Name of Person
Title or Position
Name of Company
Address (number and street)
Address (city, state, and zip)

Dear Exact Name of Person: (or Sir or Madam if answering a blind ad)

TEACHING

Principal
With this cover letter, an experienced teacher with some experience as an assistant principal is seeking an appointment as a principal.

Please accept this letter of interest for a position as Principal or Assistant Principal in the Orange County Schools as advertised in the Sunday, December 12, *Santa Barbara Herald*. My resume is enclosed and should also be on file in the Office of Personnel.

As you will see from my resume, I have served as assistant principal in Ventura County Schools. Administratively, I assisted in the planning and implementation of staff development sessions, conducted parent workshops, and coordinated an after-school Reading for Progress program. I have also scheduled and implemented computer-assisted instruction as well as face-to-face instruction in mathematics centers.

In my most recent professional activities, I have applied my expertise as a Reading Specialist for the Simi Valley Board of Education and as a BEH Consultant for Bayview County Schools. In Simi Valley, I designed a Reading Center for second grade students who were as much as 2 ½ years below their grade level in reading, and I led writing activities that helped in assessment and in stimulating literacy. I am proud of the fact that **all** of the more than 50 students increased their level of proficiency with some students increasing their proficiency by three levels!

I have extensive teaching experience in the Chapter I public and non-public school reading and mathematics programs in the New Jersey Board of Education. These programs provided opportunities for assessing the needs of the students in the schools serviced, which included working with principals, teachers, guidance counselors, social workers, psychologists, English as a Second Language (ESL) teachers, para-professionals, non-instruction computer technicians, and parents.

I am interested in being employed in the Orange County Schools as an Administrator because I am aware of the need for qualified, experienced educators in the schools. I am certain that my successful teaching and administrative experience could contribute to the vision and goals of the Orange County School system. Thank you for your kind consideration of my background and accomplishments.

Sincerely,

Sharmaine Anthony

Date

Exact Name of Person
Title or Position
Name of Company
Address (number and street)
Address (city, state, and zip)

TEACHING

Dear Exact Name of Person: (or Sir or Madam if answering a blind ad)

History Instructor

This history teacher is hoping to find a college teaching position so that he can pursue his Ph.D. in History. Aside from the fact that he would enjoy the challenge of teaching on the college level, college teaching would provide the kind of schedule he needs in order to complete the terminal degree in his field.

With the enclosed resume, I would like to make you aware of my interest in joining Georgetown University as a teaching member of the history faculty.

As you will see from my curriculum vitae, I hold an M.A. in History (GPA 3.80) in addition to the B.S. in History which I received previously at Georgetown University. I am a published author of works pertaining to state and local history. I am currently completing two books of historical fiction, and my previously published book won the Peace Book Award from the Nevada Society of Historians. I am a six-time recipient of the P.J. Sedgewick Newspaper Article Award given by the Maryland Society of Historians.

My college teaching experience includes positions as an Adjunct History Instructor at these colleges: Carson City College in Nevada, St. Mary's College in Maryland, and Baptist College in Virginia. I am currently working as a History Teacher/Coach at Alexandria Middle School, where I teach 7th grade history (Africa and Asia) while also serving as Head Football Coach and Head Baseball Coach.

While earning a reputation as a top-notch academician, I have also become recognized for my ability to stimulate, inspire, and motivate students to aim for high levels of mastery in formal classroom settings. I am confident that I could become a valuable member of your teaching faculty, and I would be honored to be associated with the institution from which I received my first degree.

My extensive writing and publishing combined with the demands of my job as a history teacher and coach for two sports have prevented me thus far from earning my Ph.D. but I am making plans to pursue the terminal degree in History.

I hope you will give me the courtesy of an interview so that I can demonstrate to you in person that I have the personal qualities and professional credentials which would make me a significant addition to your outstanding teaching faculty. Thank you very much in advance for your professional courtesies.

Sincerely,

Casey J. Stephens

Date

Exact Name
Exact Title
Company Name
Address
City, State Zip

Dear Sir or Madam:

With the enclosed resume, I would like to make you aware of my interest in teaching in a school system that can use an industrious and creative young teaching professional with a proven ability to teach, motivate, and instill a love of learning in others.

As you will see from my resume, I have taught in both wealthy school districts in the northeast as well as in a rural, poor district in the south. In most recent positions in North Carolina, I taught kindergarten and first grade in the public schools of Crawson County. I also played a key role in implementing changes recommended by a state-appointed Assistance Team that transformed elementary school student scores from low-performing to within two percent of "exemplary." Last year, I was honored by selection as Teacher of the Year at Falls Church Elementary School, where I have served as both a Kindergarten and First Grade Teacher.

In previous teaching assignments after earning my B.S. in Education in 1994, I worked as a Homebound Teacher and Substitute Teacher in Maine. My experience as a substitute teacher was valuable, because I learned the importance of planning classroom activities far in advance so that student learning is not interrupted when the regular classroom teacher is absent. I am certified to teach in Maine and North Carolina.

If you can use a enthusiastic young educator who thrives on the challenges and complexities of teaching, I hope you will contact me to suggest a time when we might meet to discuss your needs. I can assure you in advance that I could rapidly become an asset to your organization, and I can provide outstanding references.

Sincerely,

Angela Watkins

TEACHING

Teacher
This young teacher comes across in this cover letter as a highly talented hard charger with a love for children. She reports that she has been named "Teacher of the Year" at the elementary school where she now teaches, and she emphasizes her versatility by pointing out that she has taught in poor school districts and in wealthy areas.

Date

Exact Name of Person
Exact Title of Person
Company Name
Address
City, State Zip

Dear Sir or Madam:

Isn't this just the kind of person whom you would want in the classroom with your child? Through this effective cover letter, this young teacher seeking her first full-time job in teaching is able to convey her warm and caring personality as well as her dedication to her field. Here's a tip: Don't be afraid to let your cover letter reveal your personality!

With the enclosed resume, I would like to make you aware of my strong desire to become a part of your elementary teaching staff.

As you will see from my resume, I recently earned my Bachelor of Science in Education (B.S.E.) degree at the University of Georgia. Since it has always been my childhood dream to become a teacher, my college graduation was an especially meaningful event in my life.

As you will see from my resume, I recently completed a teaching assignment as a first grade student teacher, and I successfully assumed all the duties of a first grade teacher. During those two months, I wrote and completed my own professional growth and development plan, and I also planned and implemented a classroom and behavior management program.

In my previous two-month assignment as a kindergarten student teacher, I performed with distinction in planning and implementing creative lessons, communicating with teaching professionals and parents, and working with the children, whom I truly loved.

You will notice from my resume that I have expressed my true love for children through my summer and part-time jobs while in college. For four years, I was a nanny for a professional family and in that capacity I cared for three triplet newborns as well as two older children. It is an understatement to say that I refined my time management skills in that part-time job! I have also worked in a day care environment where I worked with children from infant to 12 years while learning to work effectively with people from all backgrounds.

If you can use a highly motivated young professional with unlimited personal initiative as well as strong personal qualities of dependability and trustworthiness, I hope you will contact me to suggest a time when we might meet to discuss your needs. I can provide excellent personal and professional references, and I am eager to apply my strong teaching skills and true love for children in an academic institution which emphasizes hard work and a commitment to the highest learning goals.

Sincerely,

Melanie Thompson

Date

Exact Name of Person
Title or Position
Name of Company
Address (number and street)
Address (city, state, and zip)

Dear Exact Name of Person: (or Sir or Madam if answering a blind ad)

TELECOMMUNICATIONS

With the enclosed resume, I would like to make you aware of my knowledge of and education in communications and fiber optic technology, and to express my strong interest in offering my skills to your company. I recently spoke with a former Lucent Technologies employee, Mr. Ti Wo-Chung, and he recommended that I forward my resume to your attention.

Electronics Graduate
With this cover letter, a young Electronics Technology graduate with fiber optics knowledge is seeking his first full-time job in his field. For more cover letters of people seeking their first full-time job, see the section called Seeking First Job in Field in Part I of this book.

As you will see, I have just completed my Associate's Degree in Electronics Technology. My major area of concentration was Communications and Fiber Optics. I have worked with fiber optics previously while employed by Quantum Systems on a contract job in Seattle, WA, where we installed optical module boxes and fiber optic cable along the 5-mile perimeter of a military compound.

Though my previous work experience is not highly technical in nature, I think you will see that I have proven myself to be a hardworking and reliable employee as well as a capable supervisor. Now that I have finished my degree, I am anxious to utilize my knowledge of communications and fiber optics technology. My strong work ethic, education, and technical know-how would be an asset to your organization.

If you can use a highly motivated, intelligent young communications professional with extensive fiber optics knowledge, I hope you will contact me to suggest a time when we might meet to discuss your needs and how I might serve them. I can provide outstanding personal and professional references.

Sincerely,

Tim Krepp

Date

Exact Name of Person
Title or Position
Name of Company
Address (number and street)
Address (city, state, and zip)

TELECOMMUNICATIONS

Dear Exact Name of Person: (or Sir or Madam if answering a blind ad)

Top Secret
Security Clearance

This young telecommunications professional has a lot going for her! She has one of the nation's highest security clearances—which many defense industry firms are seeking—and she offers extensive knowledge of COMSEC and SINCGARS.

I would appreciate an opportunity to talk with you soon about how I could contribute to your organization through my experience in communications-electronics, employee supervision and training, as well as operations administration.

With a Top Secret security clearance (SCI with SBI), I have excelled in extensive college-level training sponsored by the U.S. Army related to the repair and maintenance of COMSEC radio, the SINCGARS system, as well as computers, satellite equipment, and other equipment. While serving my country in the U.S. Army, I distinguished myself as a COMSEC and Telecommunications Operations and Repair Technician and was named Soldier of the Quarter. In my next job as a Radio Repair Technician, I was named Soldier of the Month and was commended for my initiative and resourcefulness in saving the organization money. I was promoted ahead of my peers to a supervisory role as Senior Radio Repairer in charge of seven technical specialists involved in radio and communications repair. In that job I accounted for more than $2 million in assets.

I am proud that I was promoted to noncommissioned officer when I was barely 21 years old and have excelled in handling operations management and employee training for the past two years. I am also proud of the significant contributions I made to the organizations for which I worked, which resulted in my receiving more than 10 medals and other honors.

Although I have been strongly encouraged to remain in the Army and continue in my unusually rapid track record of advancement, I have decided that I wish to enter the civilian labor market. I am positive that I can quickly become a valuable asset to an organization that values outstanding problem-solving skills and troubleshooting abilities, and I can provide outstanding personal and professional references at the appropriate time.

If you can use my considerable talents, skills, and abilities, I hope you will contact me to suggest a time when we might meet to discuss your needs and goals and how I might help you achieve them. Thank you in advance for your time.

Yours sincerely,

Juanita Garcia

Date

Exact Name of Person
Title of Position
Company Name
Address (street and number)
Address (city, state, and zip)

Dear Exact Name of Person: (or Dear Sir or Madam if answering a blind ad)

TELECOMMUNICATIONS

Telecommunications Manager
The military is a breeding ground for some of our most knowledgeable telecommunications professionals, and this individual proves the point. Here you see the all-purpose cover letter of a manager with digital, analog, and packet switching experience.

I would appreciate an opportunity to talk with you soon about how I could contribute to your organization through my versatile technical and supervisory skills as well as through my personal qualities and reputation for displaying initiative, self-motivation, and an energetic and enthusiastic approach.

Having advanced in rank ahead of my peers while serving my country in the U.S. Army, I offer four years of technical experience with digital, analog, and packet switching communications systems and radio systems as well as two years as a supervisor. As you will see from my enclosed resume, I have been selected for supervisory jobs and cited for my ability to train and motivate subordinates to work together as a team while building strong individual skills.

In my present assignment as a Communications Supervisor at Ft. McCoy, WI, I supervise and train signal communications technicians while applying my own technical expertise to ensure the quality of communications links for an organization with a rapid deployment mission. I control a $2 million equipment inventory which includes vehicles and power generation equipment as well as communications systems, and I handle administrative responsibilities related to maintenance and personnel records.

I am confident that I have technical knowledge, skills, and abilities which would be valuable to any organization in need of a safety-conscious and dedicated professional. I hope you will call or write me soon to suggest a time when we might meet to discuss your current and future needs and how I might serve them. Thank you in advance for your time.

Sincerely,

Bentley D. Ruston, Jr.

Alternate last paragraph:
I hope you will welcome my call soon to arrange a time for us to discuss your current and future needs and how I might serve them. Thank you in advance for your time.

Date

Exact Name of Person
Title or Position
Name of Company
Address (number and street)
Address (city, state, and zip)

Dear Exact Name of Person: (or Sir or Madam if answering a blind ad)

**Signal Communications
Supervisor**
This signal communications
supervisor with experience in
high-tech and medical
environments feels that
it is the right time in his life
to seek a suitable opportunity
in the business
telecommunications world.

I would appreciate an opportunity to talk with you soon about how I could contribute to your organization through a combination of technical knowledge of communications systems and a reputation for skill in supervising, motivating, and managing teams of technical specialists.

You will see from my enclosed resume that I have served my country in the U.S. Army. Although I have earned promotion ahead of my peers and am well-respected in my field, I feel that the time is right for new challenges and opportunities.

My extensive military training included in excess of 700 hours of course work with a concentration in signal communications operations, troubleshooting, and maintenance as well as courses designed to train maintenance managers and technical supervisors. Throughout my career I have been singled out for increased responsibilities beyond the norm for someone of my rank and years of experience.

In my present job as Communications Supervisor for a medical company at Walter Reed Army Medical Center in Washington, D.C., I have been cited for my efforts in ensuring that vital communications links are uninterrupted. I have been placed in charge of multimillion-dollar inventories of high-tech communications systems and selected for numerous special projects and extra duties. I am the recipient of three Army Commendation Medals and two Army Achievement Medals which were given in recognition of my meritorious achievements during major inspections, disaster relief efforts, and the war in the Middle East as well as for consistently high levels of professionalism, dedication, and performance.

If you are searching for a hard-working leader, I am an enthusiastic self-starter with an eye for detail and talent for maximizing available resources in order to get the job done. I hope you will welcome my call soon to arrange a brief meeting to discuss your current and future needs and how I might serve them. Thank you in advance for your time.

Sincerely,

Alton G. Loveless

Date

Exact Name of Person
Title or Position
Name of Company
Address (number and street)
Address (city, state, and zip)

Dear Exact Name of Person: (or Sir or Madam if answering a blind ad)

TELECOMMUNICATIONS

Radio Telecommunications
This young professional writes to introduce his considerable experience in installation, operation, and maintenance as well as his sharp troubleshooting skills.

With the enclosed resume, I would like to introduce myself and the extensive experience I offer in the field of radio and telecommunications installation, operation, maintenance, and troubleshooting.

While serving my country in the U.S. Army, I excelled in extensive training in the radio and telecommunications field. I became highly skilled in operating, maintaining, repairing, and troubleshooting equipment including VHF, UHF, GTE Mobile Subscriber Equipment (MSE), the SHF system for the MSE, TAC-SAT radios, COMSEC equipment, SINCGARS equipment, as well as many other devices, systems, and types of equipment.

In addition to excelling in technical areas, I was promoted ahead of my peers to supervisory roles and I became respected for my ability to train, motivate, and lead others. During a three-month training program in White Sands Missile Range, I was selected to supervise 30 personnel and led my platoon to be named "Honor Platoon." In my most recent job as a Radio Communications Supervisor at Ft. Shafter, HI, I trained, managed, and motivated a small team of radio communications specialists while controlling a $1 million inventory of communications assets. I received a respected medal for my achievements related to supporting the mission of the 82nd Airborne Division to be able to relocate worldwide within 18 hours for international crises or projects. I have become skilled at installing fixed and mobile radio equipment supporting thousands of people, and I am an experienced COMSEC Custodian. I was entrusted with a Secret security clearance.

You would find me in person to be a highly disciplined individual known for resourceful problem-solving skills as well as intense personal initiative and persistence in following through until stubborn problems are resolved. On numerous occasions, I have saved expensive downtime because of my tireless work in troubleshooting difficult equipment malfunctions.

I can provide excellent personal and professional references at the appropriate time, and I hope you will write or call me to suggest a time when we might meet to discuss your needs and how I might serve them. Thank you for your time.

Yours sincerely,

Irving Skinner

Date

Exact Name of Person
Title or Position
Name of Company
Address (number and street)
Address (city, state, and zip)

TELECOMMUNICATIONS

Telecommunications Center
Manager
A high security clearance, a
track record of promotion
ahead of his peers, numerous
honors and awards for
exceptional performance, and a
desire to make contributions to
a company's bottom line are a
few of the things this young
professional is offering. What
telecommunications industry
employer wouldn't want to
dial his number to set
up an interview?

Dear Exact Name of Person: (or Sir or Madam if answering a blind ad)

With the enclosed resume, I would like to introduce my considerable skills in the telecommunications field and make you aware of the talents which I would like to put to work for you.

While serving my country in the U.S. Army, I was promoted ahead of my peers and selected for numerous positions which were usually reserved for someone of higher rank. I enjoyed an unusually rapid promotion from Private to Sergeant in less than 2 ½ years, and I was then selected for critical supervisory roles. In one job as a Shift Supervisor in a Telecommunications Center, I managed seven military and civilian employees processing more than 160,000 messages with no security compromise. I was then selected for a job as a Telecommunications Center Manager at the U.S. Army Information Systems Command, where I supervised the upgrade of communications systems from obsolete mainframe equipment to new microcomputer terminals. In that job I received a special award for publishing a user-friendly Operator Manual which permitted message customers to prepare their own messages for transmission.

In my most recent job as Telecommunications Center Manager, I was the chief coordinator for the initial implementation of a new worldwide communications system while training and managing 10 employees. In my prior position, I acted as a Telecommunications Consultant for various organizations that needed technical assistance on the utilization of telecommunications systems and networks.

I have held a Top Secret security clearance with SCI, and I am skilled in operating COMSEC equipment and devices. I am adept at supervising, installing, operating, and performing operator maintenance in telecommunications systems. My management skills were tested and refined while serving my country. I am proud that I was able to develop and mold many junior leaders who went on to become Soldier of the Year, NCO of the Month, and NCO of the Year.

If you can use a go-getter and team player who offers a rare combination of technical expertise and management ability, I hope you will write or call me to suggest a time when we might meet to discuss your needs and how I might meet them. Thank you in advance for your time.

Yours sincerely,

Francis G. Bray

Date

Exact Name of Person
Title or Position
Name of Company
Address (number and street)
Address (city, state, and zip)

Dear Exact Name of Person: (or Sir or Madam if answering a blind ad)

With the enclosed resume, I would like to make you aware of my background as an experienced telecommunications manager and supervisor whose skills have been tested while serving in the Department of Defense.

As you will see, I have extensive experience in the operation of multimillion-dollar state-of-the-art communications systems and in developing and overseeing the performance of large teams of skilled technicians. Throughout my career with the past 12 years in management roles, I have been described as a technically proficient professional who excels in providing high-quality telecommunications support. I have served under the pressure of combat during the war in the Middle East and provided support to American troops.

Among my special skills are the proven ability to develop effective training and cross-training programs and to serve as a technical expert and advisor. I have consistently succeeded in finding ways to improve productivity and mold employees into teams which excel in every measured area of performance.

Known for my initiative, drive, and positive attitude, I have built a reputation as a talented and proficient manager who can be counted on to get the job done no matter how difficult or time consuming.

If you can use an experienced manager and supervisor who has received numerous awards for meritorious accomplishments and effective leadership, I hope you will contact me to suggest a time when we might meet to discuss your needs. I can assure you in advance that I could rapidly become an asset to your organization. I can relocate according to your needs and can provide excellent references.

Sincerely,

Aidan L. Tarbett

Telecommunications Manager
More than 12 years of experience is one of the calling cards of this industry professional. For more cover letters like this one, see the Military Transition Section.

Date

Exact Name of Person
Title or Position
Name of Company
Address (number and street)
Address (city, state, and zip)

Dear Exact Name of Person: (or Sir or Madam if answering a blind ad)

Equipment Operator

This equipment operator can use and maintain forklifts, cargo trucks, and cranes as well as numerous other vehicles and pieces of equipment in the transportation field.

I would appreciate an opportunity to talk with you soon about how I could contribute to your organization through my knowledge and skills related to the supervision and performance of cargo transfer and heavy equipment maintenance operations.

As you will see from my enclosed resume, I was selected to receive advanced training and hold supervisory roles ahead of my peers. While working for the Bechtel Corporation in locations worldwide, I was recognized with five Certificates for my professionalism and accomplishments. These Certificates of Appreciation were awarded for my contributions during special projects as well as for consistently excellent job performance.

Licensed to operate and maintain a variety of forklifts, cargo trucks, and cranes, I am skilled in troubleshooting as well as in teaching others how to carry out their responsibilities for maintaining and operating this multimillion-dollar equipment.

I offer a reputation as a fast learner, hard worker, and skilled leader who can be counted on to adapt to rapid change and adverse conditions with dedication to achieving results. If you can use a well-trained young professional who excels in motivating others to accomplish excellent results, I hope you will contact me to suggest a time when we might meet to discuss your needs. I can assure you in advance that I could rapidly become an asset to your organization.

Sincerely,

Jake Weske

Date

Exact Name of Person
Title or Position
Name of Company
Address (number and street)
Address (city, state, and zip)

Dear Exact Name of Person: (or Dear Sir or Madam if answering a blind ad)

I would appreciate an opportunity to talk with you soon about how I could contribute to your organization through my outstanding background in hazardous materials certification, management, and inspection.

As you will see from my resume, I have become as an expert in the hazardous materials field. In my most recent position as a Senior Instructor and Training Program Manager, I oversaw the training of approximately 850 people a year at the nation's premier HAZMAT training facility in Bethesda, Maryland.

In previous jobs, I applied my hazardous materials knowledge in jobs which required outstanding strategic planning, decision-making, problem-solving, and communication skills. In one job as a Transportation Operations Supervisor, I oversaw 33 specialists in a transportation terminal which handled cargo arriving and departing by air, rail, and highway. I am also skilled in overseeing the transportation of all types of materials by sea.

Throughout my distinguished military service, I received numerous medals and awards recognizing my superior management ability, hazardous materials expertise, as well as my technical logistics, supply, and transportation operations know-how. I can provide outstanding personal and professional references at the appropriate time, and I am willing to relocate and travel as your needs require.

I would appreciate your contacting me if you feel my expertise and experience could be of value to you. Thank you in advance for your time.

Sincerely,

Roland Wold

Alternate last paragraph:
I hope you will welcome my call soon when I try to speak with you briefly to see if my background is suited to your current or future needs. Thank you in advance for your time.

Date

Exact Name of Person
Title or Position
Name of Company
Address (number and street)
Address (city, state, and zip)

Dear Exact Name of Person: (or Sir or Madam if answering a blind ad)

Weapons Specialist
This individual offers
experience in loading and
transporting materials of all
types, and he is also skilled at
operating construction
equipment. With this all-
purpose letter, he can approach
companies in the
transportation and freight
distribution arena as well as
construction firms.

    I would appreciate an opportunity to talk with you soon about how I could contribute to your organization through my versatile experience and skills refined while serving my country in the U.S. Army.

    As you will see from my enclosed resume, I have been certified in hazardous material packaging, handling, and transportation and applied this knowledge as a military weapons specialist (armorer). While controlling multimillion-dollar inventories of weapons, ammunition, and explosives storage areas at sites in Korea and at Ft. Knox, KY, I earned a reputation as a young professional who could be counted on to exceed expected standards. The recipient of several U.S. Army Commendation and Achievement Medals, I was singled out on several occasions for promotion to supervisory roles ahead of my peers and to participate in sensitive overseas assignments.

    Another area of special training and interest is heavy equipment operations, a field I worked in prior to military service. I have experience as a construction foreman and am licensed to operate equipment such as DJB rock haulers, Caterpillar and John Deere track loaders, as well as forklifts and up to 5-ton trucks.

    If you can use an experienced and well-trained young professional, I hope you will contact me to suggest a time when we might meet to discuss your needs. I can assure you in advance that I could rapidly become an asset to your organization.

Sincerely,

Lee Murakami

Date

Exact Name of Person
Title or Position
Name of Company
Address (number and street)
Address (city, state, and zip)

Dear Exact Name of Person: (or Sir or Madam if answering a blind ad)

TRANSPORTATION

Long-Haul Driver
Long-haul driving can take a
person away from home for
long stretches of time. That's
what happened with this
individual, and he is sending
this cover letter and his resume
to companies that might offer
short-haul or
local-run routes.

   With the enclosed resume, I would like to make you aware of my background as an experienced tractor-trailer operator whose skills have been tested in various demanding long-haul situations.

   As you will see, I have been employed since my junior year in high school, and I have developed a strong reputation as an honest and hardworking employee. From my years of experience in various retail environments, I have developed an instinct for customer service that would be a valuable asset to your organization.

   For the last year and a half, I have driven tractor-trailers for Reliable Carriers out of Philadelphia, PA. Although I am held in high regard by my employer and can provide excellent references at the appropriate time, I am interested in finding a position that would allow me to better capitalize on my excellent customer service skills, such as a dedicated local run or short-haul position.

   If your organization can use an experienced, hard-working driver with strong customer service skills, I look forward to hearing from you to arrange a time when we might meet to discuss your present and future needs and how I might serve them.

                              Sincerely,

                              Randy Ferrell

In this section you will find answers to common questions about cover letters. Lots of "oddball" situations come up in job hunting, and you will find the answers to many of those questions in this section. In this section you will find out how to phrase the answers to delicate questions such as questions about salary.

Question 1: What is the "direct approach?"

Question 2: How do I address a letter to an ad that provides names and addresses?

Question 3: What's the best way to answer a "blind ad?"

Question 4: How do I respond to a recruiter or headhunter who has approached me?

Question 5: How do I apply for internal openings?

Question 6: How do I ask for consideration for multiple job openings?

Question 7: How do I fax my resume and cover letter?

Question 8: If I want to "drop a name" in a cover letter, what's the best way?

Question 9: If I'm relocating soon, how do I say that in the cover letter?

Question 10: If I've recently relocated, what do I say in the cover letter?

Question 11: What if I want to reopen a door that I closed previously?

Question 12: What if they ask for salary requirements?

Question 13: What if they ask for salary history?

Question 14: How do I make it clear that I want my approach to be confidential?

Question 15: How do I write a follow-up letter after an interview?

Question 16: How do I resign—gracefully?

Date

Exact Name of Person
Title or Position
Name of Company
Address (number and street)
Address (city, state, and zip)

THE DIRECT APPROACH

Question 1: What is the "direct approach?"

You need to master the technique of using the "direct approach" in your job hunt. By using the direct approach, you create an all-purpose letter, such as the one on this page, which you can send to numerous employers introducing yourself and your resume. The direct approach is a proactive, aggressive approach to a job campaign, and it sure beats waiting around until the "ideal job" appears in the newspaper (and 200 other people see it, too). Figure out the employers you wish to approach either (1) by geographical area or (2) by industry and directly approach them expressing your interest in their company. Believe it or not, most people get their jobs through the direct approach!

Dear Exact Name of Person: (or Dear Sir or Madam if answering a blind ad)

I would appreciate an opportunity to talk with you soon about how I could contribute to your organization through my extensive expertise in the financial field including my recent experience as a Financial Consultant.

As you will see from my resume, I hold the Series 7, Series 63, Series 24, and Series 65 licenses and am a Registered Member of numerous exchanges and associations of securities dealers. In 1998 I left a Wall Street firm to relocate to the South, where my wife and her family live. Since 1998 I have been working for Merrill Lynch, and after my training and licensing, I established 364 accounts and produced $5 million in managed money in my first six-month period of production. Although I am excelling in my job and have been offered a branch management position in another state, I wish to remain in the Norfolk area. Since I am not under contract with Merrill Lynch, I am exploring suitable opportunities with area firms.

Much of my rapid success as a Financial Consultant stems from my background in nearly all aspects of finance, credit, and collections, in addition to my entrepreneurial background. As Managing Director, I owned and managed a lead-based company for Dun & Bradstreet. Subsequent to that, I worked with Wall Street firms in New York City until I met my wife and she decided she wanted us to relocate to Norfolk to be near her family. I offer an extensive background in working with high net worth individuals.

I can provide outstanding personal and professional references, and I would be delighted to make myself available at your convenience for a personal interview. Thank you in advance for your professional courtesies and consideration.

Yours sincerely,

Elias Johnson III

Date

Ms. Myrtle McConnell
Clark Management, Inc.
Post Office Box 82
Virginia Beach, VA 34098

Dear Ms. McConnell:

I am writing to express my interest in the position of Manager of the Virginia Beach Resort and Tennis Club which was advertised in the *Virginia Beach Gazette* of Monday, December 18, 1999. With the enclosed resume, I would like to introduce you to my proven supervisory and guest services skills along with my track record of success as Owner/Operator and General Manager of a number of establishments.

In my most recent position in the hospitality industry, I purchased a 150-seat restaurant and 50-seat lounge from the O'Brien's chain. I changed the restaurant's name and developed a new, expanded menu while implementing higher levels of guest service. I directed the work of the front end, bar, and kitchen managers, overseeing a staff of 25 employees. In my previous position at Kasey's in Virginia Beach, we dealt with a large client base of repeat customers, arranging reservations at local golf courses as well as serving their dining needs.

For the past year, I have excelled as Business Manager of ABC Construction, helping my brother to set up his commercial contracting business. Now that his business is up and running, I am very interested in returning to the hospitality industry, and my wife and I are considering relocation to the Virginia Beach area. I feel that my strong management background and proven skills in customer service, staff development, and training would make me a valuable addition to your operation.

When we meet in person, you will see that I am a congenial professional and avid tennis player with extensive management experience that could make me an ideal candidate for this position. I offer an outstanding reputation in our industry and can provide excellent references at the appropriate time.

Yours sincerely,

Bill Adams

ANSWERING ADS

Question 2: How do I respond to an ad that provides the name and address?
It's easy enough to reply to an ad when you have the name and address of the person you're writing to, but there's more to this question than meets the eye. Read the ad carefully and tailor your letter as precisely to the ad as possible. Notice the sentence in the last paragraph where Mr. Adams mentions that he's a tennis player. He is picking up on the fact that the ad is for a tennis resort, and he is making his reader aware that he plays the game and understands the passion of the club's customers.

Date

P.O. Box 66
Dallas, TX 90345

ANSWERING ADS

Question 3: What's the best way to answer a "blind ad?"
"To whom it may concern" or "Dear Sir or Madam" is the proper salutation for a letter responding to a "blind ad" or an ad which does not reveal the company name or the name of the person to whom you are writing. Sometimes companies don't put their name in the ad because they don't want their competitors to know they are hiring. Sometimes companies don't give their name because they think it might encourage telephone calls about the job.

To whom it may concern:

With the enclosed resume, I would like to respond to your advertisement in the *Dallas Chronicle* for a Management Trainee and make you aware of the considerable office, sales, and management abilities I could put to work for you.

As you will see from my resume, I am skilled in all aspects of office activities and am proficient with WordPerfect and the Windows 95 programs including Word, Excel, and Access. I am a very cheerful and adaptable person, as has been demonstrated by my ability to adapt rapidly and become quickly productive while working in long-term and short-term temporary assignments for major corporations, small businesses, and utility companies. I am skilled at operating a multiline switchboard system.

A resourceful and enthusiastic individual, I have always found ways to contribute to increased efficiency in all of my jobs. For example, in one job with an electrical supply company, I developed ideas which resulted in increased efficiency in supply parts ordering. In another job with a prominent retailer, I was named Sales Representative of the Month and was credited with playing a key role in increasing repeat business through my customer service and sales skills.

You will also see that I offer proven management skills and personal initiative. In one of my first professional positions, I was promoted rapidly by a children's entertainment company to responsibilities which involved traveling to conventions to book shows and negotiate contracts. The youngest person ever promoted to vice president, I am still a member of the Board of Directors of that company and am respected for my business insights and marketing instincts.

If you can use a versatile young professional known for an excellent attitude as well as superior work habits including reliability, dependability, and honesty, I hope you will contact me to suggest a time when we might meet to discuss your needs. I can assure you in advance that I could rapidly become an asset to your organization.

Sincerely,

Simone Guardado

Date

Mr. John Smith
XYZ Management Recruiters
Address (number and street)
Address (city, state, and zip)

Dear Mr. Smith:

After reviewing the materials you sent me regarding the Des Moines Public Schools Superintendency, I believe that my professional and personal attributes are complementary to the needs of the school system.

In my current position as Superintendent of Fort Leavenworth Schools, I am entrusted with serving 5,700 students and supervising a staff of 660. The challenges in this district serving military dependents have been many and varied. With the cooperation of the staff and the greater school community, we have been successful in securing outstanding financial support from both the Department of Defense and Congress. As a result, we were able to open a new elementary school and expand five existing schools.

As Superintendent in Huntsville, AL, and at Fort Leavenworth, I provided the impetus for expansion of technology in the instructional program. During this past year, one of Fort Leavenworth's elementary schools was chosen as a testbed site for President Clinton's Technology Initiative (PTI). This pilot project will afford our students and staff an opportunity to share innovative programs and instructional strategies.

Believing that mutual cooperation from internal and external sources is critical for success, I am known for my ability to forge strong alliances and partnerships with community organizations. While serving as Superintendent in Huntsville, I was instrumental in forming a regional school and business alliance (SABA) which developed partnerships with the business community. Serving as Director on several boards has also provided me with opportunities to gain community support for school programs. Indeed, any professional accomplishments I have achieved during my career have been attained through the combined efforts of many people. If I were to be selected as Superintendent, I would work diligently to gain local, state, and national support in order to move the Des Moines Public Schools forward.

Thank you for your interest in my qualifications, and I look forward to talking with you soon about the next step you suggest in my formally applying for the position as Superintendent of the Des Moines School System.

Yours sincerely,

Andrew J. Foster

RESPONDING TO RECRUITERS

Question 4: How do I respond to a recruiter or "headhunter" who has approached me?
Don't take any shortcuts when responding to a recruiter who has approached you to see if you might be interested in a new situation. In Mr. Foster's case, he has been approached by a management recruiting firm handling the search for a school superintendent of a major school district. He makes sure the recruiter understands him professionally and philosophically by developing a cover letter
that fully markets his interest and background. As always, make sure your cover letter "sells" you!

Date

Exact Name of Person
Title or Position
Name of Company
Address (number and street)
Address (city, state, and zip)

**APPLYING FOR
INTERNAL OPENINGS**

**Question 5: How do I apply for
internal openings?**
We recommend sacrificing no
formality when applying for
internal promotions. As you
see from this cover letter, you
still need to "sell" your
interest and qualifications,
even when the insiders know
you.

Dear Exact Name of Person: (or Dear Sir or Madam if answering a blind ad)

With the enclosed resume, I would like to make you aware of my interest in the position of **Financial Management Analyst II with the Vermont Department of Revenue.** As you will see from my enclosed resume, I offer a background as a seasoned accounting professional with exceptional analytical, communication, and organizational skills. In my current job, I perform essentially as a Financial Management Analyst in my role as a Field Auditor and Revenue Officer with the Vermont Department of Revenue.

With the Department of Revenue, I have advanced in a track record of increasing responsibilities. In my current position as a Field Auditor, I analyze financial reports of businesses and individuals, reconciling various general ledgers as well as investment and checking accounts in order to accurately determine tax liability. Earlier as a Revenue Officer, I consulted with taxpayers to assist them in determining the validity of deductions and calculating the amount of individual income tax owed. In both of these positions, I trained my coworkers, sharing my extensive knowledge of Internal Revenue Service and Vermont Department of Revenue codes and laws while educating department personnel on correct procedures related to professional auditing and collections.

I hold an Associate of Applied Science degree in Accounting from Central Berkshire Community College and a Bachelor of Science in Business Administration from the University of Oregon at Portland.

Please favorably consider my application for this internal opening, and please also consider my history of dedicated service to the Vermont Department of Revenue. I feel certain that I could excel in this job and could be a valuable asset to the department.

Sincerely,

Kevin Strafford

Date

Exact Name of Person
Title or Position
Name of Company
Address (number and street)
Address (city, state, and zip)

Dear Exact Name of Person: (or Sir or Madam if answering a blind ad)

With the enclosed resume, I would like to make you aware of the considerable skills I could put to work for the Baltimore Family Health System. Although I would like you to consider me for any situation where my versatile skills could be of value to you, I am particularly interested in the following positions:

> Access Coordinator
> Assistant Practice Manager
> Network Analyst II (Information Systems)
> Account Analyst

You will see that I offer skills compatible with those and other business office positions. I hold a B.A. in Finance and have acquired experience in internal business auditing activities, payroll calculation and administration, computer operations, and office management. I have worked for only two companies and have been promoted to increasing responsibilities in both organizations because of my initiative, productivity, and office skills. Even in high school, I began working for Camelot Music and was promoted to Assistant Manager for a store with $1.5 million in annual sales and 15 employees. In my current job, I handle a variety of internal auditing procedures, troubleshoot accounting problems, and handle liaison with the home office. I am proficient in utilizing numerous software programs including Excel, Lotus, and many others.

With a reputation as a congenial individual with outstanding customer service and public relations skills, I can provide outstanding personal and professional references at the appropriate time. Although I am excelling in my current position and am highly regarded by my employer, it is my desire to work in a medical environment.

If you can use an energetic and highly motivated hard worker who offers versatile skills and abilities, I hope you will contact me to suggest a time when we might meet to discuss your needs and how I might serve them. Thank you in advance for your time.

Yours sincerely,

Holly M. Vargo

SEEKING MULTIPLE JOB CONSIDERATION

Question 6: How do I request consideration for multiple job openings in the organization? This individual knows the organization she wants to work for; she just isn't sure what job she wants within the organization! In such a situation, you can plainly state in the first paragraph of your cover letter that you wish to be considered for multiple job openings by name. The employer will probably be glad to learn of your versatility.

Date

BY FAX TO: Human Resources Department
910-483-2439
Reference Job Code XYZ 9034

**FAXING YOUR RESUME AND
COVER LETTER**

**Question 7: How do I
fax my resume?**

The answer is: always with a
cover letter. When you fax your
resume and the cover letter
introducing your resume, we
recommend that you put the
fax number on the top of the
letter. In this way you identify
to the receiver how you
contacted them (remember,
they may be receiving dozens
of other resumes and cover
letters), and you also have a
record of the fax number on
the top of your copy of the
letter. Never send any type of
correspondence in business
without dating it.

Dear Sir or Madam:

With the enclosed resume, I would like to make you aware of my interest in employment as a Pharmaceutical Healthcare Representative with Johnson & Johnson. I believe you are aware that Walter Freeman, one of your Healthcare Representatives, has recommended that I talk with you because he feels that I could excel in the position as Pharmaceutical Healthcare Representative.

As you will see from my enclosed resume, I offer proven marketing and sales skills along with a reputation as a highly motivated individual with exceptional problem-solving abilities. Shortly after joining my current firm as a Mortgage Loan Specialist, I was named Outstanding Loan Officer of the month through my achievement in generating more than $20,000 in fees.

I believe much of my professional success so far has been due to my highly motivated nature and creative approach to my job. For example, when I began working for my current employer, I developed and implemented the concept of a postcard that communicated a message which the consumer found intriguing. The concept has been so successful that it has been one of the main sources of advertisements in our office and the concept has been imitated by other offices in the company.

In addition to my track record of excelling in the highly competitive financial services field, I gained valuable sales experience in earlier jobs selling copying equipment and sleep systems. I have also applied my strong leadership and sales ability in the human services field, when I worked in adult probation services. I am very proud of the fact that many troubled individuals with whom I worked told me that my ability to inspire and motivate them was the key to their becoming productive citizens.

If you can use a creative and motivated self-starter who could enhance your goals for market share and profitability, I hope you will contact me to suggest a time when we could meet in person to discuss your needs and goals and how I could meet them. I can provide strong personal and professional references at the appropriate time.

Yours sincerely,

Cheri Garcia

Date

Exact Name of Person
Title or Position
Name of Company
Address (number and street)
Address (city, state, and zip)

Dear Exact Name of Person: (or Sir or Madam if answering a blind ad)

NAME DROPPING

Question 8: If I want to "drop a name" in a letter, what's the best way?
It's nice to play the "who you know" game socially and in business, and it can help you get in the door for interviews, too. If a current employee has recommended that you write to the organization, or if you have worked with members of the organization on some project, you can "drop a name" gracefully. In so doing, you will add warmth to a cover letter that will exude a very personalized tone.

With the enclosed resume, I would like to make you aware of my interest in joining your organization in some capacity which could utilize my extensive experience related to consumer lending, credit, and collections. I am responding to your recent advertisement for a Collections Assistant. I am somewhat familiar with your organization because I had the pleasure of working by telephone last year with several of your employees on matters related to skip tracing, and I was impressed with the professionalism of your personnel. Ms. Lenette Wilson, in particular, was especially helpful to me and gave me an outstanding impression of your organization.

My family and I have recently relocated to Little Rock from El Paso, TX, where I excelled in a track record of achievement as a Collections Officer. I began working for the Ft. Bliss Credit Union as a Teller, was quickly named "Teller of the Quarter," and then was promoted to handle complex responsibilities related to collections. I received numerous Customer Service Awards and achieved an extremely low delinquency rate on repossessed vehicles while maintaining the lowest possible ratios related to bankruptcies and written-off loans. I am skilled in every aspect of collections.

In addition to excelling as a Collections Officer, I became knowledgeable of consumer lending and banking while handling money orders, bank checks, IRA withdrawals, travelers checks, savings bonds, coin exchanges, night deposit posting, handling the closing of members' accounts, filing members' open-account cards, processing returned checks, as well as processing and filming checks to National Credit Union Headquarters.

If you can use a hard-working young professional who offers a reputation as a thorough, persistent, and highly motivated individual, I hope you will contact me to suggest a time when we might meet to discuss your needs and goals and how I could help you achieve them. I would be delighted to discuss the private details of my salary history with you in person, and I can provide outstanding personal and professional references.

Sincerely,

Athena Zibart

Date

Mr. Victor Graphics
Director, Franchising and Dealership Program
Chevrolet, Incorporated
234 Chevrolet Lane
Madison, WI 90257

MORE NAME DROPPING

**More name dropping —
writing to someone
you know**
You can take some liberties
when you are writing to
people you know, even about
as serious a subject as
becoming General Manager of
a major automobile dealership.

Dear Victor:

Although I have tried to retire from my career in the car business, I have discovered that I don't play golf well enough to retire! I believe you will recall that the last time I saw you was, in fact, on a golf course when we played the tournament in Virginia Beach two years ago. Hope your golf game has fared better than mine in the meantime!

Although I believe you are well acquainted with my background, I am sending you an updated resume to refresh your memory. I want you to know that I am very interested in pursuing a franchise opportunity with the Chevrolet Corporation.

I can assure you that I have the necessary capital for this business opportunity, and I believe you know that I would be an individual who could make a success out of such a franchise. I would feel honored, too, to be a part of the Handicapped Dealers Program and feel that my success would be a credit to the fine program which you direct.

I enjoyed our brief phone conversation recently, and I hope the enclosed brings you up to date on my most recent successes and accomplishments. I hope you will contact me to suggest what you think is the next suitable step in light of my desire to become associated with this program and with the Chevrolet franchise program.

Best regards to you and your family.

Warmly,

Ronald La Rae

Date

Exact Name of Person
Title or Position
Name of Company
Address (number and street)
Address (city, state, and zip)

Dear Exact Name of Person: (or Sir or Madam if answering a blind ad)

MORE NAME DROPPING

With the enclosed resume, I would like to initiate the process of being considered for employment within your organization. Mr. Jorge Villar of The Philips Group has strongly encouraged me to send you my resume.

As you will see, I am an extremely hard worker who has achieved an outstanding track record of promotion within two organizations simultaneously. While working for WZFX 99.1/WLRD 107.7 in North Carolina, I became determined to achieve the designation of Radio Marketing Associate—a designation which, as you know, only about 5% of radio sales professionals ever achieve. I set a record for first-time radio sales for the station when we billed $14,000 in one month, and I did achieve my goal of becoming an R.M.A. five years later.

At the same time that I was excelling in my chosen career field of radio sales, I was simultaneously being promoted within the Roses Department Store organization. After beginning as a stock clerk, I was promoted to Supervisor and was in charge of seven employees when I resigned to pursue my career in radio sales full-time and exclusively. The knowledge and contacts I gained while at Roses allowed me to prospect for the Roses' radio account, and through my leadership we were able to take over two-thirds of Roses' radio budget.

You would find me to be a dedicated young professional who prides myself on doing my best in every aspect of my life. I learn quickly and, on my own initiative, I have studied extensively the techniques of sales superstars including Zig Ziglar and Stephen Covington.

I can provide outstanding personal and professional references at the appropriate time, and I can assure you that I have a reputation for reliability, speed and accuracy in daily operations, as well as tact and diplomacy in customer relations. If you can use a hard worker who could become a valuable part of your organization, I hope you will contact me to suggest a time when I can make myself available for a personal interview at your convenience. Thank you in advance for your time.

Sincerely,

Jacob Edwards

Dropping the name of a mutual acquaintance
Employers will trust a job hunter a little more when he or she comes with a strong personal reference from a respected mutual acquaintance. Dropping a name in a cover letter is like presenting your references before you even get in the door. If you can "drop the name" of a respected person in a cover letter, it can play a key role in blowing the door open!

Date

Exact Name of Person
Title or Position
Name of Company
Address (number and street)
Address (city, state, and zip)

Dear Exact Name of Person: (or Sir or Madam if answering a blind ad)

With the enclosed resume, I would like to initiate the process of being considered for employment within your organization. Because of family ties, I am in the process of relocating to the Houston area by a target date of December 5. Although I already have a Houston address which is shown on my resume, it is my brother's home and I would prefer your contacting me at the e-mail address shown on my resume or at my current telephone number if you wish to talk with me prior to December 5th.

Since graduating from the University of North Carolina at Chapel Hill, I have a track record of rapid promotion with a corporation headquartered in Miami Beach. I began as an Assistant Branch Manager and Head Buyer, was cross-trained as a Sales Representative, and have been promoted to my current position in which I manage the selling process related to 3,500 different products. In that capacity, I am entrusted with the responsibility for nearly $15 million in annual expenditures, and I maintain excellent working relationships with more than 150 vendors of name-brand consumer products sold through chain and convenience stores.

In my job, rapid change is a daily reality, and I have become accustomed to working in an environment in which I must make rapid decisions while weighing factors including forecasted consumer demand, distribution patterns, inventory turnover patterns, and vendor capacity and character. I have earned a reputation as a persuasive communicator and savvy negotiator with an aggressive bottom-line orientation.

If you can use my versatile experience in sales, purchasing, distribution, and operations management, I hope you will contact me to suggest a time when we might meet to discuss your needs and how I might serve them. I can provide excellent personal and professional references, and I assure you in advance that I am a hard worker who is accustomed to being measured according to ambitious goals for profitability in a highly competitive marketplace.

Yours sincerely,

Dale P. Jensen

Date

Exact Name of Person
Title or Position
Name of Company
Address (number and street)
Address (city, state, and zip)

Dear Exact Name of Person: (or Sir or Madam if answering a blind ad)

With the enclosed resume, I would like to make you aware of the considerable sales and purchasing experience which I could put to work for your company. I am in the process of relocating to New Hampshire, and I believe my background is well suited to your company's needs.

As you will see from my resume, I have been excelling as the purchasing agent for a large wholesale food distributor with a customer base of schools, restaurants, and nursing homes throughout the southeastern United States. While negotiating contracts with vendors and handling the school lunch bid process, I have resourcefully managed inventory turnover in order to optimize inventory levels while maximizing return on investment. I have earned a reputation as a prudent strategic planner and skillful negotiator.

In a prior position as a Sales Trainer and Sales Representative with Kraft Foods in Tampa, I increased sales from $250,000 to $1.3 million and won the Captain Max award given to the company's highest-producing sales representative.

With a B.S. degree, I have excelled in continuous and extensive executive training in the areas of financial management, purchasing, contract negotiation, and quality assurance.

I can provide outstanding personal and professional references at the appropriate time, and I hope you will contact me if you can use a resourceful hard worker with a strong bottom-line orientation. I am in the Concord area frequently and could make myself available to meet with you at your convenience. Thank you in advance for your time.

Sincerely,

Barry P. Sonderfan

RELOCATING SOON

Question 9: If I'm relocating soon, how do I say that?
If you are sending your resume and cover letter in advance of your permanent relocation but you plan on being in the area soon for a visit, go ahead and say so. Perhaps you can schedule some interviews on one of your trips to your new place of residence while you're house hunting or apartment hunting. Besides, the fact that you are making advance trips to "scout things out" makes you sound very definite in your plans to relocate.

Date

Exact Name of Person
Title or Position
Name of Company
Address (number and street)
Address (city, state, and zip)

Question 10: If I've recently relocated, what do I say in the cover letter?

Sometimes you relocate back to a place where you lived and worked previously. Go ahead and say so in the letter. That tends to make the employer feel that you are more of "a local."

Dear Exact Name of Person: (or Dear Sir or Madam if answering a blind ad)

With the enclosed resume, I would like to make you aware of my interest in employment with your organization in some capacity in which you could use my strong administrative and office management skills in addition to my strong personal qualities of unlimited initiative, honesty, and reliability.

As you will see from my resume, I have recently returned to the Des Moines area with my husband, and we are glad to be back in Des Moines. We lived in Des Moines previously and, during that time, I excelled in jobs in property management, hospital purchasing, medical scheduling and insurance verification, and small business management. I also worked as the Office Manager for Budget Auto Sound. I began with the company during its start-up and I was instrumental in helping it grow into a business which produced more than $150,000 a year in revenues. In addition to handling all accounting and bookkeeping activities, I performed liaison with the company's corporate accounts for which we performed volume contract work. I have recently been re-hired by Budget Auto Sound and am again working as Office Manager.

Known for my friendly, outgoing personality and professional manner, I enjoy working with others and am skilled in handling multiple responsibilities. In one job as a Property Manager, I managed a staff of eight maintenance personnel while managing more than 100 single-family rental units.

If you can use a highly motivated self-starter who could become a valuable member of your organization, I hope you will contact me to suggest a time when we could meet to discuss your needs. I can provide outstanding personal and professional references at the appropriate time.

Yours sincerely,

Ruth Basore

Date

Exact Name of Person
Title or Position
Name of Company
Address (number and street)
Address (city, state, and zip)

Dear Exact Name of Person: (or Sir or Madam if answering a blind ad)

RECENTLY RELOCATED

With the enclosed resume, I would like to make you aware of my background in accounts management, personnel supervision, and customer service as well as my strong organizational, interpersonal, and communication skills. My husband and I have relocated back to Rochester, where our respective families are from.

While recently completing my Bachelor of Science degree, I excelled academically and was named to the Dean's List seven times. Prior to earning my degree, I excelled in both military and civilian environments.

In one job in North Carolina, I began as a Receptionist answering a 30-line phone system for a 1100-employee company which provided on-line computer services. I rapidly advanced to Accounts Manager and Shift Supervisor, which placed me in charge of eight people. In that job I made hundreds of decisions daily which involved committing the company's technical resources. In addition to dispatching technicians and managing liaison with companies such as The Bank of Chicago, United Carolina Bank, and Stein Mart, I was authorized to commit company resources valued at up to $500,000.

With my husband's retirement, we are eager to replant our roots in New York, and I am seeking employment with a company that can use a highly motivated hard worker who is known for excellent decision-making, problem-solving, and organizational skills. If you can use a resourceful and versatile individual with administrative and computer skills, I hope you will contact me to suggest a time when we can discuss your present and future needs and how I might meet them. I can provide outstanding personal and professional references, and I thank you in advance for your time and consideration.

Sincerely,

Antoinette Pardue

Question 10: If I've recently relocated, what do I say in the cover letter?
Employers like the sound of the fact that you have relocated permanently back to the place where you're from. That fact tends to communicate that you might be a permanent and stable employee in the work force of a local employer.

Date

Exact Name of Person
Title or Position
Name of Company
Address (number and street)
Address (city, state, and zip)

REOPENING A DOOR

Dear Exact Name of Person: (or Sir or Madam if answering a blind ad)

Question 11: What if I want to reopen a door I closed previously?
You can reopen a door in life sometimes. This individual was quite far along in the interviewing process for a CIA job when a relative's terminal illness forced him to abort his plans for an employment change.
He is reopening the door with this cover letter.

Over the course of the last ten years, I have tried to balance my preparations for becoming a CIA Special Agent and my personal responsibilities regarding my wife's illness. Though my wife and I had long discussions about my desire to become a CIA Special Agent, when she was diagnosed with third-stage ovarian cancer I was unable to dedicate my time towards this end. This left my goals of achieving a second under-graduate degree in Criminal Justice, a graduate degree and commission from the University of Maryland, and a law degree from Princeton University unrealized. As my wife's cancer slipped into regression I was, however, able to obtain a graduate degree and commission from a local university.

Recently with my wife's passing, I feel that it is time for me to apply for the job that she and I had discussed so many times. I appreciate your attention to my applica-tion, and I look forward to the next step in the application process of becoming a Special Agent for the Central Intelligence Agency.

To the future,

Kip Sullivan

Date

Exact Name of Person
Title or Position
Name of Company
Address (number and street)
Address (city, state, and zip)

Dear Exact Name of Person: (or Sir or Madam if answering a blind ad)

REOPENING A DOOR

As I hope you will recall, several months ago I interviewed with you for a position involving responsibility for advertising sales with the *Hartford News and Observer*. I very much appreciated your many kindnesses to me during the interviewing process.

During the time when I was interviewing with you for a position, my current employer approached me and asked if I would take on a special project which involved performing outside sales for the business. Since I had worked at Cross Roads Chrysler-Buick for five years and was very familiar with the customer base and with the company's style of doing business, he wanted me in particular to take on the project and I felt, because of his business circumstances at the time, that I had a personal and moral obligation to serve the company in that role.

For that reason I was unable to follow through with the final stage of becoming an employee of the *Hartford News and Observer*.

That project has now been completed and I feel I have loyally completed my obligation to the company in that regard. I would like to ask that you reconsider me for an advertising sales position with the *Hartford News and Observer*. I can provide outstanding personal and professional references, including from my current employer, and I can assure you that I would offer the *Hartford News and Observer* the same loyalty as I have consistently shown to my current employer.

My resume is enclosed to refresh your memory about my skills and professional qualifications. You may also recall that we first became acquainted years ago when I was attending St. Joseph's Episcopal Church.

I have a high opinion of you and of the *Hartford News and Observer* and I hope you will consider me for any position within your company which requires a positive, highly motivated individual with a proven track record of excellent performance in sales and customer service. Thank you again for your past courtesies, and I hope you will welcome my call soon when I try to contact you to see if you have needs I could fill. Best wishes for the holiday season and the New Year.

Yours sincerely,

Samantha Griggers

Question 11: What if I want to reopen a door I closed previously?
Employers can get their feelings hurt if you turn down a job they offer you. This lady had pulled out of the last round of interviews for a job with a newspaper, and months later she realized she'd made a mistake. This letter accompanying her resume reopened the door for her and led to the offer (and acceptance) of a job.

  Date

                        Exact Name of Person
                        Title or Position
                        Name of Company
                        Address (number and street)
                        Address (city, state, and zip)

WHEN THEY ASK FOR SALARY
                 REQUIREMENTS

Question 12: What if they ask
for salary requirements?
It's not in your best interests
to provide your salary
requirements in response to an
ad. It's better to discuss that
subject in person with the
employer, and always let the
employer bring the subject up.
If the employer brings up
salary, he or she is probably
interested in you and you'll be
able to negotiate your best
package. See the fourth
paragraph for the exact
wording in handling this
delicate matter.

Dear Exact Name of Person: (or Sir or Madam if answering a blind ad)

I would like to make you aware of my strong interest in the position of Training and Development Manager advertised in the *Houston Chronicle*. As you will see, I have a track record of success as an experienced instructor and training program developer as well as proven skills in employee supervision, staff development, and production management.

As you will see, I have excelled as an instructor, course developer, and technical writer. In other jobs training, overseeing the professional development of assigned personnel, and providing counseling and guidance for more junior personnel were always of primary importance.

With a versatile background which includes experience in the telecommunications field as well as aircraft and vehicle maintenance, I have been involved in most areas of operations to include logistics, planning and scheduling, and safety as well as in heavy equipment operations. I offer a reputation as a skilled communicator who has been especially effective in providing instruction in individual and group situations. I am especially proud of the associate's degree I earned while excelling in my full-time job.

With regard to my salary requirements, I would be delighted to discuss the private details of my salary history with you in person. I can assure you that I can provide excellent references at the appropriate time.

If you can use an experienced professional who is dedicated to setting and achieving high standards in all areas of performance, I hope you will contact me to suggest a time when we might meet to discuss your needs. I am confident that I could become an asset to Dickinson Associates.

                                                        Sincerely,

                                                        Chico Flores, Jr.

Date

Exact Name of Person
Title or Position
Name of Company
Address (number and street)
Address (city, state, and zip)

Dear Exact Name of Person: (or Sir or Madam if answering a blind ad)

I would like to take this opportunity to thank you for considering me for the job on June 4 as a Sales Representative for Proctor & Gamble, Inc.

I enjoyed meeting with you and being able to learn more about the company. I believe that Proctor & Gamble has a quality product line and I would be honored to represent these products.

I would also like to thank you for considering my busy schedule as a State Probation and Parole Officer and allowing me to come back for the second interview in the same afternoon. I am an extremely reliable and dependable professional, and I appreciated your professional courtesies in helping me be away from my current job as little as possible.

In response to your question about my salary history, I am currently making in the neighborhood of $35,000 with a raise anticipated within two months that could take me to close to $40,000. I enjoy a full benefits package with my current employer.

I am very interested in the position we discussed, and I can provide exceptionally strong personal and professional references at the appropriate time. Thank you for talking with me and helping me learn more about your fine company, and I hope to hear from you soon.

Sincerely,

Kim Chiang

WHEN THEY ASK FOR SALARY HISTORY

Question 13: What if they ask about salary history?
You may be asked to provide your salary history in writing, but be sure to add in everything so that the prospective employer receives a fair picture of your total compensation. Please note that we recommend that you handle a request for salary history as it is handled in the letter on page 250 rather than by providing the intimate details of your salary history in a letter.

Date

Exact Name of Person
Title or Position
Name of Company
Address (number and street)
Address (city, state, and zip)

**WHEN CONFIDENTIALITY
MATTERS**

**Question 14: How do I make it
clear I want
my approach to be
confidential?**
It's okay to ask a prospective
employer to keep confidential
your expression of interest
in the company.

Dear Exact Name of Person: (or Sir or Madam if answering a blind ad)

With the enclosed resume, I would like to <u>confidentially</u> make you aware of my interest in exploring employment opportunities within your organization.

As you will see from my resume, I have excelled in a track record of promotion within the agricultural industry and farm management. I earned my degree in General Agriculture at New Mexico State University and was awarded a Moorhead scholarship based on my high entrance exam scores. In my first job out of college, I was general manager of a small farm with two full-time workers, 15 seasonal workers, as well as a variety of crops, beef cattle, and sows.

Most recently I have been promoted to Assistant Manager supervising nine people on a 1,000-head sow farm, and I am in charge of all aspects of production as well as personnel problems and employee issues.

With a reputation as a resourceful problem solver, I have become experienced at taking care of all farm financial matters including payroll, loan procurement, accounts payable, and accounts receivable. I am also skilled at managing people and have frequently managed a staff of employees who were all Spanish speaking.

Although I am highly regarded in my current position and am being groomed for further rapid promotion, I am aware of your company's fine reputation and am expressing my interest in exploring ways in which you could utilize my expert technical knowledge as well as my proven management abilities. I have an excellent reputation throughout the industry, and I can provide excellent personal and professional references at the appropriate time. If you can use a highly motivated professional with a proven ability to make significant contributions to the bottom line, I hope you will contact me to suggest a time when we could meet in person to discuss how my experience and knowledge could be put to work for you.

Thank you in advance for your time.

Yours sincerely,

Doug Gascho

Date

Exact Name of Person
Title or Position
Name of Company
Address (number and street)
Address (city, state, and zip)

Dear Exact Name of Person: (or Sir or Madam if answering a blind ad)

WHEN CONFIDENTIALITY
MATTERS

Question 14: How do I make it
clear I want my approach to be
confidential?
Here's another example of the
wording to use when you want
to stress that you wish your
approach to be confidential.

With the enclosed resume, I would like to make you aware of my interest in the possibility of putting my strong management, production operations, and sales background to work for your company. Please treat my inquiry as highly confidential at this point. Although I can provide outstanding personal and professional references at the appropriate time, I do not wish my current employer to be aware of my interest in your company.

As you will see from my enclosed resume, I have been in the multipurpose concrete applications business my entire working life. I began in entry-level positions with Fabrico Concrete in New Orleans and was promoted to Plant Manager and Sales Manager. Then I joined Alfred Wright and Son, Inc. in Lafayette, LA, where I tripled production and transformed that company into an attractive acquisition candidate which caught the attention of Handy Concrete. When Handy Concrete Company bought Alfred Wright in 1996, I became a Division Manager and in 1998 was promoted to Regional Manager.

In my current position I manage operations at 10 divisions while supervising three Division Managers and overseeing activities of 85 people at 10 locations. I also supervise four sales and customer service professionals in addition to preparing budgets for each of the 10 divisions.

If you can use a versatile professional with a thorough understanding of all facets of the concrete applications business, I hope you will contact me to suggest a time when we might meet. Should you have ambitious goals in either the production management or sales area, I feel certain that my extensive industry knowledge and contacts could be useful.

Sincerely,

Eugene H. Dubois, Jr.

Exact Name of Person
Title or Position
Name of Company
Address (number and street)
Address (city, state, and zip)

FOLLOW-UP LETTERS

**Question 15: How do I write a
follow-up letter after an
interview?**
A picture is worth a thousand
words. This follow-up letter
after an effective interview
"closed the sale" and helped a
young restauranteur move into
the financial accounting arena.

Dear Exact Name of Person: (or Sir or Madam if answering a blind ad)

I am writing to express my appreciation for the time you spent with me on December 9th, and I want to let you know that I am sincerely interested in the position of Controller which you described.

I feel confident that I could skillfully interact with your 60-person work force in order to obtain the information we need to assure expert controllership of your diversified interests, and I would cheerfully travel as your needs require. I want you to know, too, that I would not consider relocating to Salt Lake City to be a hardship! It is certainly one of the most beautiful areas I have ever seen.

As you described to me what you are looking for in a controller, I had a sense of "déjà vu" because my current boss was in a similar position when I went to work for him in 1998. He needed someone to come in and be his "right arm" and take on an increasing amount of his management responsibilities so that he could be freed up to do other things. I have played a key role in the growth and profitability of his multiunit business, and he has come to depend on my sound financial and business advice as much as my day-to-day management skills. Since Christmas is the busiest time of the year in the restaurant business, I feel that I could not leave him during that time. I could certainly make myself available by mid-January.

If you felt you needed me to work with you during my vacation from the 26th until I go back to handle the New Year's business on the 29th, I would be happy to work with you as you close the books and handle end-of-year matters. Please note that I will be out of town from Saturday the 19th until Monday the 22nd visiting relatives.

It would be a pleasure to work for a successful individual such as yourself, and I feel I could contribute significantly to your business not only through my accounting and business background but also through my strong personal qualities of loyalty, reliability, and trustworthiness. I am confident that I could learn Quick Books rapidly, and I would welcome being trained to do things your way.

I send best wishes for the holidays, and I'd like to send a special compliment to your wife for the delicious cookies she baked!

Yours sincerely,

Jacob Evangelisto

Date

Exact Name of Person
Title or Position
Name of Company
Address (number and street)
Address (city, state, and zip)

Dear Exact Name of Person: (or Sir or Madam if answering a blind ad)

I want you to know how much I enjoyed talking with you in Sioux Falls on Friday, January 12th.

I fully understand the concept of developing retail applications in the convenience store industry. I believe you are aware that I performed essentially that job for the construction industry in a previous position. With Pathways Computer Systems, I rose from System Programmer to Director of Development as I transformed a failing operation into an efficient and profitable business.

As you are aware, I have developed expert knowledge of the convenience store industry in my current job. As Vice President of Management Information Systems (MIS), I was credited with making many major contributions to Scotchman, a 70-store convenience store chain, which made it an acquisition target of Texaco. Now that we are a part of the 1,100-store convenience store chain of Texaco, I am directing network systems development for this vastly larger organization. I understand your company's growth goals, as you explained them to me, and I feel I could become a valuable part of your strategic planning and implementation process.

One of my strengths is that I have a vast knowledge of many different areas, ranging from accounting systems and accounting development, to user interface, to putting together specifications, to the continual troubleshooting of problems and refinement of systems. It has been my responsibility to sit with technical experts in all functional areas and be able to assure the attainment of specific goals in their area of operation. I believe you already know much about my background, but I do want to reiterate that I offer expert knowledge of the convenience store industry from the user point of view, knowledge of the MMS product and system, along with expertise related to UNIX, NT, and programming. I am skilled at establishing effective working relationships at all levels.

Thank you very much for giving me so much of your time and for letting me become better acquainted with your needs. I am enclosing a copy of my mileage statement (423 miles) and a copy of the hotel statement. I believe I could become a valuable member of your management team.

Sincerely,

David R. Shelton

FOLLOW-UP LETTERS

Question 15: How do I write a follow-up letter after an interview?
Notice the last paragraph. A follow-up letter is an excellent opportunity to send your requests for reimbursement for any out-of-pocket expenses you incurred in connection with the interview.

Date

TO: John Smith
Elaine Bryant
Meredith Kleinfield

Dear Friends and Valued Colleagues:

**Question 16: How do I resign
—gracefully?**
A letter of resignation can be a
highly emotional experience,
both for the person sending it
and for the individuals
receiving it. It gives you a
formal opportunity to declare
your last day on the job and to
thank appropriate people.

It is with much sadness as well as with great personal affection for all of you that I wish to inform you that I will be leaving the Ford Motor Company. My final departure date can be worked out according to your wishes, but I would suggest Wednesday, December 20, 1999.

A sales position has become available at *The Schofield Gazette* and I believe the hours of employment will be better suited to my needs as a single parent.

Because I have been employed with Ford Motor Company since 1993, I feel as though I am "leaving home," and in that nostalgic frame of mind, it is my desire to tell you how much I have appreciated your training me, helping me, and giving me opportunities to try new things and gain new skills. I am very truly grateful to you, and I hope you know that I always gave my best effort.

I can assure you that I will continue to be a highly productive source of referrals for you even when I am gone, because I believe wholeheartedly in the products and the product line we all have represented. If I can ever help any of you individually in any way, too, please let me know.

In the meantime, please accept my sincere thanks for all the kindnesses and professional courtesies you have shown me.

Yours sincerely,

Mary Anne Murphy

Date

Exact Name of Person
Title or Position
Name of Company
Address (number and street)
Address (city, state, and zip)

Dear Exact Name of Person:

    It is with genuine sadness and many mixed feelings that I must inform you that I will be resigning from my position at Cranford, Sweeney & Co., CPAs, effective July 26.

    The firm of Hill, Gilbert & Wilkins in Spokane, also a public accounting firm, has offered me a position as a CPA at a salary of nearly $50,000 annually, and I feel it is a time in my life when I must move on.

    Leaving the firm of Cranford, Sweeney & Co., CPAs, is very difficult for me professionally and emotionally. After I passed the CPA Exam, you gave me my first job in the public accounting field, and I have thoroughly enjoyed the family atmosphere coupled with the professional style of both you and Mr. Cranford. You have taught me so much about how to solve problems, how to work more efficiently, and how to handle difficult clients. I am deeply grateful for your encouragement, professional mentoring, and strong personal example.

    Although the decision to leave Cranford, Sweeney & Co., CPAs, is difficult, I really feel that I have no choice. As a single parent who provides full financial support of my daughter, I am driven by the desire to provide a gracious standard of living for my small family. I will be placing her in a Christian school in Spokane so that she can continue learning in the same Christian environment as she has had in Tacoma.

    I hope you know that I have always given 110% to your firm in terms of my financial knowledge, intelligence, and problem-solving ability, and I hope you feel that I have made contributions to its reputation. I feel I am separating more from a family than from an employer, and I felt I wanted to put this information in writing to you as a first step because getting the words out verbally would be a difficult emotional experience for me.

    Thank you from the bottom of my heart for all you have done for me professionally and personally.

Yours sincerely,

Elizabeth J. Ritchie

LETTERS OF RESIGNATION

Question 16: How do I resign—gracefully?
Here's another example of a letter that will be an emotional experience for the people receiving it as it was for the person who signed it. Employers are often not happy when you leave them, so a great letter of resignation can ease the hurt.

ABOUT THE EDITOR

Anne McKinney holds an M.B.A. from the Harvard Business School and a B.A. in English from the University of North Carolina at Chapel Hill. A noted public speaker, writer, and teacher, she is the senior editor for PREP's business and career imprint, which bears her name. Titles in the Anne McKinney Career Series published by PREP include: *Resumes and Cover Letters That Have Worked, Resumes and Cover Letters That Have Worked for Military Professionals, Resumes and Cover Letters for Managers, Cover Letters That Blow Doors Open, Letters for Special Situations,* and *Government Job Applications and Federal Resumes.* Her career titles and how-to resume-and-cover-letter books are based on the expertise she has acquired in 20 years of working with job hunters. Her valuable career insights have appeared in publications of the *Wall Street Journal* and other prominent newspapers and magazines.

Judeo-Christian Ethics Series

BIBLE STORIES FROM THE OLD TESTAMENT *Katherine Whaley*
Familiar and not-so-familiar Bible stories told by an engaging storyteller in a style guaranteed to delight and inform. Includes stories about Abraham, Cain and Abel, Jacob and David, Moses and the Exodus, Judges, Saul, David, and Solomon. (272 pages)
"Whaley tells these tales in such a way that they will appeal to the young adult as well as the senior citizen." – *Independent Publisher*
Trade paperback 1-885288-12-3—$18.00

BACK IN TIME *Patty Sleem*
Also published in large print hardcover by Simon & Schuster's Thorndike Press as a Thorndike Christian Mystery in November 1998. (336 pages)
"An engrossing look at the discrimination faced by female ministers."– *Library Journal*
Trade paperback 1-885288-03-4—$16.00

A GENTLE BREEZE FROM GOSSAMER WINGS *Gordon Beld*
Pol Pot was the Khmer Rouge leader whose reign of terror caused the deaths of up to 2 million Cambodians in the mid-1970s. He masterminded an extreme, Maoist-inspired revolution in which those Cambodians died in mass executions, and from starvation and disease. This book of historical fiction shows the life of one refugee from this reign of genocide. (320 pages)
"I'm pleased to recommend *A Gentle Breeze From Gossamer Wings*. Every Christian in America should read it. It's a story you won't want to miss – and it could change your life."
— Robert H. Schuller, Pastor, Crystal Cathedral
Trade paperback 1-885288-07-7—$18.00

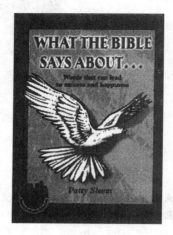

SECOND TIME AROUND *Patty Sleem*
"Sleem explores the ugliness of suicide and murder, obsession and abuse, as well as Christian faith and values. An emotional and suspenseful read reflecting modern issues and concerns." – *Southern Book Trade* (336 pages)
Foreign rights sold in Chinese.
Hardcover 1-885288-00-X—$25.00
Trade paperback 1-885288-05-0—$17.00

WHAT THE BIBLE SAYS ABOUT… Words that can lead to success and happiness *Patty Sleem*
A daily inspirational guide as well as a valuable reference when you want to see what the Bible says about Life and Living, Toil and Working, Problems and Suffering, Anger and Arguing, Self-Reliance and Peace of Mind, Justice and Wrong-Doing, Discipline and Self-Control, Wealth and Power, Knowledge and Wisdom, Pride and Honor, Gifts and Giving, Husbands and Wives, Friends and Neighbors, Children, Sinning and Repenting, Judgment and Mercy, Faith and Religion, and Love. (192 pages)
Hardcover 1-885288-02-6—$20.00

RESUMES AND COVER LETTERS THAT HAVE WORKED

Anne McKinney, Editor

More than 100 resumes and cover letters written by the world's oldest resume-writing company. Resumes shown helped real people not only change jobs but also transfer their skills and experience to other industries and fields. An indispensable tool in an era of downsizing when research shows that most of us have not one but three distinctly different careers in our working lifetime. (272 pages)

"Distinguished by its highly readable samples...essential for library collections." – *Library Journal*

Trade paperback 1-885288-04-2—$25.00

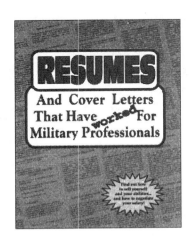

RESUMES AND COVER LETTERS THAT HAVE WORKED FOR MILITARY PROFESSIONALS

Anne McKinney, Editor

Military professionals from all branches of the service gain valuable experience while serving their country, but they need resumes and cover letters that translate their skills and background into "civilian language." This is a book showing more than 100 resumes and cover letters written by a resume-writing service in business for nearly 20 years which specializes in "military translation." (256 pages)

"A guide that significantly translates veterans' experience into viable repertoires of achievement." –*Booklist*

Trade paperback 1-885288-06-9—$25.00

RESUMES AND COVER LETTERS FOR MANAGERS

Anne McKinney, Editor

Destined to become the bible for managers who want to make sure their resumes and cover letters open the maximum number of doors while helping them maximize in the salary negotiation process. From office manager to CEO, managers trying to relocate to or from these and other industries and fields will find helpful examples: Banking, Agriculture, School Systems, Human Resources, Restaurants, Manufacturing, Hospitality Industry, Automotive, Retail, Telecommunications, Police Force, Dentistry, Social Work, Academic Affairs, Non-Profit Organizations, Childcare, Sales, Sports, Municipalities, Rest Homes, Medicine and Healthcare, Business Operations, Landscaping, Customer Service, MIS, Quality Control, Teaching, the Arts, and more. (288 pages)

Trade paperback 1-885288-10-7—$25.00

GOVERNMENT JOB APPLICATIONS AND FEDERAL RESUMES:
Federal Resumes, KSAs, Forms 171 and 612, and Postal Applications *Anne McKinney, Editor*

Getting a government job can lead to job security and peace of mind. The problem is that getting a government job requires extensive and complex paperwork. Now, for the first time, this book reveals the secrets and shortcuts of professional writers in preparing job-winning government applications such as these:
The Standard Form 171 (SF 171) – several complete samples
The Optional Form 612 (OF 612) – several complete samples
KSAs – samples of KSAs tailored to jobs ranging from the GS-5 to GS-12
Ranking Factors – how-to samples
Postal Applications
Wage Grade paperwork
Federal Resumes – see the different formats required by various government agencies. (272 pages)

Trade paperback 1-885288-11-5—$25.00

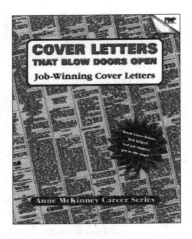

requesting reinstatement to an
academic program, Follow-up letters
after an interview, Letters
requesting bill consolidation, Letters
of reprimand to marginal employees, Letters requesting financial
assistance or a grant, Letters to
professionals disputing their
charges, collections letters, thank-
you letters, and letters to accompany resumes in job-hunting. (256
pages)
Trade paperback 1-885288-09-3—
$25.00

**COVER LETTERS THAT BLOW DOORS
OPEN** *Anne McKinney, Editor*
Although a resume is important, the cover
letter is the first impression. This book is
a compilation of great cover letters that
helped real people get in the door for job
interviews against stiff competition.
Included are letters that show how to
approach employers when you're moving
to a new area, how to write a cover
letter when you're changing fields or
industries, and how to arouse the
employer's interest in dialing your number
first from a stack of resumes. (272 pages)
Trade paperback 1-885288-13-1—$25.00

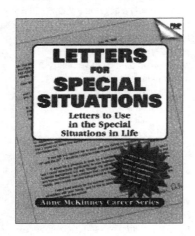

LETTERS FOR SPECIAL SITUATIONS *Anne
McKinney, Editor*
Sometimes it is necessary to write a
special letter for a special situation in life.
You will find great letters to use as
models for business and personal reasons
including: Letters asking for a raise,
Letters of resignation, Letters of
reference, Letters notifying a vendor of a
breach of contract, Letter to a Congress-
man, Letters of complaint, Letters

PREP Publishing Order Form

You can order any of our titles from your favorite bookseller! Or just send a check or money order or your credit card number for the total amount*, plus $3.20 postage and handling, to PREP, Box 66, Fayetteville, NC 28302. If you have a question about any of our titles, feel free to e-mail us at preppub@aol.com and visit our website at http://www.prep-pub.com

Name: _____

Phone #: _____

Address: _____

_____

E-mail address: _____

Payment Type: ☐ Check/Money Order   ☐ Visa   ☐ MasterCard

Credit Card Number: _____ Expiration Date: _____

Check items you are ordering:

☐ $25.00—RESUMES AND COVER LETTERS THAT HAVE WORKED. Anne McKinney, Editor

☐ $25.00—RESUMES AND COVER LETTERS THAT HAVE WORKED FOR MILITARY PROFESSIONALS.
   Anne McKinney, Editor

☐ $25.00—RESUMES AND COVER LETTERS FOR MANAGERS. Anne McKinney, Editor

☐ $25.00—GOVERNMENT JOB APPLICATIONS AND FEDERAL RESUMES: Federal Resumes, KSAs,
   Forms 171 and 612, and Postal Applications. Anne McKinney, Editor

☐ $25.00—COVER LETTERS THAT BLOW DOORS OPEN. Anne McKinney, Editor

☐ $25.00—LETTERS FOR SPECIAL SITUATIONS. Anne McKinney, Editor

☐ $16.00—BACK IN TIME. Patty Sleem

☐ $17.00—(trade paperback) SECOND TIME AROUND. Patty Sleem

☐ $25.00—(hardcover) SECOND TIME AROUND. Patty Sleem

☐ $18.00—A GENTLE BREEZE FROM GOSSAMER WINGS. Gordon Beld

☐ $18.00—BIBLE STORIES FROM THE OLD TESTAMENT. Katherine Whaley

☐ $20.00—WHAT THE BIBLE SAYS ABOUT... *Words that can lead to success and happiness.* Patty Sleem

_____ **TOTAL ORDERED (add $3.20 for postage and handling)**

PREP offers volume discounts on large orders. Call us at (910) 483-6611 for more information.

THE MISSION OF PREP PUBLISHING IS TO PUBLISH
BOOKS AND OTHER PRODUCTS WHICH ENRICH
PEOPLE'S LIVES AND HELP THEM OPTIMIZE THE
HUMAN EXPERIENCE. OUR STRONGEST LINES ARE
OUR JUDEO-CHRISTIAN ETHICS SERIES AND OUR
BUSINESS & CAREER SERIES.

Would you like to explore the possibility of having PREP's
writing team create a letter for you similar to the ones in this
book?

For a brief free consultation, call 910-483-6611
or send $4.00 to receive our Job Change Packet to
PREP, Department COV, Box 66, Fayetteville, NC 28302.

QUESTIONS OR COMMENTS? E-MAIL US AT PREPPUB@AOL.COM